Russell Kelso Carter

Divine Healing

Russell Kelso Carter

Divine Healing

ISBN/EAN: 9783337779238

Printed in Europe, USA, Canada, Australia, Japan

Cover: Foto ©Lupo / pixelio.de

More available books at **www.hansebooks.com**

DIVINE HEALING

OR

THE ATONEMENT

FOR

SIN AND SICKNESS.

BY

CAPT. R. KELSO CARTER.

For Twenty Years of the Pennsylvania Military College, Author of "Pastor Blumhardt," "Miracles of Healing," "Supernatural Gifts of the Spirit," Editor of "The Kingdom," Etc.

NEW EDITION, REWRITTEN AND ENLARGED.

———

New York:
JOHN B. ALDEN, PUBLISHER.
1888.

DEDICATION.

I LOVINGLY DEDICATE THIS BOOK TO ONE WITHOUT WHOSE AID IT WOULD NOT HAVE APPEARED; TO ONE FOR WHOSE TENDER CARE, PATIENT INSTRUCTION, AND GENTLE, LOVING LIFE I SHALL THANK GOD THROUGH TIME AND THROUGH ETERNITY; TO ONE WHO HAS BEEN EVER TO ME THAT WHICH IS PUREST, AND SWEETEST, AND HOLIEST IN CHRISTIAN HUMANITY; TO HER WHO FIRST TAUGHT ME THE ALL-CONQUERING NAME OF THE MIGHTY JESUS: MY MOTHER,

MARY ESTHER (KELSO) CARTER.

CONTENTS.

	PAGE
INTRODUCTION.—From The Century Magazine	9

Explanation. The Authority—God's Word. Cases Not the Proper Foundation. The Doctrine. Ancient Medical Knowledge. Specialist Physicians in Egypt. God's Covenant with Israel. Promises of Health in Exodus and Deuteronomy. Health to the Obedient Jew. Abraham, Isaac, Jacob, David, Solomon, Ahaziah, Asa, Hezekiah. Isaiah's Promises. Jesus Christ's Work. Unbelief the Limit. The Apostles' Work. The "Body for the Lord." The Earnest of Our Inheritance. The Promise in James. Medical Knowledge in the Days of the Apostles. Dean Alford's Comment on Jas. v. 14, 15. The Oil Sacramental, not Medicinal. Death. The Practice.

CHAPTER I.—Pardon of Past Sin 21
Promises of Scripture. Half-hearted Christians. Absurdity of Pardon for Future. Modern "Indulgences."

CHAPTER II.—Kept from Falling 23
Different Schools. Dr. Hodge. Mr. Moody. John Wesley. Unqualified Promises. Salvation a Finished Work. Sickness and Sin Not Mentioned as Absent from Heaven.

CHAPTER III.—Healing of Bodily Disease 26
The Atonement for the Body as Well as for the Soul. Special Cures in Answer to Prayer. The General Doctrine. My Own Case. Carl Reed *vs.* His Own Father. Similarity of Evidence for Healing of Soul and of Body. Skepticism in the Church. Explaining Miracles. God Works by Scientific Law Always. Henry Varley and the Cyclone. "God Said." The Case of Sarah. Abimelech's Household. Rebekah. The Exodus. The Decalogue. Promises in Deuteronomy. The Wilderness. The Philistines and the Ark. Solomon's Vision. Naaman and Hezekiah (page 35). Healing in the Psalms. Proverbs. Isaiah's Atonement Chapter. Young's Translation. Hegstenberg's. Isaac Leeser's. Jesus Not Sick Inwardly. Sickness and Natural Law. Why Christ Bore Our Diseases. Healing and Spiritual Blessing. Promises in Jeremiah. Suffering and Disobedience. Ezekiel. The Woe to the Shepherds. Micah, Habbakuk, Malachi. The New Testament (page 48). The Name Jesus. Christ's Temptation. Satan's Foreknowledge. Feeding on Christ. Conditions of Christ's Miracles. The

CONTENTS.

Commission to the Twelve. The Seventy. Faith in the Promise Essential. An Ignorant Objection. Jesus Came to Save Men's Lives. As thou hast sent me, even so send I them. The Apostles' Prayer. Corinthians—The Gospel of the Body. Members of Christ. The Laws of Health. Eating and Drinking. The Promises, Yea and Amen. Members of His Body. The Curse of the Law (page 56). Christ Our Life. The Purpose of the Miracles. Thomas Erskine. Admiral Fishbourne. Argument from History and Analogy. The Whole a Type of Its Parts. Preparation for the Second Advent. Satan's Trump Card.

1. SICKNESS FROM THE DEVIL.. 63
Rev. Samuel Wakefield. Scripture Declarations. God's Part in the Matter. The Atonement and Satan's Work. Hymeneus and Alexander. Reasons for such terms as "God Smote Him." Miss Havergal's Faulty Logic. Our Dear Ones. God's "Hired Razor."

2. THE IMPORTANCE OF THE BODY.. 71
The Body not a Cage. The Real Source of Sin. Paul's Opinion of his Body. "The Old Man." The Body for the Lord. The Body of Moses.

3. A SANCTIFIED DIET.. 77
Esoteric Buddhism. The Atonement for Child-birth. Law of Leprosy. Law of the Priesthood. Wakefield on Physical Atonement.

4. WHO MAY BE HEALED.. 82
The Word "Physician." Bible Neglect of Doctors and Medicine. The Direction to the Sick in Jas. v.

5. THE SIN UNTO DEATH.. 86
Sins Forgiven, but Punishment not Remitted. The Case of Moses. The Wilderness Life for the Body. Abuses of the Body. Appetites. The Marriage Relation.

6. THE PERFECT MEANS... 90
Simple Faith and Obedience. Visible Means may be used. Healing and Forgiveness.

CHAPTER IV.—KEPT FROM SICKNESS 93
Importance of Conditions. Some Difference Between Soul and Body. Sickness not Always a Proof of Sin. A Thousand Generations. Christ Fulfills the Law. Jacob, the First Recorded Case of Death-sickness. The Day of Small Things. Little Sins. Criminal Ignorance of Health Laws. Statutes. Scoffers. Dr. Buckley. Sickness a Disgrace. Paul's Testimony. Walking in the Light. Job's Case. Sickness sometimes a Means of Grace. The Lord's Prayer. God's Will.

CHAPTER V.—OBJECTIONS AND QUESTIONS..................................... 101

1. THE "VILE BODY"... 101
2. TROPHIMUS... 101
3. PAUL'S THORN 102
A Messenger of Satan. Its Exceptional Character. The Thorn Healed.
4. THE MAN BORN BLIND... 108
5. LAZARUS... 109
The Roaring Lion. How God Sends Evil.
6. DEATH APPOINTED TO ALL... 112

CONTENTS. vii

                            PAGE

7. FOR THE APOSTOLIC AGE... 113
   The Promises and the New Covenant. Why the Apostolic Gifts Disappeared.
8. THE DAYS OF MIRACLES HAVE PASSED.................................. 115
   A Negative Proposition. Epochs. Prophecy.
9. THE USE OF MEANS... 119
   Timothy. Hezekiah. The Blind Man. Naaman. Paul and Silas. Was Oil a Medicine? Ancient Medical Knowledge. Nothing new under the Sun. Oil as a "Cure-all." Why God has allowed the discovery of medicine. Symbolism of Jas. v. 14, 15. The Doctors Speak.
10. WHO ARE THE ELDERS?.. 127
11. GIFTS OF HEALING 128
    Dr. Cuyler's Views. My Own Call. A Case of Healing.
12. CASTING OUT DEVILS.. 132
    Dr. Forbes Winslow's Opinion of Demoniacs. Modern "Possession."
13. MODERN THORNS... 134
14. ROMANIST MIRACLES... 136
    A Case by an Eye-witness. True Faith Always Rewarded.
15. GLORIFYING GOD IN SICKNESS.. 138
    Possible Obstinacy. Discipline. Uses of Sickness. Job xxiii. Elihu and James. Every One Will not be Healed. Sickness not a Dart, but a Wound. Kissing the Rod.
16. GOD'S WILL TO HEAL.. 144
    Trying to Defeat God's Will. Thy Will be Done.
17. THAT REVIEW ARTICLE... 146
    Epochs. Modern Revivals and Miracles. Signs not Following Those who Disbelieve in Signs. Raising the Dead. The Lord's Supper. The Imagination. Cheap Miracles. Post-millenniumism.
18. THE CENTURY ARTICLES.. 152
    Dr. Buckley's Error in Philosophy.
19. WHY INFANTS SUFFER.. 153
    Inherited Disease. The Pains of Motherhood.
20. WHY NOT INSTANTANEOUS... 155
    Miriam. Shunamite's Son. Hezekiah. Job. David. Blind Man. Nobleman's Son. Blind Man at Siloam. Lazarus. Epaphroditus. Trophimus.

CHAPTER VI.—FULL SALVATION... 159
  The Fourfold Gospel. Quadrangular Christians. Unbelief. The Church Preparing for Translation. Chinese Missions and Healing.
CHAPTER VII.—REVIEW AND CONCLUSION.................................... 165
APPENDIX A.—JOHN WESLEY ON DIVINE HEALING............................. 174
APPENDIX B.—THE CASE OF MRS. REBECCA FRAVEL.......................... 176
APPENDIX C.—THEOSOPHY AND ESOTERIC RELIGIONS, MIND CURE, CHRISTIAN SCIENCE, etc... 177
APPENDIX D.—MY CONFESSION... 179
  Reasons for Writing this Book. My Healing. Calvinism and Arminianism.
GLOSSARY OF SCRIPTURE TEXTS.. 182

INTRODUCTION.

As the briefest and most comprehensive synopsis of the doctrine advocated in this book, I have decided to place as an introduction the article written for the *Century Magazine*, and published, in a much reduced form, in that journal for March, 1887. In presenting the original draft of that article, the attitude of the *Century* editor and managers toward it will be understood in a moment, when I state that they allowed me but four pages, while Dr. Schauffler and Dr. Buckley, for their attacks on divine healing, occupied altogether some thirty pages.

By way of explanation, it may be said that the writer has been most intimately associated with the "faith-healing" movement ever since it first began to attract public attention in this country. Seven years ago he was healed of a stubborn case of organic heart disease, after the best physicians, and the most favorable climate and manner of life had alike signally failed to afford relief. At that time the literature concerning this subject was limited to the life of Dorothea Trüdel, and a small volume of Faith-Cures by Dr. Cullis, besides such more general works as Horace Bushnell's Nature and the Supernatural. During these seven years, and especially in the last four, the subject of healing through faith has risen into general prominence, and the literature now forms quite a small library. All of these writings are not new, but in many instances are largely composed of quotations from the early fathers, and other prominent Christians, all along the history of the church. In the perusal of this mass of writing, and in the contributions which he has himself made to the library mentioned, the writer of this article has necessarily been placed in a position to speak with authority on the question, What is the doctrine and practice of Divine Healing, as presented by its most prominent advocates? It may be added that there is hardly a single individual who has been brought prominently forward in this movement with whom he is not acquainted, either personally or through some form of correspondence.

One other explanation is needed. There are two classes of believers in Divine Healing. First, those who hold that God does heal individuals frequently, according to His sovereign will in the case, and in answer to prayer; but that there are many cases in which it is not His will to heal, not merely because of failure in the individual to exercise faith or meet some divine condition, but over and above all this. The second class believe that the atonement of Jesus Christ has provided a salvation which covers the body as well as the soul, and offers the possibility of deliverance from the inward power of sin and sickness in this life, *provided* we do meet all the divine conditions. Both classes agree that means may be used, or left untouched; it being always conceded that these, like the clay and spittle upon the eyes of the blind man, would have been entirely inadequate to the results obtained. It is in the interest of the second class mentioned, which class embraces all the prominent advocates of "faith-healing," that this article is written.

The object of this paper is simply to bring before the reader the real nature and ground of the doctrine, as far and as clearly as is possible in such limited space as that offered by a brief magazine article. The difficulty of the task will be surmised when it is known that a book of three hundred pages has proved insufficient to cover all the ground desired.

THE AUTHORITY.

The only authority to which any real recognition is accorded is found in the Bible. To the Word of our God we bow with absolute submission. What God says we propose to believe, whether we have been so fortunate as to prove it in our own experience or not. With Daniel Webster, we "believe religion to be not a matter of demonstration, but of faith. God requires us to give credit to the truths which He reveals, not because we can prove them, but because He declares them." This does not mean that we are always unable to offer any reasonable proof of our belief, but simply emphasizes the thought that the ground for our belief is not found in the proof, but in the Word of God alone. The thoughtful reader will now be prepared for the following statement, which I formulated years ago. It is this:

Individual cases of healing, or phenomena, are absolutely worthless as to the question before us. All the cases in the world have nothing whatever to do directly with the doctrine of Divine Healing, for the very simple reason that they are not and never have been made the basis, or ground of that doctrine. The only foundation is the Word of God, and hence the examination of cases *per se* has no direct bearing upon the subject. Failures in cases may serve to throw light upon defects in the practice of healing, but not upon the doctrine itself. The only source of light, and the only true battle-ground, lie therefore in the Scriptures of truth. Some people seem to be saved instantaneously, so to speak, while many others appear to grow gradually into salvation all the way along to the grave; and others still, who profess a desire to be saved, do not receive salvation at all, but die in their sins. No Christain, however, thinks of making these facts the basis for the doctrine of salvation through faith; that is found exclusively in the promises of the Word. Should the whole world fail to be saved, we would still teach the gospel of salvation; and if all fail to be healed, we must hold to the gospel of healing, provided only that these be found in the Word. And after all has been said, on

INTRODUCTION. 11

the human side, one success establishes a possibility in the face of a thousand failures.

THE DOCTRINE.

Passing rapidly over the time when Abraham, Isaac, and Jacob each sought the Lord as the direct healer of physical disorders (see Gen. xx. 17; xxv. 21; xxx. 2), we come to the date of the Exodus, when God specially undertook the salvation of His people. But before reading the Word, here let us inquire whether human skill had anything to offer in the way of medical treatment. Presumptive evidence upon this point is very strong. The antediluvians, with the opportunities afforded by their long lives, must have carried scientific matters to a very high point. Their knowledge was brought across the waters of the flood by Shem and his brothers; and be it remembered that he was alive until about the time of Jacob's birth. Egypt received and developed therefore all the knowledge of the world which survived the deluge; and with this view of the case we can see that it is no empty comparison when we are told that "Solomon's wisdom excelled the wisdom of all the children of the east country and all the wisdom of Egypt." The wise king is expressly stated to have been filled with knowledge far beyond any other man, before or after him; hence the comparison with the wisdom of Egypt greatly exalts the latter. Now Clement of Alexandria, who lived in the second century, mentions six hermetic books of Egyptian medicine, one of which was devoted to surgical instruments. Besides this, there are now in existence various Egyptian papyri, which testify strongly to the skill and fame of the medical men of the day. The learned George Ebers, in Uarda, chap. iii, says: "Whoever required a physician sent for him, not to his own house, but to a temple (for each was attached to a priestly college). There a statement was required of the complaint from which the sick person was suffering, and it was left to the principal of the medical staff of the sanctuary to select the master of the healing art whose special knowledge appeared to him to be suited for the treatment of the case." Herodotus also testifies to the same purpose.

Here, then, we see that the Eyptians possessed medical knowledge and skill of a very high degree. But the Scriptures inform us that "Moses was learned in all the knowledge of the Egyptians," hence Moses must have possessed the highest medical information. Notwithstanding all this, when the pathway was opened through the sea, the Lord gave the following unmistakable promise at the very beginning of their new life. In Ex. xv. 26, we read: "If thou wilt diligently hearken to the voice of the Lord thy God, and wilt do that which is right in his sight, and wilt give ear to his commandments, and keep all his statutes, I will put none of these diseases upon thee, which I have brought upon the Egyptians: for I am the Lord that healeth thee." (or, I am the Lord thy healer).

Need we remark, in passing, that this promise was tested again and again? They were healed and kept in health as long as they rendered perfect obedience. Moses prayed for leprosy (Num. xii. 13), and Aaron for the plague, (Num. xvi. 47,48). The serpent's bite found its cure solely through faith (Num. xxvi. 9), and the pestilence vanished when David sacrificed (2 Sam. xxiv. 25). The Psalmist declares that when the children of Israel walked through the wilderness "there was not one feeble (sick) person among their tribes," (Ps. cv. 37); and Solomon reminds the people that there had not failed one word of all the promises given through Moses, (1 K. viii. 56). Joshua, also, before he died, said to the people, "Ye know in all your hearts, and in all your souls, that not one thing hath failed of all the good things which the Lord your God spake concerning you: all are come to pass unto you, and not one thing hath failed thereof," (Josh. xxiii. 14).

We are therefore confronted with the fact, that instead of sending the people to Moses for the benefit of his learning, they were referred only to God, and were actually preserved in physical health so long as they obeyed the divine commands. But let us read the health covenant more fully. In the fifth commandment we find the most explicit promise of physical life, conditioned on obedience to parents. Passing on, we read passages like the following, which cannot be disputed on any ground whatever: "Oh, that there were such an heart in them, that they would fear me, and keep all my commandments always, that it might be well with them, and with their children forever." (Deut. v. 29). (This will reach down to our day and generation). "Ye shall walk in all the ways which the Lord your God hath commanded you, that ye may live, and that it may be well with you, that ye may prolong your days in the land which ye shall possess" (v. 33). "If thou shalt indeed obey his voice, and do all that I speak . . . I will take sickness away from the midst of thee." (Ex. xxiii. 22-25). "If ye shall despise my statutes, or if your soul abhor my judgments, so that ye will not do all my commandments, but that ye break my covenant; I also will do this unto you; 1 will even appoint over you terror, consumption, and the burning ague, that shall consume your eyes and cause sorrow of heart." (Lev. xxvi. 15, 16). "If ye hearken to these judgments, and keep and do them, . . . the Lord will take away from thee all sickness, and will put none of the evil diseases of Egypt, which thou knowest, upon thee; but will lay them upon all them that hate thee." (Deut. vii. 12-15). "If thou wilt not observe to do all the words of this law that are written in this book, . . . then the Lord will make thy plagues wonderful, and the plagues of thy seed, even great plagues, and of long continuance, and sore sicknesses, and of long continuance. Moreover, he will bring upon thee all the diseases of Egypt, which thou wast afraid of, and they shall cleave unto thee. Also every sickness and every plague which is not written in the book of this law, them will the Lord bring upon thee, until thou be destroyed. And ye shall be left few in number." (Deut.

xxviii. 58-62). Manifestly, if "every sickness" was to come only if they disobeyed, they would be absent if they were obedient.

Certainly there will not be found a man who will attempt to deny, in the face of all this, that the Jew was promised entire deliverance from all manner of sickness by the power of God alone, and that the only condition was perfect obedience. We have already seen that the Jews understood this, even from the days of Abraham. The case of that patriarch has been cited, as well as those of Isaac and Jacob. The history of the march through the wilderness is full of illustrations. When they obeyed they were healthy. When they disobeyed they were afflicted, but were always cured by prayer. David has left the most abundant testimony to his understanding of the matter. Hear him: "The Lord is the strength of my life." (Ps. xxvii. 1). "O Lord, my God, I cried unto thee, and thou hast healed me." (xxx. 2). "O Lord, thou hast brought up my soul from the grave, thou hast kept me alive, that I should not go down to the pit." (xxx. 3). "The Lord will strengthen him upon the bed of languishing: thou wilt make all his bed in his sickness." (xli., 3). "He that dwelleth in the secret place of the Most High shall abide under the shadow of the Almighty. Surely he shall deliver thee from the snare of the fowler, and from the noisome pestilence. Thou shalt not be afraid for the terror by night; nor for the arrow that flieth by day; nor for the pestilence that walketh in darkness; nor for the destruction that wasteth at noonday." (xci. 1, 6). "Bless the Lord, O my soul, and forget not all his benefits: who forgiveth all thine iniquities; who healeth all thy diseases; who redeemeth thy life from destruction . . . so that thy youth is renewed like the eagle's." (ciii. 2, 5). Many more quotations could be given, but these will suffice.

When Solomon dedicated the temple, he prayed that God would heal "whatsoever plague or sickness there may be," when the sufferer should pray towards that house, and the Lord distinctly promised to do so. "If my people, which are called by my name, shall humble themselves, and pray and seek my face, and turn from their wicked ways: then will I hear from heaven, and will forgive their sin, and will heal their land." (2 Chr. vii. 13, 14).

When David's child was sick we read of no physician in the case; the prophet brought the word of the Lord. Even the mighty sinner Jeroboam knew where to send when disease struck his child, and so we find his wife going to the prophet of the Lord. And later on the stern rebuke and inexorable sentence of the Almighty are given to Ahaziah, because he sent to enquire of Baalzebub, and forgot that there was a God in Israel. Finally, on this line, the case of Asa stands out as the greatest lesson of the whole inspired record. He had been severely rebuked for trusting in the king of Syria instead of the Lord; but when he fell ill the lesson was not remembered, for we read, "And Asa was diseased in his feet, until his disease was exceeding great; yet in his disease he sought not to the Lord, but to the physicians. And Asa slept with his fathers and died." (2 Chr. xvi. 12, 13). Two hundred years later Hezekiah prayed earnestly, and the Lord miraculously healed him, employing as his messenger an inspired prophet, and not a physician, and in answer to the king's prayer the people also were healed. (2 Kings xx. 1-11, 2 Chr. xx. 15).

There is no mistaking the sense of the Word in these two instances. Asa failed to put his case in the Lord's hands, and sought human help instead. For this he died. But Hezekiah besought the Lord to heal him, even when the sentence of death had been pronounced, and for this appeal and manifestation of faith he lived; yet, when Hezekiah failed to clearly testify of God's healing to the Babylonish ambassadors, the judgment of heaven fell upon him also. (2 Chr. xxiii. 31, and 2 K. xx.12). Before leaving this period let the reader turn to Job xxxiii. 14-30, and see what a clear declaration it makes concerning God's purpose in sickness; and then we will be ready to take the next step in the argument.

So far we have builded on a rock. Divine healing for the Jew can not be disputed for a moment. But now, having traced it clearly in the Word to the closing days of the kingdom, it becomes necessary to show that it bridges the gulf between the kings and the advent of the Messiah. We have just seen Isaiah employed as an agent in a "faith-cure." Let us read what he has to say upon the subject. The great atonement chapter of the Old Testament gives us the following literal readings: "A man of pains and acquainted with sickness." (Verse 3). "Surely our sicknesses he hath borne, and our pains he hath carried them." (4). "And by his bruises there is healing to us." (5). "And Jehovah hath delighted to bruise him, he hath made him sick." (10). The above is Dr. Robert Young's translation, made of course without the faintest idea of assisting modern "faith-healers." Dr. Isaac Leeser gives a significant rendering of the fourth verse: "But only our diseases did he bear himself, and our pains he carried." Now in view of the facts developed in the preceding argument, what sort of mind would it have required in a Jew to say that this chapter only referred to spiritual blessings? But we are not left to human argument here. Without spending further time on such passages as Jer. xvii. 5-14, and xxxii. 2.; Ez. xxxiv. 2-16; Micah vi. 13, and Mal. iv. 2, we pass at once to the time of Christ.

From the very beginning of His ministry, Jesus Christ joined the body with the soul; and we read that He healed "all that had need of healing." In Matt. viii. 16, we find a commentary written by the Holy Spirit, which cannot possibly be explained away. "When even was come, they brought unto him many that were possessed with devils; and he cast out the spirits with his word, and healed all that were sick: that it might be fulfilled which was spoken by the prophet, saying: Himself took our infirmities, and bare our sicknesses." Here, then, the Holy Ghost informs us that the words of Isaiah did refer to the body. But the apostle Peter also quotes these same words for the soul, when he says: "Who his own self bare our sins in his own body on the tree." (1 Pet. ii. 24). Let him who can disprove the following:

If Peter can be relied on for the present day and generation, so can Matthew. And if Matthew's quotation has no force to-day, then neither has Peter's.

The Jew believes in a material kingdom; the Christian in a spiritual dominion. We claim that both are right in what they receive, and both are wrong in what they reject. The truth concerning salvation embraces the entire man, spirit, soul, and body. In the new dispensation we have not lost anything. There has not been a subtraction, but an addition. Jesus Christ did not abolish the decalogue, nor the moral law; the ceremonial only passed away. He came to fulfill, not to destroy. Our spiritual advantages in the dispensation of the Holy Ghost are not offset by a corresponding loss on the physical side. We are not playing at see-saw with the Jew. The laws of health and of healthy food have not changed since the days of Moses. We find trichinæ in pork, tape-worms in the hare; and equally good scientific reasons have been discovered for accepting nearly or quite all of the bill of fare laid down three thousand years ago. But let us follow the New Testament teaching on the subject.

Jesus Christ never turned away from those who sought healing at His hands. He specially commissioned the twelve to heal as well as to preach; and later the same commission was given to the seventy. (Luke ix. 1-6; and x. 1-19). The only limit to these benefits was unbelief, as is plainly declared in Mark vi. 5; and Luke, iv. 27. His last words, according to Mark, contain a positive promise of the "signs" which should "follow them that believe;" among which we find the healing of the sick through the laying on of hands. This was not a promise to the apostles, but to "them that believe". Some who have written against this doctrine have been so short-sighted as to point to the absence of these signs among certain prominent teachers, as proof that the day of such manifestations has passed. They are sadly illogical. The only correct inference is that these persons are troubled with unbelief, at least on this point; and their candid confession fully sustains such a conclusion.

The apostles took up the work of healing as a very important part of the gospel. "Such as I have give I thee," said Peter at the beautiful gate of the temple. Let us recall the significant words of the old Romish prelate, when his companion remarked, as he gave alms to a beggar, 'The church can no longer say with St. Peter, 'silver and gold have I none'," "True father, but neither can she say 'in the name of Jesus Christ of Nazareth, rise up and walk'." In those days a man, who like Stephen was full of the Holy Ghost and of faith, almost of necessity did great signs and wonders among the people; and simple healings abounded everywhere. When the unbelievers raged against them, the apostles did not merely ask for more grace to bear it, but actually prayed for "signs and wonders, in the name of Jesus." (Acts iv. 29).

In 1 Cor. vi. 13, Paul asserts that "the body is for the Lord, and the Lord for the body;" and in chap. xi. 30, he tells us of some who were sick, and others who died because of sin. Continuing his explanations to the Corinthians, we find several chapters devoted to the "gifts of the Spirit," among which "gifts of healing" are prominent. A little simple logic at this point will be of assistance. These gifts have precisely the same apostolic warrant as the "word of wisdom" or the "word of knowledge." The church has not thrown away "governments," indeed she is well nigh governed to death in these days; but the apostle, in verse 28, chap. xii. ranks this "gift" far below "healings," if there be any discrimination in the order of statement.

Again, the Holy Spirit brings to us "the earnest of our inheritance," (Eph. i. 14,). Part of this inheritance is to have "our mortal bodies quickened by his Spirit." (Rom. viii.11). "He that hath the Son hath life," and it is therefore concluded that "Christ formed within you the hope of glory" must or may give an earnest of the "purchased possession" not merely on one side—the spiritual, but on the physical as well. The body is to share in the glorification, hence the "earnest" includes the body. An impartation therefore of the Divine Life is looked for, in the body as well as in the soul, enabling the man to perform any and all God-directed work until the day of his departure arrives, or Christ comes the second time.

Finally, we have the unanswerable direction to the sick in Jas. v. 14, 15. "Is any sick among you? (among you believers) let him call for the elders of the church; and let them pray over him, anointing him with oil in the name of the Lord: and the prayer of faith shall save the sick, and the Lord shall raise him up; and if he have committed sins (as a cause of the complaint) they shall be forgiven him." Concerning this passage John Wesley remarks, in his Notes on the New Testament, in accord with Bengel, ("This single conspicuous gift, which Christ committed to His apostles, remained in the church long after the miraculous gifts were withdrawn. Indeed it seems to have been designed to remain always, and St. James directs the elders, who were the most, if not the only gifted men, to administer it. This was the whole process of physic in the Christian church, till it was lost through unbelief." This statement of Wesley's brings up the question as to the progress made in medical science in the time of Christ. A very few quotations will suffice.

We find in the Homeric poems abundant evidence that, at that early day, medicine as a science was by no means a new thing. "And there is no sign given of the subordination of medicine to religion, nor were priests charged with medical functions . . . circumstances which throw grave doubts on the commonly received opinion that medicine derived its origin in all countries from religious observances." (Enc. Brit.) Hippocrates the Great (B. C. 460) was a voluminous writer, a close observer, and a skillful physician. He mentions no less than two hundred and sixty-five drugs in his various works, besides many dietary and surgical remedies or methods. In all chronic cases he chiefly relied upon diet, exercise and such natural methods. After him arose two schools under Herophilus of Chalcedon, a profound anatomist and a renowned physician, and his rival Erasistratus. (Doctors disagreed in those days as well as at present). Alexandria, the seat of learning, received the followers of both, and was the scene of a long controversy between them. Erasistratus and his disciples employed a "great variety of drugs." (Enc. Brit.) After these arose the Empiric school (280 B. C.) whose physicians were "extremely successful in practical matters, especially in surgery and the use of drugs, and a large part of the routine knowledge of diseases and remedies, which became traditional in the times of the Roman empire, is believed to have been derived from them." (Enc. Brit.) Asclepiades, the friend of Cicero, (124 B. C.) founded a system known as "Methodism." His knowledge of disease and surgical skill was very considerable. In the treatment of sickness he laid great stress upon "diet, exercise, passive movements or frictions, and the external use of cold water;" in short, a modified athletic training. This is surely sufficient to convince the most skeptical that oil was only one of hundreds of remedies current among the physicians of the time.

Before leaving this passage in James let us read no less an authority than Dean Alford. He says, " 'shall save' . . . already here, considering that the forgiveness of sin is afterwards stated separately, *sosei* can *only* be used of *corporeal healing*, not of the salvation of the soul . . . The anointing was not a mere human medium of cure, but had a sacramental character. (The same words are used of baptism, Matt. xxviii. 19; Acts ii. 38; x. 48; xix. 5.) . . The apostle is enforcing the efficacy of prayer in afflictions, verse 13. Of such efficacy he adduces one special instance. In sickness, let the sick man inform the elders of the church. Let them, representing the congregation of the faithful, pray over the sick man, accompanying that prayer with the symbolic and sacramental act of anointing with oil in the name of the Lord. Then the prayer of faith shall save (heal) the sick man, and the Lord shall bring him up out of his sickness; and even if it were occsasioned by some sin, that sin shall be forgiven him. Such is the simple and undeniable sense of the apostle, arguing for the efficacy of prayer. . . . Observe the promises here made of recovery and forgiveness are unconditional, as in Mark xvi., 18 al. . . And pray for one another that ye may be healed in case of sickness, as above. The context here forbids any wider meaning."

Death is a consequence of sin, and is unmistakably a part of the curse of the law. But "Christ hath redeemed us from the curse of the law," Gal. iii. 13), and a logical conclusion leads us to believe in translation, were it not for the special scripture which steps in on this point, as it certainly does not in the case of sickness, and declares that: "It is appointed unto men once to die." (Heb. ix, 27). Read also Rom. viii. 10-23; 1

Cor. xv. 23-32; Col. iii. 4; Heb. ii. 8; and ix. 28. These texts withhold the boon of translation from the direct covenant, and retain it in the special providence of God, except for the living, waiting saints at the second advent. They have its sure promise.

"Jesus Christ, the same, yesterday, to-day, and for ever," is a tremendous declaration. Now we have seen that the promises of God most undeniably contain the assurance of physical health, conditioned on obedience. These promises have not been outlawed by time. We cannot throw them away without sacrificing the decalogue itself and all the moral law. An unbroken line of leaders, kings and prophets carry them down to the gospel dispensation in which we live. These promises of God then are ours to-day. But upon what is their efficacy based? In 2 Cor. i. 20, we read, "For all the promises of God in Him are yea, and in Him amen, unto the glory of God by us." These are included in the "all;" therefore, they are yea and amen in Christ. And this simply means that they owe their existence and power entirely and solely to the vicarious atonement of our Lord and Saviour. There is no escape from this conclusion. The atonement gives life to the promises; and the promises, beyond all dispute, provide physical health, as well as soul healing. The conditions to-day are the same as of old. We must believe, and obey. Belief is faith, and obedience is works. "Faith without works is dead;" so belief and simple obedience cannot be separated. When Naaman joined his obedience to his belief, and dipped in Jordan, faith and works were united, and salvation resulted. It is ever so.

THE PRACTICE.

1. "Faith-healers" believe in the use of means. The Scriptural means are always employed:—1. Laying on of hands. 2. Anointing with oil. 3. The prayer of faith. They believe in occasional special leadings of the Spirit to employ other means, which may be inherently efficacious or not.

2. No one is advised to lay aside all medicines, by any prominent teacher or leader, unless he can do so with perfect spontaneity. A forced abstinence from drugs is mere will power, not faith.

3. Faith in the patient is regarded as necessary when the individual is responsible. Even the man borne by his friends, and let down through the roof, had to obey the command, "Rise, take up thy bed." Special exceptions to this are known, where the individuals have not even been aware of the prayer offered in their behalf. These would be included under a promise like that in Jas. v. 16, "Pray one for another that ye may be healed," as general answers to prayer. They are certainly conclusive against the supposition of a "mental subjective condition" in the patient.

4. A perfect consecration of the whole spirit, soul and body, as a "liv-

ing sacrifice," is strongly urged. All are taught that it is almost blasphemous to ask for healing with any other view than the entire devotement to God of the renewed powers. Hence the universal experience of spiritual blessings in those seeking healing.

5. Inquirers are instructed to believe they do receive, *when* the Spirit witnesses within that their consecration and obedience are complete, and the prayer has been offered. They are to believe this on the simple warrant of the Word. "What things soever ye desire, when ye pray, believe that ye receive them, and ye shall have them." This is in precise accord with the method pursued with those seeking salvation. "Believe and receive" is the formula that always applies. A man acts out his real belief; hence the patient is told to act as if he were well, (if he can do so in faith). The leaders in this movement have themselves received life and health while following this same plan of action; and therefore give this advice with all knowledge and honesty.

6. The laying on of hands, or prayer and anointing, are distinctly taught to be of no efficacy in themselves, any more than Jordan was to Naaman. But it is held that "to obey is better than sacrifice."

7. God has chosen to save men through the "foolishness of preaching," yet all who hear are not saved. In precisely the same way, all for whom prayer is offered are not healed: This, however, affords no excuse for the abolition of either preaching or praying. Lists of failures are not kept in either case; and the real reason lies in the fact presented in the beginning of this article, that the doctrines of Christianity are not founded upon phenomena, but upon the Word of God alone.

8. All who intelligently weigh the meaning of words, counsel the use of such expressions as will clearly convey the correct idea. A man who is exercising faith, but finds his symptoms continue, is advised to say, I believe I am healed, on the warrant of the promise. He is told not to say he feels, but he believes.

9. It is taught that Satan can tempt to sickness, precisely as he can tempt to inward sin; by producing a symptom. He can consistently advise the use of a medicine to one who is striving to fix his faith on God's power alone, especially when he thinks that the remedy will accomplish nothing. (In any case it is as consistent as the actions of those good people who profess to believe that it is the will of God for them to suffer, and at the same time spend time and wealth on every conceivable medicine in the attempt to defeat that will by getting well.)

10. Finally, it is distinctly taught that Divine Healing, like every branch of salvation, is a matter for personal experience, and as such is not susceptible of perfectly logical explanation to the unbeliever. To him all such things are "foolishness," but "to us who believe" they become "the power of God." Every saved or healed man can testify from his heart, "One thing I know, that whereas I was blind, now I see," though he may utterly fail to convince the Scribes and Pharisees.

DIVINE HEALING.

True or false, there is no belief rising more swiftly before the churches everywhere than that of Divine Healing. There are over thirty "faith-homes" in America to-day. In England, and on the continent of Europe, can be found a large number; some of them commodious institutions with a history of many decades of years. In June 1885 an International Conference on this subject assembled in London, composed of delegates from all parts of the world, and the great Agricultural Hall was taxed to its utmost to accomodate the serious crowds that flocked to hear. During the last two seasons a number of conventions have been held in New York, Brooklyn, Philadelphia, Baltimore, Pittsburg, Detroit, and elsewhere, in all of which Divine Healing has claimed an important part. The mass of evidence offered, the multitude of witnesses arising and the words of Scripture on the subject demand at least a respectful hearing, and invite the closest scrutiny into the doctrine and practice of Divine Healing.

DIVINE HEALING.

CHAPTER I.

PARDON OF PAST SIN.

"Who his own self bare our sins in his own body on the tree, that we, being dead to sins, should live unto righteousness."—1 Pet. ii. 24.

It is hardly necessary to attempt to show that the Atonement was intended to cover committed sin. This little book is written primarily for Christians, and of course there is not a Christian on the face of the earth who does not believe that the death of our Lord provides a full and free pardon for all our past sins, and all our past unrighteousness. Nevertheless it may be well to quote Scripture on this point, that the whole argument may be presented together.

"Who was delivered for our offences, and was raised again for our justification."—Rom. iv. 25.

"For all have sinned, and come short of the glory of God; being justified freely by his grace through the redemption that is in Christ Jesus; whom God hath set forth to be a propitiation through faith in his blood, to declare his righteousness for the *remission of sins that are past*, through the forbearance of God."—Rom. iii. 23-25.

"By him all that believe are justified from all things."—Acts xiii. 39.

"All we like sheep have gone astray; we have turned every one to his own way; and the Lord hath laid on him the iniquity of us all."—Isa. liii. 6.

"Thou wilt cast all their sins into the depths of the sea."—Micah vii. 19.

"I, even I, am he that blotteth out thy transgressions for mine own sake, and will not remember thy sins."—Isa. xliii. 25.

"I have blotted out, as a thick cloud, thy transgressions, and as a cloud, thy sins; return unto me; for I have redeemed thee."—Isa. xliv. 22.

"He made intercession for the transgressors."—Isa. liii. 12.

"Bless the Lord, O my soul, and forget not all his benefits: who forgiveth all thine iniquities."—Ps. ciii. 2, 3.

"And he shall redeem Israel from all his iniquities."—Ps. cxxx. 8.

Of course we could consume hours in simply reading the Scriptures upon this point. Jesus Christ came into the world to save sinners; and every Christian believes, if he believes at all, that the Atonement covers all his past sins and all his past unrighteousness, up to the present moment. He who does not believe this, directly confesses that he would be lost if he should instantly die. The pardon of past sin is, of necessity, the first boon to the sinner. He feels condemned; his offenses are like mill-stones about his neck, and he cries unto God for release from the death sentence, which he can feel hanging over his head. Having obtained pardon, the soul feels justified by faith, and has peace with God, through our Lord Jesus Christ. Christ becomes the Elder Brother, and "Our Father" rises to the lips, and thus, Adoption is realized.

Many Christians live for years on the very first round of the ladder. They have received pardon for past offences, and nothing more. They do not feel fully justified up to the present moment; have very little peace, and do not dare to declare their adoption into the family of the Lord. Are you a Christian? is answered with evident reluctance by the hesitating, "I hope so." But all such are fully aware of their privilege and duty in the premises. They know that they ought to have peace, to feel sure of their pardon, and to know the family to which they belong well enough to declare their relationship without any misgivings. This full experience and faith constitute justification.

Just here I call special attention to the fact that justification, in the very nature of the case and of the word, has reference only to the past. Even Dr. Charles Hodge frankly acknowledges the "apparent solecism" in speaking of the pardon or justification of future sins. To most men's minds such language is an actual solecism. My own common sense tells me that I can not be pardoned to-day for sins that will be committed to-morrow. The Romanist buys an "indulgence" for future sin; but even the daring presumption of a John Tetzel never ventured to call these licenses by the name of pardon. And I most earnestly maintain that the man who teaches that, at conversion, the soul is justified from all the sins of the past, and from all the sins of the future, is just as much preaching an indulgence for sin, as ever did the famous monk of Reformation times. Hear Ezekiel:

"But when the righteous turneth away from his righteousness, and committeth iniquity, and doeth according to all the abominations that the wicked man doeth, shall he live? All his righteousness that he hath done shall not be mentioned: in his trespass that he hath trespassed, and in his sin that he hath sinned, in them shall he die."—Ezek. xviii. 24.

"The righteousness of the righteous shall not deliver him in the day of his transgression; neither shall the righteous be able to live for his righteousness in the day that he sinneth."—Ezek. xxxiii. 12.

The Church needs a radical reformation to-day on this point. There are too many indulgences sold. The successors of John Tetzel proclaim to-day you can not live without sin; therefore the Atonement pardons you in advance for the unavoidable transgressions of the morrow.

Ezekiel is not read, and a false theology paralyzes the activities of many souls. My brother, realize the truth. Pardon refers to the past. Justification establishes your present standing, not your future actions. Jesus Christ grants no indulgences for sin. But learn that there is a wider and deeper experience than this. Something more is included in the Atonement. Open your eyes; reach forth your hands; go boldly on, and you shall obtain.

CHAPTER II.

KEPT FROM FALLING.

"Unto him who is able to keep you from falling, and to present you faultless before the presence of his glory with exceeding joy, to the only wise God our Saviour, be glory and majesty, dominion and power, both now and ever. Amen."—Jude 25.

There are many precious promises of Scripture given to "him that overcometh," and every true Christian struggles manfully to overcome sin, both outward and inward. We are told by the large majority of the Church, that it is possible to get the victory over all outward transgressions, so that we will give no visible display of anger, resentment, malice, envy or uncharitableness; that this can be accomplished through the agencies of constant prayer and unceasing watchfulness; but that we can not hope to avoid all inward sin, much less to be free from the taint of the natural heart. Dr. Charles Hodge, representing the more rigid school, assures us that an "advanced Christian" will find himself "sinning, even daily, in thought, word and deed." Mr. Moody may be cited as the leading representative of a school that believes that God's grace is sufficient for all trials and temptations, and that by this grace we can have the victory always in thought, word and deed; but that this is always a victory over a real enemy who dwells *within* the soul to the very hour of death. In other words, this latter theory does not accept the entire extermination of the inbeing of sin, but maintains that the roots are still within the heart, and require the most constant repression to prevent sprouting.

It may be said that this last is surely all that is necessary, since it certainly embraces the idea of being actually "kept from falling." Undoubtedly it is much superior to the others; but I maintain that even this theory *positively limits the Atonement of Christ.* The Wesleyan theory, however, presents as possible, to every believer who will fill the conditions of absolute consecration, unhesitating faith, and constant confession, an experience of Christ's saving power, deep enough to root up every trace of inbred depravity, and to utterly exterminate the inbeing of sin. In this experience there is a war, it is true, an unremitting conflict with the power of darkness; but it is a battle in which, like God's people of old, we "stand still and see the salvation of the Lord." We "do not need to fight in this battle," but simply trust Jesus to do it all for us. We "shout for the Lord *hath given* us the city," and do not lift a finger in the struggle, except in the exercise of our faith in the perfect work of Jesus.

There is a very important element of faith and of doctrine contained in this last idea of the Atonement, which is practically wanting in each of the others. Only in the Wesleyan view of the matter is the Atonement believed to be *instantaneous* in its application to unrighteousness, or inward depravity. Even the Moody, or Plymouth Brethren, theory, grand as it is, looks upon the Atonement as incapable of relieving the soul from the load of inherited evil disposition until the very hour of death. Perhaps the word "incapable" would be rejected; but it does not alter the sense in the least to say that the Atonement was not designed to cleanse the soul completely before the hour and article of death. The practical result to the experience of the soul is that Jesus' sacrifice *can not* remove the troublesome roots of sin.

The Scripture being the *only* authority, let us notice a few points:

To the tempted I quote: "God is faithful, who will not suffer you to be tempted above that ye are able; but will with the temptation also make a way to escape, that ye may be able to bear it."—1 Cor. x. 13.

"Now thanks be unto God, which *always* causeth us to triumph in Christ."—2 Cor. ii. 14. If the dread of sins of thought rise before you, read, "For the weapons of our warfare are not carnal, but mighty through God to the pulling down of strongholds; casting down *imaginations*, and every high thing that exalteth itself against the knowledge of God, and bringing into captivity *every thought* to the obedience of Christ."—2 Cor. x. 4, 5. And if this seem impossible, remember the challenge of the Almighty, "Is anything too hard for the Lord?"—Gen. xviii. 14; and the specific promise, ringing down from the ancient times. "And the Lord thy God will circumcise thine heart, and the heart of thy seed, to love the Lord thy God with all thine heart, and with all thy soul, that thou mayest live."—Deut. xxx. 6. Read also, Ezek. xxxvi. 25-29; 1 Jno. i. 7; Jude 24, Heb. vii. 25.

Now this little book is founded entirely upon the grand central truth, that ample provision was made upon Calvary for the actual and practical destruction of the works of the devil—sin and sickness. When Jesus cried

"IT IS FINISHED"

He expressed this fundamental fact. He came to "destroy the works of the devil;" and when He said that mission was accomplished, I propose to believe Him. I am not shutting my eyes to the fact that death is a work of the devil. Undoubtedly it is, but we have this provided for in Scripture, and are told that "death the last enemy *shall be* destroyed." I read in Revelation that in the eternal city there shall be no sorrow or sighing, no tears or tribulation, and no night; but I do not read that there shall be no sin or sickness. Now if it be a fact that we must sin and sicken up to the moment of our entrance into glory, why did not the Revelator mention the new and wondrous experience of the glorified saints in heaven? He thought it worth while to write down the exemption from sorrow and tears. Ah! John remembered the words of Jesus, "In the world ye shall have tribulation;" "Blessed are ye, when men shall revile you, and persecute you, and shall say all manner of evil against you falsely, for my sake. Rejoice, and be exceeding glad: for great is your *reward in heaven*." John knew well that no saint would ever be free from these things, while in the flesh, and so he pictures the delights of the holy city when "God shall wipe away all tears from their eyes; and there shall be no more death, neither sorrow, nor crying, neither shall there be any more pain;* for the former things are passed away." And he it was who wrote, "whosoever is born of God doth not commit sin," for "if we walk in the light, as He is in the light, we have fellowship one with another; and the blood of Jesus Christ, His Son, cleanseth us from all sin." He, of all others, clearly taught that the Christain should be entirely free from sin, in this life; and therefore he did not mention the exemption from sin in heaven, for this would be nothing new to the soul that is completely washed in the blood. It may be suggested that the absence of temptation in the new Jerusalem is not specified either. To this I reply that, where there is no sorrow, no crying, no tears, no death and no devil, there could not be any temptation. Of course a perfectly pure heart could not be tempted from the inside; temptation must come from without, as in the case of Eve; and when "death, the last enemy" has been destroyed, and Satan eternally consigned to his prison home, manifestly there could be no temptation. It goes without saying. Besides, we may easily claim that "sorrow, crying, tears." etc., obviously include the idea of temptation; for what Christian does not know, that a sorrow, which does not present the *temptation* to doubt God in some way, is not worthy of the name?

I have thus briefly defined the true doctrine of the Atonement for the soul. It embraces pardon from past sins and past uncleanness; and cleansing from all traces of inherited depravity, as well as the keeping power against sin in any form, outward or inward. The Atonement of Jesus Christ is a finished sacrifice, once for all, for my sins of commission and of omission, and for inbred sins; and of course provides for a maintenance of cleanness in my soul. As this is the familiar branch of the subject, I will not write more upon it: but will refer the reader to such works as

---

* This word, in the original, is *ponos*. The primary meaning of this word, as given by Robinson, by Pickering and others, is *work, labor, toil, travail, etc.* The secondary meaning may be pain, but more the in sense of distress, trouble, misery, injustice, etc. The word is derived, by Robinson, from *peno*. It is thus abundantly proven that the idea of disease is not suggested at all.

Wesley's Sermon on Perfection; his Plain Account of Christian Perfection; Bishop Foster's Christian Purity; Geo. D. Watson's Holiness Manual; Wm. McDonald's Scriptural Views of Holiness; the first Epistle general of John, and St. Paul's letter to the Hebrews. The latter is a regular, systematic treatise on the doctrine of Entire Sanctification, and anyone who reads it honestly, before God, will surely find "the way into the holiest." Praise the Lord!

CHAPTER III.

HEALING OF BODILY DISEASE.

"Who healeth ALL thy diseases."—Ps. ciii. 3.

By the grace of God I expect to show that the Atonement has provided for the body all it has provided for the soul. As this is a feature of Christ's sacrifice which has been largely buried beneath a mass of skepticism, doubts, unbelief and forgetfulness, it will require much more space than has been devoted to the preceding chapters.

Of course every true Christian readily admits that God can cure bodily sickness; and that He has often done so, and done it in answer to prayer. There are few families in the land who can not point to some incident of this kind. A dear one had come nigh unto death; physician's skill was exhausted, and no hope remained. But in their extremity they called upon God, and suddenly the symptoms changed, and the patient recovered. A single sample will suffice. The young son of a Methodist minister was slowly but surely choking to death with membranous croup. The father gathered together several brother ministers, and together they knelt about the bed and besought God to spare the child. While they thus prayed, a spasm of coughing seized him, a hard mass of phlegm was dislodged, and the boy recovered. This was many years ago, and he is still living. Of such a case as this the doubter exclaims—"Why he was going to cough anyhow, and the result was merely a happy accident;" but the Christian readily yields the glory to God. Everyone knows that such occurrences as this are without number in the history of the Christian Church.

Now I wish to call special attention to the fact that such a case can never be cited as an illustration of the special power of God, without the fear of contradiction, based upon apparent reason. The unbeliever either in or out of the church, says that we cannot possibly prove any interference with the laws of nature. The physician was on hand, and his medicine had been administered. The very tendency of these remedies was to clear out the throat; and when this very result was accomplished, why not credit it to the physician? Even in the case of a remarkable physical transformation, as the straightening of a curved spine, the same reasoning prevails; for have not physicians often succeeded in such cases? The devout Christian is perfectly willing to concede that God did the work potentially, and that the patient would have died without the divine interference; but he believes that it was done through the legitimate channels of the means used by the nurse and physician.

With none of these theories and beliefs have we anything whatever to do. The position to be stated and sustained in this chapter is, that *God now heals bodily sickness, precisely as He now heals soul sickness, by His power alone, unaided by any means whatever; and that He does it through and by virtue of the perfect Atonement of Jesus Christ.*

I do not propose to burden this little work with numerous instances of healing. Any one who is skeptical is referred to "Pastor Blumhardt," "Faith Cures," "The Great Physician," "Dorothea Trüdel," "Healing of Sickness by Scriptural Means," "Prayer of Faith," etc., all of which can be obtained from the Willard Tract Repositories in Boston, New York, or Philadelphia. I can never speak or write upon this subject, however, without giving my personal testimony. Three able physicians in Baltimore, and two in Philadelphia, agreed in pronouncing my trouble to be heart disease, and incurable; although they all hoped to benefit me. In this respect, however they all failed. After seven years of sickness I consecrated all to God, believed His word, called upon His servant, Dr. Chas. Cullis, and was prayed with according to James v., 14, 15, with the laying on of hands and the anointing with oil in the name of the Lord. From that day to this—over eight years—I have never touched any form of medicine or remedy. Praise the dear Lord alone! I am well. I do more work than I ever did before, look to Him alone for strength and health, and He never leaves me nor forsakes me. For full particulars of my case, see "Miracles of Healing" and the Appendix to this book. Of course I understand that the doubter will say that there is no absolute proof of miraculous intervention. While it is true the doctors can not get the glory, yet my imagination, force of will, etc., did the thing for me; and probably the doctors were mistaken in their diagnosis, as they often are.

For those who ask for still more convincing evidence of modern miracles of healing, I suggest the reading of the case of a broken arm,*

---

* This case has gained considerable notoriety through the attempted denial of its correctness by the subject himself, Dr. Carl H. Reed, of Philadelphia. This denial is published in a little pamphlet against "Faith Cures," issued by Dr. James Hendrie Lloyd, of the Pennsylvania University. The young man says:

"DEAR SIR: The case you cite, when robbed of all its sensational surroundings, is as follows:

"The child was a spoiled youngster who would have his own way, and when he had a '*green stick*' fracture of the forearm, and having had it bandaged for several days, concluded he would much prefer going *without* a splint. . . .

"To please the spoiled child the splint was removed and the arm carefully adjusted in a restored in a single night, recorded in "The Great Physician," and "Dorothea Trüdel," and of the numerous cases found in the "Life of Pastor Blumhardt," and in the two volumes of "Faith Cures," by Dr. Cullis.

These will suffice. I unhesitatingly assert that the evidence for the miraculous healing of disease through faith in Jesus, is every whit as clear and undeniable as is the evidence of the conversion of any soul in the last eighteen hundred years. How do you come to believe that a soul is truly converted? By the profession of faith in Jesus, and by the visible change in the outward life. How do you know that a sick body has been healed by the power of Jesus? By the evident change in the physical life, and by the profession of faith in the Healer. *The evidence is precisely the same.* "One thing I know, that whereas I was blind, now I see," is a kind of testimony that never has been and never can be successfully answered. The Lord takes care to provide such overwhelming manifestations of His power that even the "magicians can not do so with their enchantments." In our day, however, men, and Christians, even, have found a way of "withstanding," that exceeds Jannes and Jambres themselves. They refuse to accept the more ordinary testimonies of healing, attributing the results to the power of will and imagination.* They incredulously ask for absolute physical evidence, such as the reuniting of a broken limb, but when this is given, as above, the prompt reply is a flat 'I don't believe it." †

---

sling. As a matter of course, the bone soon united, as is customary in children, and being only partially broken, of course all the sooner. This is the miracle!

"Some nurse, or crank, or religious enthusiast, ignorant of matters physiological and histological, evidently started the story, and unfortunately my name—for I am the party—is being circulated in circles of faith curites, and is given the sort of notoriety I do not crave.

"I have been pestered with letters on the subject from ministers and members of the fraternity, who seek to rob us of our patients, but have consigned all such letters to my waste-basket. . . . I take pleasure in giving you these few notes, trusting they will satisfy your mind in regard to this example of faith-cure.

"Very respectfully yours, "CARL H. REED."

The feeling of foolish shame which so obviously animated the writer of this note is to be sincerely mourned by every Christian reader of the simple narrative of the wonderful cure as related in the two books referred to; and the rashness of the denial will be most painfully apparent when I state that the "nurse, or crank, or religious enthusiast, *ignorant of matters physiological and histological,*" who "started the story," was his own father, himself a physician of wide experience, who personally related the incident, a short time after its occurrence, to Dr. Cullis, just as it is recorded in "Dorothea Trüdel," and to Dr. Boardman, just as it is found in "The Great Physician."

* The new school of "mind physicians" in Boston, and elsewhere, is already referred to by Christians as proof that healing is only the result of mental power.

† I once said to a prominent Presbyterian clergyman of Philadelphia : Doctor, what would you say if I told you that for seven years I suffered from chronic heart disease, and that for seven years I have been well, in answer to the prayer of faith?

He promptly replied, "I say that if you had the heart disease, I don't believe you are well, and if you are well, I don't believe you ever had it."

Such unbelief as that is simply invincible. Even the Pharisees of Peter's day did not go quite so far. They admitted that a great miracle had been done, and could not be denied; but studied to prevent the spread of the new faith. See Acts iv. 17.

HEALING OF BODILY DISEASE. 29

This is the root of the whole opposition—unbelief. The absolute tendency of the natural heart is to oppose God at any and every possible point. This is the real secret of the partial acceptance of the wretched and absurd theory of evolution by so many Christians. A so-called natural cause is assigned for a result, previously accredited to the miraculous power of God. In fact it may be safely asserted that the leading tendency of the world to-day, is to minify God's power. We are living in an age when it is fashionable and popular to favor any *anti-miraculous* theory that can possibly trumped up. The devil has forced upon the world a pet phrase, until it has become a proverb: *The days of miracles have passed.* And most people regard this proverb as much more authentic than any old King Solomon ever wrote. We find recorded in the sayings of the wise man, such as these: "My son, attend to my words: . . . For they are life unto those that find them, and health to all their flesh." Prov. iv. 20, 22. "For by me thy days shall be multiplied, and the years of thy life shall be increased." Prov. ix. 11. "Why shouldest thou die before thy time?" Eccles. vii. 17. But the number who are willing to take God's word at its face value, without any discount, is exceedingly small. A man, who calls himself a minister of the gospel, recently stated in his pulpit that "nobody nowadays, *except the unintelligent*, thinks of believing the Bible to be an inspired book."

> Men don't believe in a devil now,
>   As their father's used to do;
> They've forced the door of the broadest creed,
>   To let his majesty through."

expresses the sentiment of a large portion of the "intelligent" church goers of our day. Truly the tree of knowledge has always proved a dangerous possession.

In face of all this skepticism, however, there are many Christians who will freely admit that God has done many wonderful things in answer to prayer, and that the like may be expected to occur again. But they assure us that such cases are sporadic, and do not afford the least foundation for the belief in a general theory of healing through faith. They even seek to explain these events by the supposed operations of certain natural laws.

Now let us honestly consider this matter of seeking to explain miracles. I do not hesitate to pronounce any such attempt as radically wrong, and as very dangerous to the spirit of childlike faith, without which, Jesus said, we cannot enter the kingdom. When the late General O. M. Mitchell delivered his eloquent astronomical lectures throughout the country, he sought to present a possible scientific theory for the miracle of the sun's stoppage at the command of Joshua. He showed that it could have been done without arresting the revolution of the earth, by simply condensing the atmosphere, and thereby vastly increasing its refractive powers. I do not wholly condemn such a theoretical explanation, but on the contrary, heartily approve of it, *provided* it is used in its legitimate place. The only real use for any of these so-called reconciliations of science and Scripture, is to prepare the way in the natural heart of an *unbeliever* for the faith that must follow, and to afford the Christian a confirmation of the truth that God is perfect harmony. Most men stumble over their heads with such persistency that they must be knocked down, like Paul, upon their own chosen pathway, and positively stricken blind or dumb, before they can receive the simple truth. But the moment any soul that has been to the fountain of cleansing for the pardon of sin, and has been adopted into the family of God, seeks to find a more intimate knowledge of God, and to see more of His deep things, all such "explanations" must be thrown away. "The entrance of thy word giveth light," is the only efficacious recipe. *A "son of God," must be content to take his Father's word without any endorsement.**

It is entirely possible and even extremely probable, that all the miracles of the Bible were performed by God, through laws just as absolute and infallible as the attraction of gravitation itself. I have no doubt whatever that, if the Lord saw fit to explain to me just how He severed the lower waters of the Jordan from those that came down from above, I would understand it just as clearly and as scientifically as I do the statement that, "the Lord caused the Red Sea to go back by a strong east wind all that night." Divine wisdom saw fit to tell us the *modus operandi* of this miracle, but not of the other. When Henry Varley went into Captain Black's cabin and, kneeling down with him and his officers, prayed God to stop the terrible cyclone, which threatened them with speedy death; who could have imagined any natural law, by which the natural results of those terrific waves could be averted? Yet, while he prayed, a mighty hail-storm beat the dashing billows as smooth as though they were covered with oil, and the terrible wind fell calm. Even so, I believe that the opening of the deaf ears, the raising of the dead, the healing of the broken arm, and all the list of miraculous works of God are certainly and clearly explicable by natural laws, and that there is no such thing in God's universe as the temporary abolition of His established principles. In order to stop those waves God did not annihilate the laws of momentum and inertia, but actually used these very principles to accomplish the result. Left to themselves those waves would have continued to break long enough to demolish the vessel; but Omnipotence used the momentum of the frozen hail to check the momentum of the liquid water. God can insert an unseen key in the great clock of the stars and wheel them backwards in their orbits, as easily as I can in the same manner, reverse the hands of my watch. The natural law of gravity ordains that the boat shall float with the stream, but the natural law of the steam's expansive force propels the

---

* When a Christian reads such grand "explanations" as Prof. Vail's "Annular Theory of the Creation and Deluge," and receives therefrom new ideas of God's wonderful power and perfectly harmonious work, all is well.

HEALING OF BODILY DISEASE.

vessel in the opposite direction. The natural law of motion insists that a body shall move in a straight line, yet the natural law of the peculiar twists imparted to the base-ball, actually causes it to curve, first to the right and then to the left; and for a similar reason the twisting rifle-ball turns from its proper course. Every time a bird flies, an animal moves, or a piece of machinery is put in motion, we have before our eyes just as much a "violation" of natural law, as when God's hand parted the crystal gates of the sea for the marching hosts of Israel. In other words, *we see an example of one natural law dominating another.*

But, all this being admitted, I still insist that any attempt at an explanation of a miracle, which God has not seen fit to explain, is dangerous to an advancing faith. We should of course settle the great fact that "all things are possible with God," but it is not necessary to stumble over apparent or imaginary contradictions in order to reach a little of the "all things possible to him that believeth." We are to believe God blindly it is true—that is faith—but we are not required to believe unreasonably. I am asked, how can the Lord heal a fatal case of sickness without flying in the face of law? I answer, how. could he stop a cyclone? My belief thus becomes perfectly reasonable, while it is perfectly blind, *as all absolute faith must be.* Nicodemus has an enormous family, who are always betraying their descent by the question, "How can these things be?" When the doubting ministers said, "How can we hope to accomplish anything in India;" the soldier Duke of Wellington, replied, "That is none of your business. You have your marching orders, 'Go ye into all the world, and preach my gospel to every creature.' You have nothing to do with the results; obey your orders." Nicodemus was not an infidel, but a godly man; and whenever the true Christian asks Nicodemus' question after God's word, he is sure to miss the power of that word.

Many a Christian almost indignantly resents the imputation that he does not believe God just as much as any other man; but of course his belief is absolutely governed by his light. If I say to him, I believe what God says; he responds, so do I. But when I adduce certain promises of Scripture for faith healing, he immediately insists upon confining them to the Apostolic age, or gives them a forced spiritual interpretation, entirely at variance with the plain sense of the language. Yet he says he believes God as much as I do. Manifestly, if I am right, he does not believe as much as I, but stops short at the limit of the light he has received. I always praise the Lord for that word of Holy Writ, "Knowing this first that no prophecy of the Scripture is of any private interpretation. For the prophecy came not in old time by the will of man (no prophecy ever came by the will of man, Rev. Ver.): but holy men of old spake as they were moved by the Holy Ghost." 2 Pet. i. 20, 21.

We thus come face to face with those words of power and executive ability first recorded in Gen. i. 3. "God said." When Jesus was tempted of the devil, his only answer was, "It is written," and so Paul only gives us a single weapon of offense—"the sword of the Spirit, which is the word of God." We need various pieces of armour for defense; the helmet, shield, and breast-plate; but when we seek to advance from one battle-field to another, when we sally forth to win a new victory over the foe, we need a sword, and that sword is always the same that formed from chaos the rolling worlds—"God said." This "Word was in the beginning with God, and the word was God," and "in Him was light and the light was the life of men." This is the Word whose "entrance giveth light." Let us always remember the simple recipe for faith—"Faith cometh by hearing, and hearing by the Word of God." Rom. x. 17.

We now come, in logical sequence, to the question, what hath God said on the subject of healing bodily disease? Let it be borne in mind that I am not writing this chapter merely to prove that some people have been healed, but to show that the Atonement of Jesus Christ actually embraced sickness as well as sin: in short, that God is ready to heal any disease through faith, just as He heals sin through faith.

In Gen. xviii. we read of God's promise to heal Sarah of a physical infirmity; and, although twenty-five years elapsed before the work was accomplished, yet it was done "through faith." See Heb. xi. 11. In Gen. xx. 7–17, we find God directing Abimelech to go not to the physicans, but to the prophet Abraham for the prayer of faith; and in answer to that prayer his whole household was healed. Some years after we read of Isaac's prayer for his wife, "and the Lord was intreated of him." Gen. xxv. 21; and later still Jacob indignantly rejected the thought that anyone but God could act as a physician. See Gen. xxx. 1, 2.

After two hundred years their descendents passed through the crystal gates of the Red Sea, and sang God's praises for the greatest national deliverance in all history. Here, upon the very threshold of their new life Jehovah gave them a distinct promise which for clearness cannot be excelled in Scripture. "If thou wilt diligently hearken to the voice of the Lord thy God, and wilt do that which is right in his sight, and wilt give ear to his commandments, and keep all his statutes, I will put none of these diseases upon thee, which I have brought upon the Egyptians. For I am the Lord that healeth thee (or, the Lord thy healer)." Ex. xv. 26.

After a short time, during which the Israelites proved that even in battle God alone is the disposer of results, for only when Moses' hands were held up did they prevail; they came to Sinai, and received the decalogue. Here we find a distinct promise of health and life, *conditioned on obedience.*

1. "Honor thy father and thy mother, as the Lord thy God hath commanded thee; that thy *days may be prolonged,* and that it may go well with thee, in the land which the Lord thy God giveth thee."—Deut. v. 16. "The first commandment with promise," promises what? Simply physical life as a consequence of obeying God in honoring our parents.

HEALING OF BODILY DISEASE.

But physical life and our experience " in the land" are under the " natural laws." Here then in the decalogue itself we find the fundamental truth that God will physically preserve the *obedient*. I praise the dear Lord for this grand evidence that the remission of sickness was included in His plan. The *only* commandment that carries a distinct promise, assures us that life and prosperity alike are from God alone.

2. Deut. v. 33: "Ye shall walk in all the ways which the Lord your God hath commanded you, *that ye may live*, and that it may be well with you, and that ye may *prolong your days* in the land which ye shall possess." See also Deut. iv. 40; xii. 25–28; xxii. 7. Eph. vi. 3. After reading all these texts we certainly see that physical life was most emphatically promised to God's obedient children. Much could be said upon this, but we pass on.

3. Deut. vii. 12–15. "Wherefore it shall come to pass, *if ye hearken* to these judgments and keep and do them, that the Lord thy God shall keep unto thee the covenant and the mercy which he sware unto thy fathers: And he will love thee, and bless thee, and multiply thee; he will also bless the fruit of thy womb, add the fruit of thy land, thy corn, and thy wine, and thine oil, the increase of thy kine, and the flocks of thy sheep in, the land which he sware unto thy fathers to give thee, * * there shall not be male or female barren among you, or among your cattle. And the *Lord* will take away from thee *all sickness*, and will put none of the evil diseases of Egypt, which thou knowest, upon thee; but will lay them upon all them that hate thee."

Here we have a general collection of physical benefits to be directly conferred by the Lord. Surely barrenness, corn, wine, oil and the increase of flocks are all under "natural laws"; yet here we find them placed absolutely *under the great law* of love and obedience. The fifteenth verse is specially conclusive. "The Lord shall take away from thee all sickness." Could anything be plainer than that? It is absolutely certain that the Israelites had a *law* of entire exemption from sickness. But God is the same to-day; and *the only ground for any benefit to fallen man lies in the Atonement of Jesus Christ.*

4. Deut. xxviii. 15–61. "If thou wilt not hearken," etc., ... "the Lord will make thy plagues wonderful, and the plagues of thy seed, even great plagues and of long continuance and *sore sickness* and of long continuance. Moreover he will bring upon thee all the diseases of Egypt which thou wast afraid of; and they shall cleave unto thee. Also *every sickness*, and every plague, which is not written in the book of this law, them will the Lord bring (*cause to ascend*: margin. Query. Ascend from the pit of hell?) upon thee until thou be destroyed." See entire chapter, as also xxix. 22–24. These lengthy declarations of the great Jewish lawgiver are certainly conclusive. Again and again was the plain law of physical health laid down; and the language admits of no alteration, or turning from the literal sense. If they served God, He would by His

power keep off the *evil* diseases of every kind, whether named or not. If they served Satan and the flesh, He would "cause" sickness " to ascend" upon them. (The great trouble to-day is that so many people believe we have a different God, and that the great *principles* of His government passed out of use with the Mosaic ritual.) This law of health was not ritualistic, it was a *fundamental principle* based upon the eternal equity of an unchangeable God. (And He who "hath reserved better things for us," is " the same yesterday, to-day and forever.") This entire charge from the lips of Moses, is wonderfully forcible and clear upon the point that God meant to take care of the body as well as the soul.

The narration of the wanderings furnishes us with some marked illustrations of this close parallel. The wonderful promise just quoted from Exodus xv. 26, was given immediately after the wonderful deliverance at the Red Sea. At Sinai they greatly sinned, and were plagued accordingly; but were healed in answer to the prayer of Moses. Again, they lusted for flesh, and pestilence fell upon them. Miriam sinned and was stricken with leprosy, only to be healed through prayer. In the thirteenth and fourteenth chapters of Numbers we have a most significant history. The people had come to Kadesh-barnea, the spies went out and returned with an evil report. The nation believed the skeptics and doubted God, and as a consequence were condemned to wander and die in the wilderness, while the plague destroyed the fearful spies. Then follows that marvellous dramatic picture in Numbers 16th, when Korah and his followers sank into the earth, and Aaron stood "between the dead and the living," with swinging censer, obeying Moses' order to *"make an atonement"* for the congregation; *" and the plague was stayed."* In Numbers xxi, we have the story of the Brazen Serpent. The people sick and dying with bodily pains, were told to look and live. Here we have the Atonement most strongly and beautifully set forth. "As Moses lifted up the serpent in the wilderness, even so must I be lifted up, that whosoever believeth in me, should not perish but have everlasting life." These were types to be sure; but were they only types, and nothing more?

5. In Deut. xxxii : 39, we find a most unequivocal declaration. Jehovah contrasts himself with the gods of the heathen, and as a distinguishing mark of his supremacy he says; " see now that I, even I, am he, and there is no God with me: I kill and I make alive; I wound, and I heal." And a little further we find the significant expression concerning strict obedience to Gods laws: "For it is not a vain thing for you: *because it is your life:* and through this thing he shall prolong your days in the land." In the same sense we read 1 Sam. ii. 6: "The Lord killeth and maketh alive; he bringeth down to the grave, and bringeth up." Well could Moses close his wonderful prophetic blessings with the assurance, " The Eternal God is thy refuge, and underneath are the everlasting arms, and he shall thrust out the enemy from before thee; and shall say, Destroy them. Israel then shall dwell in safety. . . . Happy art them, O Israel; who is like unto

thee, O people *saved by the Lord, the shield of thy help*, and the sword of thy excellency."

6. Even the Philistines seem to have comprehended that the God of Israel was the great Physician, for when they sent back the ark "they said, if ye send away the ark of the God of Israel, send it not empty ; but in any wise return him a trespass offering; then ye shall be healed, and it shall be known to you why his hand is not removed from you." 1 Sam. vi. 3. This is strong testimony from the surrounding heathen, that the Jews sought and received physical healing from the Lord, and through a " trespass offering."

7. God made a specific promise to Solomon of life, conditioned on obedience. "And if thou wilt walk in my ways, to keep my statutes and my commandments, as thy father David did walk, then I will lengthen thy days." 1 Kings iii. 14. Again in 2 Chron. vii. 12–14, we read, "And the Lord appeared to Solomon by night, and said unto him, I have heard thy prayer, and have chosen this place to myself for an house of sacrifice. If I shut up heaven that there be no rain; or I command the locusts to devour the land, or if I send pestilence among my people. If *my people which are called by my name* shall humble themselves, and pray, and seek my face, and turn from their wicked ways ; then will I hear from heaven, and will *forgive their sin*, and will heal their land." Two things in this gracious promise suggest the words of James. The assurance is given to " my people," just as the Apostle says "any among you" (the believers in the "twelve tribes scattered abroad"); and the connection between the healing and the forgiveness of sin. "I will forgive their sin, and will heal their land," is exactly parallel to "the Lord shall raise him up, and if he have committed sins they shall be forgiven him." The forgiveness of sin turns solely upon the Atonement; and here the inference is very plain, that the sickness should be removed in the same way and for the same reason that the sin was forgiven. The condition prefixed makes this still more forcible. "If my people . . . . shall humble themselves and pray and seek my face, and turn from their wicked ways." Now we know that when a man humbles himself, turns from his sins and seeks God's face, he is forgiven. But how? Solely through the merits of the vicarious Atonement. But here we see the same conditions set for bodily healing. How irresistible then the conclusion that bodily healing was based upon the same wonderful sacrifice?

8. NAAMAN AND HEZEKIAH. The cases of these two men serve to illustrate the scripture doctrine of Divine Healing in a striking manner. The great general must needs learn the lesson—always so hard to remember—of simple unquestioning obedience. He who was accustomed to issue orders the most peremptory, whose disobedience he would have punished by death, had to step down into the same humble sphere, and dip in Jordan, not because there was any healing property in it, but simply because God said, do it. When he surrendred unconditionally, self died, and the

divine touch gave health and strength. Many a general upon the field of polemics to-day finds the laying on of hands and the anointing with oil, much greater stumbling-blocks than the muddy Jordan was to Naaman. Would that they might profit by his example.

In the case of Hezekiah we have the significant fact at the beginning that even after an inspired prophet brought the message "thou shalt die," importunate prayer speedily prevailed to the extent of a complete reversal, and the Lord wrought a miracle in nature, and a miracle of healing for the good king. But, we read that "Hezekiah rendered not again according to the benefit done unto him," in that when the King of Babylon "had heard that Hezekiah had been sick," and "sent unto him to *enquire of the wonder that was done in the land*," he did not testify as he should have done to God's healing power, but entertained the ambassadors with the spectacle of his own wealth and greatness. 2 Chr. xxxii. 31.

The lesson is very sharp and clear as read in these two biographies. The most absolute self-renunciation and simple obedience in order to receive. The most perfect humility and lifting up of God alone in order to retain. "Some great thing" gives opportunity to display our strength and skill; but a baby can simply obey without understanding the reason. (Great wealth, gifts, or scientific skill brings man to the front, but only the child can innocently ignore self and say, "my father did it all.")

9. The 33d chapter of Job is very strong and clear, but as it is referred to elsewhere, we will omit an analysis here.

10. David knew a great deal about faith-healing. Hear a few of his utterances upon the subject. Ps. vi. 2, "Have mercy upon me, O Lord; for I am weak: O Lord, heal me; for my bones are vexed." Verse 5 shows that he spoke of physical trouble. "For in death there is no rememberance of thee: in the grave who shall give thee thanks?" Then in verse 9 he gives this experience. "The Lord hath heard my supplication; the Lord will receive my prayer." Again in Ps. xli. 2. "The Lord will strengthen him (he that considereth the poor;) thou wilt make all his bed in his sickness." In Ps. lxxviii. 20-22, we find the idea suggested that God expects us to use the means, and only the means, which He has commanded. Moses smote the rock when God said "speak ye to the rock," and David declares, "therefore the Lord was wroth . . . because they believed not in God, and trusted not in his salvation." The best medicine I can use is the simple word in Jas. v. 14, 15; and when I do as God commands, I trust only in His salvation and best honor him. As Dorothea Trüdel so beautifully wrote: "we honor God most by believing His word."

11. Ps. xci.; What Christian does not love to read this magnificent poem? But how many Christians dare to believe it? I declare my firm conviction that no honest man can sit down and study this psalm in the light of what we have already considered, asking himself honestly the question, what does it really mean? without being satisfied that he has

not realized the literalness of God's salvation as fully as he ought. I give Young's translation in full; but do not fail, dear reader, to compare the regular version with it.

1. "He who is dwelling
   In the secret place of the Most High,
   In the shade of the Mighty lodgeth habitually,

2. "He is saying of Jehovah,
   My refuge and my bulwark, my God, I trust in Him,

3. "For He delivereth thee from the snare of a fowler,
   From a calamitous pestilence.

4. "With His pinion He covereth thee over,
   And under His wings thou dost trust,
   A shield and a buckler is His truth.

5. "Thou art not afraid of fear by night,
   Of arrow that flieth by day,

6. "Of pestilence in thick darkness that walketh,
   Of destruction that destroyeth at noon,

7. "There fall at thy side a thousand,
   And a myriad at thy right hand,
   Unto thee it cometh not nigh.

8. "But with thine eyes thou lookest,
   And the reward of the wicked thou seest,

9. "(For thou, O Jehovah, art my refuge,)
   The Most High thou makest thy habitation.

10. "Evil happeneth not unto thee,
    And a plague cometh not near thy tent,

11. "For his messengers He chargeth for thee,
    To keep thee in all thy ways,

12. "On the hands they bear thee up,
    Lest thou smite against a stone thy foot.

13. "On lion and asp thou treadest,
    Thou trampest young lion and dragon.

14. "Because in Me he hath delighted,
    I also deliver him—I set him on high,
    Because He hath known My name.

15. "He doth call Me, and I answer him,
    I am with him in distress,
    I deliver him, and honor him.

16. "With length of days I satisfy him,
    And I cause him to look on my salvation."

DIVINE HEALING.

Now in the light of reason and common sense, what did the Psalmist mean by all this? When we read "A shield and buckler is his truth," we say, certainly, we believe that. "Thou art not afraid of fear by night;" we believe that. "Of pestilence," or "a plague cometh not near thy tent;" well, that is a *figure of speech*. Is this the way to read God's Word! What can be said of "With length of days I satisfy him, and I cause him to look on my salvation?" The last part is not a figure; then is the first? We might very profitably discuss the entire pslam, one verse at a time; but I do not wish to do more than bring clearly before the mind the great fact that this glorious psalm distinctly promises physical health and immunity from sickness to—and here is the great point—the man who "is dwelling in the secret place of the Most High, in the shade of the Mighty *lodgeth habitually*." These wonderful promises then are to him who is always dwelling and always abiding in Christ, or "under the shadow of the Most High." Just here we see the weakness of the devil's famous quotation of Scripture to the tempted Saviour. "He will give his angels charge concerning *thee*, and in their hands they shall bear *thee* up lest thou dash thy foot against a stone." Who is the "thee" referred to? He who *abideth continually* in God. If any man ventures to disregard all the laws of God concerning health and safety, expecting to be kept from injury, he is guilty of gross presumption, and does exactly what Satan tempted Jesus to do. The moment anyone presumes upon a promise of God, that moment he steps out from the "shadow of the Most High," and the 91st Psalm is not for him. So we must be exceedingly careful not to let an excess of zeal persuade us to act in defiance of the laws of a well proportioned physical endurance. There are times and seasons when God lays extraordinary work upon His servants, but in such cases extraordinary strength is granted, and the Spirit makes the necessity very clear. Moses fasted forty days upon two occasions, and Philip was caught away from the Eunuch, while Elijah "girded up his lions and ran before Ahab" to the gate of Samaria. But these are rare exceptions, and must be left entirely in the sphere of the special guidance of the Spirit—a sphere at once the most delicate and dangerous to ambitiously explore,—*or criticise*.

12. Ps. ciii. 1-5. The third verse is best rendered as in Young,

> "Who is forgiving all thine inqiuities.
> Who is healing all thy diseases."

David calls upon his soul to bless the Lord, because he forgiveth all his iniquities. How does God forgive sin? Of course, through the Atonement of Jesus Christ. But the Psalmist, in the same breath, blesses God because He heals all his diseases. How does God heal sickness? O, by the skill of human physicians! A perfectly candid mind must allow that there is not the least *a priori* evidence in the text for any such conclusion. On the contrary, the whole weight of evidence clusters about the clear parallelism—iniquities and diseases, all healed by Jehovah. No man, without the natural prejudices of education, would dream of necessarily calling in an agent in one case, any more than the other. If God forgives the iniquities, then God heals the diseases. The only agent needed is the blood of Christ.

13. Ps. cvii. This entire psalm may be read with profit. The head lines declare that it speaks of "God's providences over travelers, over captives, over sick men, over seamen, and in divers varieties of life." In verse 6, we read of the travelers "Then they cried unto the Lord in their trouble, and he delivered them out of their distresses." In verse 13, we read precisely the same words of the captives. In verse 28, the same words speak of the deliverance of seamen. Now surely all these are literal and not figures of speech. But verse 19 gives exactly the same deliverance to the sick. As if this were not enough the Psalmist adds another assurance, not given to traveler, captive or sailor. In these cases the deliverance is declared, but the manner of that deliverance is not specified. When he speaks of the sick, however, the method and means of healing are distinctly pointed out. "*He sent his word and healed them*, and delivered them from their destructions." Praise the Lord! for this straightforward statement. The traveler is "led forth"; the captive "brought out"; the seamen "brought unto the haven;" but not a word is said of the means employed. But when the sick are "saved out of their distresses," then we have the way set forth. "He sent his word and healed them." How well this accords with the declaration of *John* of the Eternal Word, that "In him was life; and the life was the light of men." John i. 4. Again we read, "And this life is in his Son. He that hath the Son hath life." 1 John v. 11, 12. All agree that Jesus will give life to the body eventually, but fail to see the privilege of present life in the sense of health.

This psalm enforces another point. "Fools because of their transgressions, and because of their iniquities are afflicted." What plainer statement could we have that sickness is the consequence of sin in some form? This being so apparent, how can we fail to grasp the comforting promise that if these same "fools" "cry unto God" even from "the gates of death," "he saveth them out of their distresses"? And this is followed directly by the declaration that the healing comes by "His Word." (Yet this does not say that every sickness proves a fool and a transgressor.) David's testimony is just to the point here, for he declares in Ps. cxix. 50, "This is my comfort in my affliction; for thy word hath quickened me."

14. David's son seemed to have an idea that there is health in the Word, for he wrote, "My son, attend to my words; incline thine ear unto my sayings. Let them not depart from thine eyes; keep them in the midst of thine heart. For they are *life* unto those that find them, and *health to all their flesh*." Prov. iv. 20-22. In chap. iii, 7, 8, he says,

"Fear the Lord, and depart from evil. It shall be health to thy navel, and marrow to thy bones." The two words rendered *health* are given in the margin, *medicine*. Dr. Young gives *healing*. The idea is evidently expressed by the words restorative, remedy, healing, medicine. The wise man wrote again, "In the way of righteousness is life."—Chap. xii., 28.

In quoting such verses as this last I do not mean to argue that physical life alone is meant, but that it is certainly included in the text. "The fear of the Lord is a fountain of life, to depart from the snares of death." —Chap. xiv. 27.

"When a man's ways please the Lord, he maketh even his enemies to be at peace with him."—Chap. xvi., 17. Is not disease, as the work of the devil, an enemy? If I am sick I am at once anxious lest that some action, word or thought, or some failure to see the Spirit's leadings does not "please the Lord." "Wisdom giveth life to them that have it."—Ec. vii. 12. "Why shouldest thou die before thy time?"—vs. 17. Evidently Solomon believed it possible for life to be lengthened by conformity to the will of God, for he wrote: "By me thy days shall be multiplied, and the years of thy life shall be increased;" and again, "The fear of the Lord prolongeth days."—Prov. ix. 11, and x. 27.

Who will not admit the truth of the last declaration? Even the statistics of life insurance prove that piety is conducive to long life. But how? Is it answered, through the beneficial result of natural laws more carefully observed because of religion? I reply that even this is purchased for us by the blood of Christ. The actual state of probation into which all men are born depends upon the Atonement, for only by virtue of this was and is judgment suspended.

15. In Isaiah xxxiii. 24, we read of a time when in Zion "the inhabitant shall not say I am sick; the people that dwell therein shall be forgiven their iniquity." Here it avails nothing to claim a reference to the Millennium for the coupling together of healing with forgiveness is too marked to be overlooked. And then we find that glorious promise, "He giveth power to the faint; and to them that have no might he increaseth strength. Even the youths shall faint and be weary; and the young men shall utterly fall: but they that wait upon the Lord shall renew their strength; they shall mount up with wings as eagles, they shall run and not be weary; and they shall walk and not faint."—xl. 29–31. (What earnest Christian does not know that again and again this supernatural renewal of strength is given under the most terrible trials of life, and therefore, that the body as well as the soul is included in the promise?)

16. In Isaiah liii. 4, we read, "Surely He hath borne our griefs and carried our sorrows." It can not be questioned that this statement is just as clear, comprehensive, and emphatic as, "He was wounded for our transgressions, he was bruised for our iniquities." In fact, were I disposed to stickle for a mere grammatical construction, I might claim that the former is the stronger of the two. It is a fact that the church has com-

HEALING OF BODILY DISEASE.

monly read this verse as if the words "griefs" and "sorrows" have reference to afflictions of the mind and spirit; and few have ever gone farther than to believe that they might apply to the comforting and sustaining grace given in bodily sickness. It may therefore be a matter of surprise to many devout Christians to be told that neither of these words has reference to spiritual matters, but to bodily sickness alone. One of the ablest Hebraists of our country recently sent me this translation, without having an idea of the use to which it was to be put.

"Surely our sicknesses hath he taken upon him, (lifted up, as a load,) and our sorrows, he hath carried them."

Albert Barnes says of this verse, "In the 53d chapter of Isaiah is fully stated the doctrine of the Atonement, or that the Messiah was to suffer for sin. In the verse quoted (Matt. viii. 17; Isaiah liii. 4), he states the very truth which Matthew declares. The word translated *griefs* in Isaiah, and *infirmities* in Matthew, means, properly, in the Hebrew and Greek, *diseases of the body.* In neither does it refer to the diseases of the mind, or to sin. To bear those *griefs*, is clearly to bear them *away*, or remove them.

"*Our sorrows.*" Perhaps the proper difference between this word and the word translated *griefs* is, that this refers to the pains of the *mind*, that of the *body;* this to anguish, anxiety, or trouble of the soul, that to bodily infirmity and disease. * * * The phrase therefore properly seems to mean that He took upon himself the mental sorrows of men. He not only took their diseases and bore them away, but He also took or bore their mental griefs. That is, He subjected himself to the kind of mental sorrow which was needed in order to remove them."

Archbishop Magee, in his great work on "The Atonement," assigns the same meanings to the words, and quotes many Scripture verses where the same original Hebrew word is so translated. The reader is referred to any standard commentary for additional testimony upon this point. But a still better authority remains. In Matt. viii. 16, 17, we read, "He healed *all* that were sick: That it might be fulfilled which was spoken by Esaias the prophet, saying, Himself took our infirmities, and bare our sicknesses." Here we have an inspired commentator, plainly declaring that the verse has reference to bodily ailments. We ought to render special praise to Jesus for this divine interpretation, for without it there might be some show of reason in the opposition to the doctrine herein set forth. These able scholars agree with Matthew that Jesus actually lifted up, as a load which we could not carry, our diseases and pains of body and mind. Barnes says: "*bore them away.*" The clear meaning is, that Jesus did take upon Himself our diseases and our mental troubles, in precisely the same way that he "bore our sins in his own body on the tree."

But this fourth verse is only a portion of the evidence found in this wonderful chapter. We find the word "grief," in verses 3, 4, and 10.

In each case the real meaning is *sickness* or bodily pain. The learned translator, Dr. Robert Young, in his version of the Bible, thus renders these verses:

3. "He is despised, and left of men,
A man of pains (Heb. Makob), and acquainted with sickness (*Choli*),
And as one hiding the face from us,
He is despised and we esteemed him not.

4. "Surely our sicknesses (*choli*) he hath borne,
And our pains (*makob*) he hath carried them,
And we—we have esteemed him plagued,
Smitten of God and afflicted.

5. "And he is pierced for our transgressions.
Bruised for our iniquities,
The chastisement of our peace is on him,
And by his bruise there is healing to us.

6. "All of us like sheep have wandered,
Each to his own way we have turned,
And Jehovah hath caused to meet on him,
The punishment of us all.
* * * * * *

10. "And Jehovah hath delighted to bruise him,
He hath made him sick (chalah)
If his soul doth make an offering for guilt,
He seeth seed—he prolongeth days.
* * * * * *

12. * * "With transgressors he was numbered,
And he the sin of many hath borne,
And for transgressors he intercedeth."

There is no escaping the force of this accurate translation. Dr. Young was not laboring to prove a doctrine of faith-healing, but he more than confirms Albert Barnes in the quotation from the latter, just given. The word *makob*, rendered *sorrows* in verses 3 and 4, means *pains*. But, as Barnes says, it seems to refer to "anguish, anxiety, trouble of soul," or to mental pain. But the words *choli* and *chalah*, mean respectively, *sickness, weakness, pain*, and, *to make sick*. Verse 3 is very strong. In it the prophet distinctly states that Jesus Christ was "*a man of pains, and acquainted with sickness.*" No Christian living would object to the idea that he was a man of pains (mental sorrows), in that He actually suffered and endured the pangs of anguish or sorrow, even to a much greater extent than we ever knew. When "He sweat as it were great drops of blood," did He not bear and feel the real weight of deadly sorrow? Of course no one will think of objecting to this. But the rest of the verse just as distinctly avers that He was "acquainted with sickness." As long as the word in English is put "grief," the ordinary reader is not mystified, and passes on; but the scholar finds reason for reflection. When, however, we see that the real meaning is "*sickness, weakness, pain,*" and not grief at all, in its ordinary sense, even the common mind

HEALING OF BODILY DISEASE.

will naturally ask, what does this mean? I reply that if the first part of the line means that Jesus endured mental sorrow, the latter part means that He actually experienced the pangs of sickness. If this is not true, then there is no use for God to tell us anything in language, for we can not possibly believe Him to mean what He says.

One of the most learned and able Hebraists of the old country is E. W. Hengstenberg, doctor and professor in the theological department of the University of Berlin, Germany. He says in his three most excellent volumes, "Christology of the Old Testament and Commentary of the Messianical Prophecy," *that we have no right and no Scriptural grounds to say* that the Hebrew word "*choli*," German "*Krankheit*," *i. e.*, sickness (grief) is here to be taken as figurative or typical. The word "*choli*," sickness, (grief) includes also the wound-and-bruise pains. (1 Kings xxii. 34-35. Jeremiah vi. 7; x. 19. 1 Peter ii. 24.) "And through his wounds we are healed." (German translation.) The 10th verse in Isaiah 53 refers to it, as it reads in Dr. R. Young's translation. "Yet it pleased the Lord to bruise (wound) him; He hath made him sick."

Dr. Isaac Leeser, the able translator of the Hebrew English Bible, renders these verses as follows:

3. "He was despised and shunned of men:
A man of pains and acquainted with disease.

4. "But only our diseases did he bear himself,
And our pains he carried.

5. "And through his bruises was healing
granted to us.

10. "But the Lord was pleased to crush
him through disease."

Now let the objector sit calmly down and face these clear translations. What will you do with them? It is a noticeable fact that in the three years that have elapsed since the first edition of this book was issued, not one of its many opponents have ventured to discuss this chapter, or to attempt a refutation of the argument here advanced. Indeed it may be said that none of the critics have ever attempted to follow the Scriptural logic, but have contented themselves with attacking the counterfeits and excrescences which have sprung up around and upon the doctrine of Divine-healing. Calvinists, studying cases or "phenomena" are many. Arminians, facing the open promises are few.

Many devout hearts will be horrified to think that Christ was ever sick. But let us look upon it. (Certain it is that Jesus never knew the *inner principle of disease* within the system, any more than He was ever actually poisoned with the indwelling *principle* of sin. There is no Scripture to warrant for a moment the thought that sin ever resided in the Son of God as a *root* or inward fountain of pollution.) He was so absolutely pure and perfect that there was no place or spot wherein sin could find a lodgment for an instant. Just so no disease could ever lurk within His body. Notwithstanding all this, Jesus certainly did bear our sins. He certainly did feel and know the *power* of sin, and endure the essence of its consequences and penalties; and there is precisely the same language to warrant our belief that He also felt and endured the pangs or pains of sickness. The Apostle tells us "He was made sin for us, who knew no sin," and the Prophet says that Jehovah "hath made him sick." Peter writes: "Who his own self bore our sins in his own body on the tree," and Isaiah declares, "Surely our sicknesses he hath borne, and our pains—he hath carried them." But as Leeser, translates "only *our* sicknesses did he bear."

Again, what are the punishments of sin? All will admit that sin is punished by soul-condemnation, remorse, mental anxiety, and frequently by sickness. Now of course Jesus took upon Himself the condemnation, anxiety, and mental and moral anguish. All admit this, and believe that these punishments are at once remitted the moment we are pardoned, and that they are remitted because of the vicarious Atonement. Then by what rule of Scripture or of reason is the last mentioned punishment severed from the rest? Mark the Prophet's words. "Jehovah hath caused to meet on him *the punishment* of us all." Now confessedly, sickness is part of that punishment. Hence it is demonstrated, by the immutable Word, that sickness is included in the vicarious Atonement.

It may be claimed that sickness cannot be included, because it is under "natural law." (It is surely about time for Christians to learn that "natural law" is God's law. Now what law can be cited, in the realm of physics, which is more universal and more inexorable, than that which declares that sin will surely cause anguish, anxiety, remorse and soul sickness? Is not this law just as truly "natural" as that which governs bodily disease? And if God chooses to cancel the sin and remove its mental effects, by grace through faith; what Christian will dare say that He can not just as easily remove the sickness? Is it true that God will always, and *at once*, give deliverance from every penalty and consequence of sin, except one? and that this one must inevitably remain to the bitter end? Away with such a thought! Isaiah affirms that the entire punishment of us all was caused to meet on Him. Oh! glory to His name! He testified "It is finished." There was nothing incomplete about the work of our mighty Jesus.

We might follow every verse in this remarkable chapter with profit. "He is pierced for our transgressions." What does that mean? Of course that Jesus bore the penalty of our offences, so that we do not have to bear it. But is the language a whit clearer than "Himself bore our sicknesses?" "The chastisement of our peace is upon Him," is surely not quite so plain as "by His bruise there is healing for us." "He was numbered with the transgressors" gives light to many a despairing sinner; but is it more explicit than, "He hath made him sick?" Surely, nothing but the blindest prejudice can close the eyes, in the light of these facts, to the great truth that sickness is included in the vicarious Atonement, every whit as emphatically as sin, in this great proof chapter of Isaiah.

It may be well to caution the reader against any such blunder as that perpetrated by a prominent divine when he recently wrote very slightingly of an attempt to prove faith-healing by means of Isaiah liii, intimating that the whole thing is so figurative that we cannot be sure of any special interpretation. Let every one remember that this wonderful chapter is the very pith and marrow of the Old Testament proof for the vicarious sufferings of our Lord, and has been so regarded by the church in all ages. It is a chapter which, of all others, most troubles the Jew and delights the Christian. Albert Barnes certainly did not seek to prove faith-healing when he said, "In the 53d chapter of Isaiah is *fully stated* the doctrine of the Atonement." And again he said, speaking of the phrase "bore our sicknesses,"—"To bear these 'griefs,' is clearly to *bear them away, or to remove them.*" Yet he had just affirmed that the word "griefs" meant only "disease of the body," and did not refer at all to the mind. One thing I fearlessly maintain, that if the Atonement for sickness is not taught in this chapter, then the Atonement for sin cannot be found in it. I praise the dear Lord, it is all there! A perfect work; embracing mental pains and physical disease for the body; and transgressions and inbred iniquity for the soul.

Now, why did He thus bear our sicknesses? Was it for His own chastisement, reproof or correction? Did He *need* to bear the load of disease any more than the load of sin? Then, why did He do it? We have the fact that He did bear both. Why was it? Everyone must admit that 1 Pet. ii. 24 and Matt. viii. 17 are equally plain and positive; and the candid mind must be struck with the close analogy between them. But Peter gives us the reason for sin-bearing—"that we, being dead to sins, should live unto righteousness." That is, that we, being free from the necessity, as well as the guilt of sin, should live in soul health. Is it then stepping beyond the plain rules of analogy to say that Jesus bore our sicknesses that we, being dead to disease, should live unto bodily health? Be cool and deliberate and let your logic come to the front. Does not Matthew say as much? He tells us that Jesus "healed all that were sick" in order to fulfill the Scripture, which of all others plainly speaks of the Atonement. Paul says, in Eph. v. 23, "He is the Saviour of the body," * and we all believe that the complete fullness of salvation will never be realized until that wonderful day, when the reunited soul and body shall be glorified with Him at his appearing. The man who believes that the soul can never be free from sin in this life is entirely consistent in believing that there is no such thing as exemption from sickness of the body. But

* This word is used 135 times in the New Testament, and in nearly every instance refers to the physical body.

he who finds in Jesus the perfect cleansing of the soul, and the keeping power against all sin, can be equally consistent in placing his body beneath the same wonderful salvation.

In this connection it is a remarkable fact, that no one has been known to seek the healing power for the body, without receiving a distinct spiritual baptism; and further, that every one known to the writer (a very large number), who has been *entirely healed* in body, is or has become a believer in and professor of entire sanctification of soul. For over eight years I have closely and constantly studied this subject, and observed a very large number of cases. It has often appeared that, after the first joyful experience of the healing power and the accompanying baptism of the Spirit, the Lord has evidently striven to lead the awakened soul into that absolute self-surrender which brings the full revelation of a whole Saviour. But this leading has been resisted. The individual has drawn back, and said, I cannot do this, I cannot go there, I will not believe God wants me to be willing to act thus and so. At once the healing power of the body has been arrested, and very often a speedy relapse, either in whole or in part, has followed. This is the plain secret of a great many apparent failures in-faith-healing. If I start out to take Jesus Christ for a whole Saviour, there must be no possible reservation. I must be willing to *confess* and to *profess, to be, to do, or to suffer* anything, anywhere, in any way whatever, without a particle of hesitation.

It is noticeable that a text which is often quoted for the soul, "This is the will of God, even your sanctification,"—1 Thess. iv. 3, has no reference to spiritual matters, but to those bodily sins which, of all others, most frequently induce severe bodily disease.* This closely agrees with the old promise to Israel, "If thou wilt diligently hearken to the voice of the Lord thy God, and wilt do that which is right in his sight, and wilt give ear to his commandments, and keep all his statutes, I will put none of these diseases upon thee, which I have brought upon the Egyptians. For I am the Lord that healeth thee (or the Lord, thy healer)."—Ex. xv. 26. Here we see, distinctly joined together, the entire consecration and devotion of soul, with the health of body. What could be plainer? So we find God speaking frequently to His people:—"I will take sickness away from the midst of thee."—Ex. xxiii. 25. "The Lord will take away from thee all sickness."—Deut. vii. 15. "I make alive . . . and I heal."—Deut. xxxii. 39. That these promises were literally fulfilled, we have the word of the Psalmist, who tells us of the wandering people of God: "There was not one feeble (sick) person among their tribes."—Ps. cv. 37. "He

---

* If a text be desired that expresses God's will for sanctification from all sin, take Heb. x. 9, 10: "Then said he, Lo, I come to do thy will, O God. . . . . By the which will we are sanctified, through the offering of the body of Jesus Christ once for all." There can be no doubt in this case as to the application of th. word. The whole Epistle to the Hebrews is, in fact, a clear, consecutive treatise and argument on entire sanctification.

HEALING OF BODILY DISEASE.

sent His word, and healed them."—Ps. cvii. 20. When they sinned, sickness came. When they repented, sickness departed.

When the types of the Old Testament taught healing, as the brazen serpent, the swinging incense "between the living and the dead," the cleansing of the leper, etc., it is certainly a retrograde step to curtail the antitype and place it on lower ground. It is at once illogical and unwarranted.

Before leaving Isaiah we must read God's promise to the penitent, "I have seen his ways, and will heal him. I will lead him also, and restore comforts unto him and to his mourner.—" lvii. 18. And again we read: "Then shall thy light break forth as the morning, and thine health shall spring forth speedily; and thy righteousness shall go before thee; the glory of the Lord shall be thy reward.—" lviii. 8. When is this to be? "If thou take away from the midst of thee the yoke, the putting forth of the finger, and speaking vanity." In other words, if you wholly obey God. The condition is plain, and always the same.

17. Jeremiah prayed, "Heal me, O Lord, and I shall be healed; save me and I shall be saved."—xvii. 14. Here again we see the health of soul and body coupled together, and the true power of restoration attributed to God alone.

"Is there no balm in Gilead? is there no physician there? why then is not the health of the daughter of my people recovered?"—viii. 22. We have only to read the context to see that disobedience was the only cause.

"Thus saith the Lord; cursed be the man that trusteth in man, and maketh flesh his arm, and whose heart departeth from the Lord. Blessed is the man that trusteth in the Lord, and whose hope the Lord is."—xvii. 5, 7. Will anyone maintain that this only refers to spiritual matters? Do we not often see professed Christians clinging to physicians with the most abject *abandon*, and literally praying to man to save life? The prophet emphatically points to the great Physician when he says "Heal me O Lord, and I shall be healed."—xvii. 14. He records the declarations, "I will restore health unto thee, and I will heal thee of thy wounds, saith the Lord."—xxx. 17. "Behold, I am the Lord, the God of all flesh : is there anything too hard for me?"—xxxii. 27. "Behold I will bring it health and cure, and I will cure them, and will reveal unto them the abundance of peace and truth."—xxxiii. 6. "In vain shalt thou use many medicines." xlvi. 11.

These utterances can hardly be twisted out of all reference to the body* and let it be remembered that Jeremiah lived and wrote in degenerate days, when disobedience and sin were national. This effectually disposes of the objection that these health promises required national righteousness

---

*Read the many passages in Jeremiah where God distinctly promises to remove physical punishments if the people would only turn to Him, keep the Sabbath and obey His laws. And the emphatic avowal that "because" of their disobedience all their suffering came.

before the individual could be cured. The weeping prophet's words ring with the challenge "Is anything too hard for me."

18. Ezek. xxxiv. 4, 16. "The diseased have ye (the shepherds) not strengthened, neither have ye healed that which was sick," etc. . . . . . "I will strengthen that which was sick." The whole chapter is weighted with reproof to the shepherds of Israel for neglecting their duty. When we read, "neither have ye sought that which was lost." . . . . . "I will seek for that which was lost," we assent at once to its plain meaning; but when we read of healing the sick we begin to think of "figures of speech." When, however, we remember Jesus' commission to the twelve and to the seventy—"preach the gospel and heal the sick," we see that the old prophet may have been more literal than we have been educated to believe. Possibly the modern shepherds have missed a great blessing in not claiming and enjoying the privilege granted in James v. 14–15, to the "elders of the church." I say nothing of possible reproof. In all love I say to the shepherds, brothers do not imagine that all these reproofs and terrible threatenings of Ezekiel, Zachariah and other prophets, were meant only for the possible priests of a period in Jewish history not thoroughly understood. Are you leading the sheep in the best possible pastures, are you preaching a *full* gospel? Are you afraid Jesus Christ may become a little too supernatural, and get a little too much glory? Are you fearful that the discoveries, skill and science of man may not be sufficiently honored? Are you ready to be "little children" before the Lord? O divine Master? let Thy truth enter and give light!

19. Micah vi. 13, is exceedingly clear as to the connection between sin and sickness. "Therefore, also will I make thee sick in smiting thee, in making thee desolate because of thy sins."

20. Habbakuk, iii. 19, declares, "The Lord God is my strength, and he will make my feet like hinds' feet, and he will make me to walk in high places."

21. The Old Testament canon is about to close and to close with a promise. Will the God of the wonderful past forget the body? Hear him. "But unto you that fear my name shall the Sun of righteousness arise with healing in his wings."—Mal. iv. 2. I ask, what kind of healing did He bring? Was it not physical as well as spiritual? Then why not seek to reinhabit the "desolate heritage?" Why not use the wealth left us in our Father's will?

22. Matt. i. 21. "And thou shalt call His name Jesus, for he shall save his people from their sins." This distinctive office was thus prominently set forth in the annunciation; and so comprehensive and sweeping is it that all evil would be included were it not for the express provisions of Scripture, which specially mention death, afflictions, tribulations, testings and other fiery trials. The very name of Jesus calls up this fundamental promise. He is a SAVIOUR. Not merely an *alleviator*. The theology of our day largely lowers the Saviour of men in to the role of a great philanthrop-

HEALING OF BODILY DISEASE. 49

ist, visiting and comforting the prisoners, but leaving them in jail for life. It is this that paralyzes the arm of the church and makes it a figure-head where it should be a flaming power. Jesus came to save from sin, and to save now.

23. The first temptation presented to Jesus in the wilderness was a purely physical one. There is a deep and powerful significance here. Many suppose that the devil was not sure of the divinity of Christ. Be this as it may, he was sure that Jesus had a man's body and a man's physical nature; and long experience had confirmed him in the belief that a man can be approached most easily through the body. This Man had fasted forty days, and was hungry. Satan knew the almost resistless power of awakened appetite and physical desire, and so he suggested the immediate provision for a natural want. But the temptation aimed at another thing. The possible doubt as to the identity of Jesus led to the keen insinuation upon that point; or if this be not true, the sneering tempter reminded Him of omnipotent power.

I incline to the former belief. There is too much credit given to the devil entirely. What better advantage could he ask than to have men endow him with transcendent powers? He likes to wield the lash of a master, and if he can get a soul to believe it to be impossible to fight against him, his battle is already won. He always turns away people's minds from that declaration "Resist the devil and he will flee from you;" and whispers, you cannot hope to fight against him; he was next to God in heaven, and his power is almost unlimited. So it comes about that men are willing to ascribe a slightly limited omnipotence and omniscience to Satan. Nearly everybody supposes him to possess foreknowledge, and even gives gives him credit for having an intimate acquaintance with God's plans and purposes. Dear reader, this is all manufactured in hell. Are we to suppose that He, before whom archangels veil their faces, is visible to the personification of sin? Are God's ways which "the angels desire to look into" open reading to the prince of darkness? Will God, who allows glimpses into the future to come now and then to His most favored servants, give foreknowledge freely to His greatest enemy? Depend upon it Satan only knows the future as revealed in prophecy. Undoubtedly he may often interpret it better than man; but he knows nothing to come, of himself. He cannot tell the destiny of a single soul till God declares it; hence his unremitting war to the last. His hope of success endures to the very gates of death, and he never spares an effort. What he most likes to hide from us to-day is that *he is a beaten foe.* Christ overcame him, defeated him, whipped him at every point; and Christ is ready to give the same victory to the true believer. Oh! how Satan dreads the discovery of this great secret! how carefully he guards against it, and how he howls with disappointment and rage, when a soul perceives it, through faith in the blood.

But to return. Satan presented his first temptation to the worn out physical powers of Jesus. It was a literal trial. "If thou be the Son of God, command that these stones be made bread." (*Even the devil admits that the miracle of creation demonstrates God.* Let infidelity profit by his example). But he evidently based his hope of success upon the weak body which was calling loudly for food. To this literal, physical temptation, Jesus replied "It is written, man shall not live by bread alone, but by every word that proceedeth out of the mouth of God."—Matt. iv. 4. See Deut. viii. 3. Moses told Israel that God fed them on manna in order to make them know that man should live upon the words of God, as well as upon his natural food. The devil desisted at once, and tried another spot in the armor. As Judge Lowe has beautifully said, "'It is written' was enough for the devil, and only the devil will ever say it is not enough."

I feel that I am treading upon holy and delicate ground. Yet I am persuaded that Jesus' words did not want in literal signification. I remember Elijah in his forty days' march across the desert "*to* Horeb, the mount of God." I recall Moses, as for nearly three months he abode in God's presence. The scene in the wilderness of the Jordan rises before me, and another scene as well. Upon a silent mountain top a man *continues* all night in prayer to God. In the early morning watch, in the strength which came not from physical food, but from ·conversation with His Father, He walks upon the tossing sea (the great symbol of the surging sin of our souls), calms the tempest, *not by slow methods of gradual subsidence*, but by a word; and when He reaches the other shore, so strong is the faith within Him that "as many as touch the hem of His garment are made perfectly whole."—Matt. xiv. 36. "The water that I shall give him shall be in him a well of water springing up into everlasting life."—John iv. 14.

With loving gratitude, I, with many others, testify for Jesus in this matter. More and more I am coming to realize that my whole life, physical as well as spiritual, hangs upon the Word of God. "His words are sweet to my taste," and "I esteemed the words of his mouth more than my necessary food," have a significance beneath the "figure of speech." I know that "the life which I now live *in the flesh* I live by the faith of the Son of God, who loved me and gave himself for me." Jesus brought my soul out of the pit of sin. Jesus brought my body out of the pit of fatal disease. Jesus keeps my soul, and Jesus keeps my body. These have become great thrilling facts in my experience. Again and again, when weary and tired with physical work, I have found rest and strength in the "words of his mouth," and been more refreshed than if I had eaten or slept. "The words that I speak unto you, they are spirit, and they are life."—John vi., 63. A few minutes on my knees, alone with God, have given me more actual physical strength, not to mention spiritual vigor, than hours of idleness. I do not mean to say that we are to disregard all the laws of nature and press beyond the bounds of reason. Quite the reverse. I speak of times when work was to be done, which while trying, was not at all unreasonable. I do not throw away my reason, but only make it dependent upon, and co-laborer with faith. Many an outbreaking, God-defying sinner endures much more physical effort every day than I do, or ever did. That is not the point. The distinction lies in this. I was prostrated through disease. Jesus restored me. But now my physical nature and experience often demonstrate, to my entire satisfaction, that, but for the living Word, I would not be alive, much less in health and comfort. I am made to feel vividly my constant dependence upon Jesus, and am always conscious that every breath I draw for body, soul, or spirit, comes straight from His hand. I am thus sweetly aware that I belong entirely to my Saviour, and I praise Him for all I am, and all I have. Praise the Lord!

One thing is certain. Jesus met a temptation which involved the question of physical life and health, by the positive statement that these do not depend upon the human means of sustenance alone, but upon the Word of God. To contend that He referred only to spiritual comfort would be to say that the Son of God used Scripture where it was not applicable. This would be blasphemy.

24. The miracles of healing wrought by our Lord were all on conditions that are closely identified with redemption and the gospel. "Believe ye that I am able to do this?" "Thy faith hath saved thee." These were the conditions always. And who has not noticed that not one was ever refused. "He healed them that had need of healing."—Luke ix. 56. It was not as important as healing the soul; and it seemed to be less difficult, for we are told that in Nazareth, "He could do there no mighty work, save that he laid his hands upon a few sick folk and healed them."—Mark vi. 5.

25. The commission to the twelve apostles is significant. Matt. x.: "He gave them power against unclean spirits, to cast them out, and to heal all manner of sickness and all manner of disease." After conferring this power,* He said: "as ye go, preach, saying, The kingdom of heaven is at hand. Heal the sick, cleanse the lepers, raise the dead, cast out devils; freely ye have received, freely give." Mark vi. 12, 13, tells us: "And they went out, and preached that men should repent. And cast out many devils, and anointed with oil many that were sick, and healed them." (We are not told that they secured many converts, but are assured of the success attending their healing ministry. See Luke ix. 1, 2, 6. "He gave them power and authority over all devils and to cure diseases. And he sent them to preach the kingdom of God, and to heal the sick. And they departed, and went through the towns, *preaching* the Gospel, and *healing* everywhere." Again in Luke x. 1, 9, 17, 18, 19, we read: "The Lord appointed other seventy also, and sent them two and two before his face . . . and said unto them . . . into whatsoever city ye enter . . .

---

*How did they know they had the power? I imagine only because Jesus said so.

hea.. the sick that are therein, and say unto them the kingdom of God is come nigh unto you. And the seventy returned again with joy, saying, Lord, even the devils are subject unto us through thy name. And He said unto them, I beheld Satan as lightning fall from heaven. Behold I give unto you power to tread on serpents and scorpions, and over all the power of the enemy; and nothing shall by any means hurt you."

These quotations prove, that Jesus gave His first preachers a double commission, for souls and bodies. (They prove that these diseases, or at least some of them, were the direct work of the devil.) They prove that all such power is "through thy name," the name of Jesus; which is simply another way of saying that the *benefits of such power rest solely upon the vicarious Atonement.* And they prove that to these first teachers He also promised a continuance of health in their own persons; even in spite of "serpents," "scorpions" and all the "power of the enemy." The inference is not unreasonable, that the poison from a serpent's bite, in its operation upon the human body, belongs to the "power of the enemy," "he that hath the power of death,"—the devil.

26. I here trespass a little upon the following chapter, because of the connection. In Mark xvi. 17, 18, we read, "And these signs shall follow them that believe; In my name shall they cast out devils; they shall speak with new tongues; they shall take up serpents; and if they drink any deadly thing, it shall not hurt them; they shall lay hands on the sick, and they shall recover." In this last utterance to His disciples Jesus promised all these signs "to them that believe." I elsewhere discuss the absurdity of the argument which predicates anything upon the fact that these signs have not followed good Christian men and women, who had no belief in or expectation of these signs. But here is the promise. Notice that it includes the assurance of personal *exemption* from physical injury, as well as the extension of benefits to others. Upon what could these benefits be based, save upon the Atonement? No twist of the language can possibly alter the plain fact that Jesus directly promised miraculous preservation, and miraculous powers to "them that believe." * When the apostles felt the need of "power from on high," they deliberately united in asking God to stretch forth His hands to heal, "and that signs and wonders may be done by the name of thy holy child Jesus."—Acts iv. 29, 30. Note that this prayer was offered in an age of faith in the supernatural and amongst a people whose whole history abounded in the miraculous. Is there less need to-day, when we are surrounded by a materialism in the world and *in the church,* which holds that God has not stepped outside the barrier of "natural law" for centuries, and that He cannot or will not do so?

Are the words "*If ye have faith,* nothing shall be impossible unto you"

---

* For conclusive evidence of the existence of everyone of these signs in modern times, see "Supernatural Gifts of the Spirit."

of no real force in our day? Is it true that "if two of you shall agree on earth as touching anything that they shall ask, it shall be done for them of my Father which is in heaven?"—(Matt. xvii. 20 and xviii. 19).

But, thank God, these promises hold to-day, for though "Heaven and earth shall pass away, my words shall not pass away."—Matt. xxiv. 35. The conditions of absolute faith, and sometimes of "prayer and fasting," (Mark. ix. 28, 29,) must be fulfilled. If we fail in the smallest fraction of our duty we need not wonder that the answer is withheld. It could not be otherwise.

A distinguished literary Christian, ridiculing the doctrine of this book, says: "I can tell you the reason of these cures; it is the *faith*. Destroy that and the disease will return. I met a man who had been cured, and when I explained it to him, his sickness returned. He said he did not know whether it was better to be ignorant and well, or to have the knowledge and be sick."

A more pitiable exhibition of ignorance in an able man would be hard to find. Certainly "it is the faith." But there is nothing ridiculous about that. Most assuredly, if you destroy the faith the disease returns. How could it be otherwise? And yet this learned man appears to be persuaded that he expressed a brilliant argument against "faith-healing" in the above words. How infinitely obtuse! Did not Jesus say "according to your faith"? One of the healed was specially warned to "sin no more lest a worse thing come upon thee"; and when we remember that "whatever is not of faith, is sin," we at once see the logical reason for a return of the disease if faith fail. Peter only walked upon the sea while his eye was fixed on Jesus.

27. Luke ix. 56. "For the Son of man is not come to destroy men's lives, but to save them." Is this not conclusive? Did he save the physical lives of those diseased multitudes? Then do not these words at least include the body? Of course the *conditions* are always to be remembered, and they are very searching. "If ye abide in me, and my words abide in you,"—*emphasize this a thousand times*—"Ye shall ask what ye will, and it shall be done unto you."—Jno. xv. 7. The great cause of trouble lies in the fact that we will emphasize the latter half, because it holds up the desired objects, while we forget the conditions.

28. "As thou hast sent me into the world, even so have I also sent them into the world."—Jno. xvii. 18. Ponder and pray over these words. He was sent, a perfect man, holy, harmless, undefiled. He was free from sin, and from inward disease. He bore the weight of other's sins and sicknesses. There was no evil within Him, but He was almost overwhelmed by the evil from without. "Even so" our Lord sends us into the world. Even so He sends His own who are wholly consecrated to Him. Cleansed from all sin, and strengthened by His own divine life,—the life of Jesus in our mortal flesh quickened by His Spirit; we are to go forth bearing the reproach of the cross, and enduring every form of evil from *without;*

but not from *within*. There God's image is to be constantly seen, and God's perfect peace to perpetually reign. In this view we can see a positive answer to that marvelous prayer "I pray not that thou shouldst take them out of the world, but that thou shouldst keep them from the evil."—Jno. xvii. 15. Not from the evil of persecution, of trial, of nakedness, of peril, of sword; for "in the world ye shall have tribulation." Jno. xvi. 33. But from all touch of "evil" upon or in the personality of the individual. In close accord with this we find John declaring, years after, "We know that whoever is born of God sinneth not; but he that is begotten of God keepeth *himself*, and that wicked one toucheth him not."—1 Jno. v. 18. Have God's hedges all withered since the days of Job and David? (Job i. 10, Ps. xxxiv. 7.)

29. Acts iv. 29, 30. "And now Lord . . . grant unto thy servants, that with all boldness they may speak thy word, by stretching forth thy hand to heal, and that signs and wonders may be done by the name of thy holy child, Jesus." The full significance of this remarkable prayer seems to have been strangely overlooked. The Apostles, after a most extraordinary "miracle of healing" had been called in question on this very point of cure, and had declared that it had all been done in Jesus' name and "by faith in his name." Remember that Peter had said to the man "such as I have, give I thee." And then see them uniting in a prayer which most undeniably couples miraculous healing of the body with the proclamation of the word; thus plainly declaring that the "signs and wonders by the name of thy holy child, Jesus," were distinctly an integral part of that word which they so desired to "boldly" proclaim. And God confirmed their understanding of the matter by signs, and great power in spiritual matters; sending Stephen and Philip, "full of *faith*, and the Holy Ghost," to proclaim this word and to be the instruments in the cures.

30. Corinthians may almost be called the gospel of the body, for it so abounds in physical directions, admonitions, and advice. In 1 Cor. ii. 5, we read, "Your faith should not stand in the wisdom of men (what of physicians when God has said 'I am the Lord thy healer'?—Ex. xv. 26), but in the power of God." In chapter iii. 16, 17, the Apostle declares that we are the temple of God, that the Spirit of God dwells in us, and that if we defile the temple, God will destroy us. Who will dare to deny that this includes the body and the laws of health? In chapters v. and vi., after discussing a physical sin, Paul asks, "Know ye not that your bodies are the members of Christ?" Having just stated that "The body is for the Lord, and the Lord for the body." Beyond controversy, the physical body alone is here indicated. How is the body "for the Lord?" Of course to serve Him. But how is "The Lord for the body," except to save it and preserve it? And how can the Lord save any part or portion of a man, except through the Atonement? And how can the Atonement be applied for anything which was not contained in the divine plan of that sacrifice?

If our bodies are "the members of Christ," and He "bore our sicknesses," there is certainly the possibility of our exemption; and we can glorify God by meeting the conditions and enjoying this privilege, for the Apostle says, in chapter vi. 19, 20, "What, know ye not that your body is the temple of the Holy Ghost which is in you, which ye have of God and ye are not your own? For ye are bought with a price (body and all); therefore glorify God in your body and in your spirit, which are God's." How can we glorify God in our spirits? By letting Him save them, and keep them from sin; and by serving Him spiritually. How can we glorify Him in our bodies? By letting Him save them and keep them from sin, (this includes all offenses against the laws of health and physical morality) and by serving Him physically.

Certainly it is plain that if the body be held in strict subjection to the laws of health, and no physical sins be committed, that sickness is extremely improbable. (Recall the case of the old Venetian Admiral who reformed at forty years of age, after a life of beastly drunkenness, and then lived in perfect health until past one hundred, through habits of mathematical rigidity and abstemiousness.(We have seen that the Jews were promised health and strength if they lived in perfect obedience. Paul knew this well, and he wrote several chapters in Corinthians on those physical sins of lust and appetite, which so commonly bring the punishment of disease, in order that they might be avoided, God glorified and the individual benefited. With great emphasis he declares: "I keep under my body and bring it into subjection." He fully appreciated the close relation between physical sins, and physical effects. But if these abuses of the bodily functions were avoided, the results would be also. In the same spirit he alludes to a great physical sin and its retribution (chapter x, 8) and then declares, "Now all these things happened unto them for examples; and *they are written for our admonition*, upon whom the ends of the world are come."

If the church would obey the injunction of verse 31, "*Whether therefore ye eat or drink, or whatsoever ye do, do all for the glory of God*," *and obey it in the last and least particular*, *the doctors would have to look to the world for support.*

I cannot swell this book to an unwieldy size, and must therefore be brief; simply remarking that a volume as large as this can easily be prepared on the subject of Divine Healing in the Epistles alone. But passing on I note that the "natural body," 1 Cor. xv. 44, is under sentence of death, but let us remember that there was never any sentence of sickness pronounced, except as a result of disobedience, and this was coupled with a strong promise of health, if obedient. These things are too plain. They must be overturned or admitted.

2 Cor. i. 20. "For all the promises of God in him are yea, and in him amen, unto the glory of God by us." Having used this in the introduction, I simply say, read the abundant promises of God concerning

obedience and health, and then deny if you can, that the Atonement brings us health of body, "in him, unto the glory of God by us."

And finally, "We walk by faith, not by sight" (2 Cor. v. 7.) was written just in the midst of a pointed discussion of the physical body. Read it and ponder.

31. In Eph. v., we read of physical sins which bring physical disease; and we are warned not to be deceived, but to remember that "because of these things cometh the wrath of God upon the children of disobedience." Passing on, Paul touches the relation of husband and wife, and declares that Christ is "the saviour of the body." The word "saviour" means preserver, and the word "body" is the one that is always used when the physical man is indicated. True, a comparison is made between the church and wives; but the following language gives distinct support to the idea that the physical is meant. "Men ought to love their wives as their own bodies," and "no man ever yet hated his own flesh," are distinctly physical in their import.

Then follows the tremendous declaration. "For we are members of his body, of his flesh, and of his bones." Well may Paul add, "This is a great mystery." Thank God! many mysteries become plain when we are walking with Jesus. Even this is not wholly a blank. This wonderful union with Christ; just what is its nature and how it is brought about; who can tell? But may we not believe in the union itself as an actual fact, and not merely a figure? "Members of his body, of his flesh, and of his bones." The life of Jesus in me, coursing through my veins, and thrilling my soul and spirit; how can it be mine, save through the merits of His atoning sacrifice? "He that eateth me, even he shall live by me."—Jno. vi. 57. "Doth this offend you," beloved? Beware how you ask "How can this man give us his flesh to eat"? The answer will only be the yet stranger statement, "Except ye eat the flesh of the Son of Man, and drink his blood, ye have no life in you." Remember, "He that eateth my flesh and drinketh my blood, *dwelleth in me and I in him*." I do not attempt to explain, but can only say these words have a meaning now to me that is new and strange and wonderful.

32. Gal. iii. 13. "Christ hath redeemed us from the curse of the law, being made a curse for us; for it is written, cursed is every one that hangeth on a tree." This is a tremendous assertion, and it clearly involves the vicarious Atonement for sickness or disease. These afflictions are indisputably the attendants and results of sin. That they are emphatically included in the "curse of the law," can not be denied for a moment. Refer again to the numerous quotations already made from Exodus, Leviticus, Deuteronomy, etc., for the repeated and lengthy declarations of Moses upon this point. (In fact there is vastly greater evidence that sickness and disease constituted the "curse of the law" than that spiritual death was indicated. This may appear startling, but it is most positively true.) Of course I do not for a moment belittle the spiritual side of the question, but

HEALING OF BODILY DISEASE.

I do point to the fact that the "law" most specially and repeatedly declares bodily sickness to be directly included in the "curse," and to form a very important element thereof. But Paul positively affirms that "*Christ* HATH *redeemed us from the curse of the law*," the whole of it, of course, for who will dare say the work of redemption is not finished. But how hath He redeemed us? By "*being made a curse for us.*" Let us put this argument in its simplest form.

1. All forms of sickness and disease were included, and *even mentioned particularly*, in the "curse of the law."—Ex. xv.; Ex. xxiii.; Lev. xxvi.; Deut. vii.; Deut. xxxii., etc., etc.

2. "Christ *hath* redeemed us from the curse of the law." Therefore, Christ *hath* redeemed us from all sickness and disease. There is no future tense about it, the work is finished. Again,

1. Christ redeemed us from sin by His vicarious Atonement; that is, "He was made sin for us."

2. Christ redeemed us from the "curse of the law," by "being made a curse for us."

Therefore we are redeemed from all the "curse of the law," body, soul and spirit, solely through His vicarious Atonement. Praise the Lord! Search the Scriptures, and see whether these things be so.

33. In Colossians i. 27 and ii. 4, we find two phrases "Christ in you," and "Christ our life," that most beautifully and wonderfully express the doctrine of physical health in Christ, just as much as they express our spiritual life. The idea is that Christ is formed within us; that He indeed becomes the life of the body as well as the soul; so that we are enabled, "as we have received Christ Jesus the Lord"—by faith for soul and body—to "so walk in him" (chap. ii. 6) for the performance of all the work He may have for us to do on this earth; and this I believe to be the experimental fulfillment of the petition recorded in chap. iv. 12, in which Epaphras prayed, "that ye may stand perfect and complete in all the will of God." The last utterances of Israel's great lawgiver contain this same truth, very clearly expressed, "For he is thy life, and the length of thy days."—Deut. xxx. 20. This cannot be misconstrued, for the expression "length of thy days" forbids any meaning other than a physical one. Yet of this physical existence Moses says of Jehovah, "he is thy life." Joining this with Paul's words, "Christ who is our life," we have the full gospel for soul and body.

One single case will be quoted here from Scripture. In Heb. xi. 11, we are distinctly informed that it was "through faith" that Sara received the healing from a purely physical deficiency, and that it was "because *she* judged him faithful who had promised." Plainly, her faith was necessary, and was exercised before the healing came. And it was certainly a clear case of "gradual" healing by faith.

34. As we read the life of Christ, we are struck with the continued stream of healing miracles that flowed from Him wherever He went.

"He healed *all* that were sick." 'As many as touched were made perfectly whole." This record begins with His ministry, and terminates in Gethsemane with the act of healing power in restoring the ear of the high priest's servant. When the great prophet, Elisha, was laid to rest, the dead bones of a man sprang into life at the touch of his body but when Jesus died *many* graves opened, and the risen dead walked the streets of Jerusalem. Truly the Atonement made provision for the body.

But it is contended that these numerous miracles of healing were wrought in order to establish the divinity of our Lord. Now, it is true Jesus himself said that His works testified of the Father, and at another time, He exhorted His hearers to "believe Him for the very work's sake." But surely the latter clearly hints at the fact that such was not the primary intention. "I work the works of Him that sent me," gives us the idea that Jesus *continuously* bore the sins and sickness of lost souls and bodies. He said not "I have worked;" that would admit the construction of an intended demonstration of His divinity; but "I work," is present and unlimited. Let us remember in this connection, that His name, given to Moses, proclaims the unchanging character of His nature and His work— I AM. There is no past or future, properly speaking, with our Master and Lord. Glory to His name! Rather should we see, in these miracles, the natural outcome of that love wherewith He loved us. He healed because, in a sense, He could not help it. He that wept over the city, could not withhold the touch of health from the citizens who came to Him honestly, believing in His power to heal.

Thomas Erskine wrote, "Until Christ's ascension He did not receive gifts for men*; the power of the Holy Ghost was not lodged in Him as the Head of the body, and so that power could not flow *internally* from Him into the members. The inflow of the power into them was a witness to the world of the exaltation of the Head. The great and common mistake with regard to the gifts is, that they were intended merely to authenticate or to witness to the inspiration of the canon of Scripture, and that therefore when the canon was completed, they should cease; whereas they were intended to witness to the exaltation of Christ as the Head of the body, the church. Reader, do you not feel that if these things be so, then there is a nearness to God, and a walking in him, and a down-breaking of the creature in real Christianity of which you as yet know nothing." †

A very strong proof that the miracles of Christ were not merely intended to demonstrate His divinity is found in the fact that the Bible always avoids any such thing. God's existence and nature are always presupposed. The first words of the sacred writing " In the beginning God created the heavens and the earth," assume all that can be imagined of

---
* Eph. iv., 8.
† See "Supernatural Gifts of Spirit," p.19, from Erskine's "Brazen Serpent."

the miraculous power of the Creator. When the threats of vengeance were sent to Pharaoh the words were spoken "He shall know that I am God," etc.; but of course we see that the primal object was the deliverance of the chosen people. The convincing of the Egyptians was a secondary result. Had this been the object of the miracles why were they not wrought for the doubters when they asked for one? They were performed only for those who had faith, or for pure benevolence, as in the case of feeding the five thousand.

Admiral E. Gardiner Fishbourne, of the English Navy, endorses the idea of Thomas Erskine, just quoted. He says; in answer to the question, why these miracles now?*

"In mercy God is opening men's eyes to their past unbelief as to His power and love in Christ, ...

"He is endorsing real theology, and condemning the unreal imputative, merely speculative and powerless systems. . . . .

"He is generating faith in the supernatural by witnessing to its reality, and proving that Christianity is not *effete* or less potential than it was in apostolic times, and showing that those who argue that it is so, and who limit the Holy One of Israel by teaching that divine joy, divine holiness, and divine healing were confined to apostolical times, have been, and are, doing irreparable damage to their own souls, while they destroy the unity of the church and its power over heathendom.

"These cures are to prove that Christ's love is not less than it was when He tabernacled in the flesh in Judæa, and *that His power is even greater now that He is enthroned at the Father's right hand;* and that it is now, as it was from the beginning, His desire to enthrone Himself by His Spirit, in the hearts of all believers.

"To prove to those who, in child-like faith, accept it, that the Word of God is inspired by the Holy Ghost, and can be understood by those who seek His enlightenment, *while it is a sealed book to all who are without His teaching*, however deep and extended is their human knowledge.

"To prove to this money-grubbing, God-denying and unspiritual age, that there is neither progress nor profit when the soul is not fully saved and sanctified.

"To prove to the false philosophers and unbelieving divines that the God, in whom we live and move and have our being, is known to, and knowable only in the Lord Jesus Christ by faith, while the reality of His presence, love, and power is demonstrated to reason by faith healing."

Erskine has the clear idea—the witnessing to the risen Christ as the living Head of the body. This will always be seen whenever the members evince that consecration and faith which allows the inflow and outflow of supernatural power.

* Small pamphlet "Wholeness, or Holiness and Health through Faith in the Lord Jesus Christ." London : Elliot, Stock & Houghton.

One very important point has been entirely overlooked. Those people came very close to Jesus; much closer than most persons do to-day. Note that He did not heal at a distance, except where the messenger came specially on behalf of the patient. "*As many as touched* were made perfectly whole." He did not cast the devils out of a man while the sea of Galilee rolled between them, but when they actually met. This obvious fact has blinded men to a glorious parallel. We are told that this is the very reason why miracles of healing are not to be expected to-day. Jesus is not here, as He was then. Ah! is it so? "Lo I am with you alway, even to the end of the age," was spoken almost in the same breath with the promise of the signs and wonders to "follow them that believe."* Men have failed to see the wonderful truth that it is actually possible, in this century of grace, to draw just as near to Jesus Christ as it ever was when He walked the streets of Jerusalem. The door of faith may be narrower than the door of sight, but it is wide enough to admit any soul that has resolutely laid aside "every weight, and *the sin* which doth so easily beset us." Eighteen centuries ago no sick man ever went to Jesus for healing, and at the same time left part of his body at home. He had to go with a whole purpose and a whole action. Just so to-day. If you will take all you are or hope to be, all your doubts, all your fears, all your dread of men and men's opinions, and go to Jesus in an absolute and irrevocable consecration of soul and body, you will get near enough to "touch the hem of His garment;" and it is true to-day that "as many as touch are made perfectly whole." But you can't touch Him through a reservation, any more than you can receive the electrical current through a thick glass plate. Judas and John were both near to Christ. Judas had his doubts, his greed, his selfish desires, and he was repelled from the divine presence of the Master, and died a victim of sin and death. But John, with earnest purpose and honest love, drew so near that he leaned on Jesus' breast, and the pulsing of that eternal heart imparted love and light and life: so that he lived a century, and was spared a death from violence. Moses lived to one hundred and twenty, a perfect physical man: Enoch walked with God three hundred years, till God took him; and Elijah, who like Moses, talked with God upon the mount, passed up in a chariot of fire. But each of these saints "knew God face to face," and there was no power in the hands of Satan to hurt them, in soul or body. My brother, if you press as near to Jesus as those men did, the life-power of His glorious nature will expel all the Judas elements of your entire being, while the John characteristics will bloom and blossom into marvelous and supernatural beauty. *Have you ever tried to touch Jesus?*

---

* Prof. J. Rendell Harris, of the Johns Hopkins' University, has done good service, through his studies of the mechanical measurements of the Greek text, in showing that the discredit cast by the Revisers on the closing verses of Mark, the story of the woman taken in adultery and other passages, is entirely a mistake.

35. There is one general argument from Scripture which is of great importance. It is the argument from analogy, and from history. When Jesus ascended he left two great promises; the coming of the Holy Ghost, and his own return. Both of these are necessary to the establishment of the kingdom on earth; and hence we find the two constantly united in the Apostolic epistles.

In Christ's own history we find Him begotten as the Son of God, but unknown to His own nation. We find Him baptized with the Holy Ghost, and immediately working as never man worked. And we see Him raised from the dead, a glorified being, and ascending to God. The first was foreshadowed in the types of the Mosaic ritual. The second was indicated by His encounter with the doctors in the temple. And the third was betokened by His transfiguration.

At or before each stage the devil specially sought to arrest further progress. He strives to kill the infant Jesus; to cause His downfall in the wilderness; and to destroy Him on Calvary.

Now there is one great principle which governs the universe. It is this: the history of the whole is the history of its parts and *vice versa.*

The history of the church is the history of the individual. The history of the type is the history of the antitype. Hence we find the natural physical world clearly teaching the same truths. God visits the earth with a flood destroying all past sin and sinners, just as Jesus Christ came to give the washing of regeneration, casting all our sins into the depths of the sea.

The second time He will come with fire, destroying the very roots and seeds of evil, and making "all things new," just as He comes the "second time without sin" unto those who seek for Him, and with the fiery baptism "with the Holy Ghost" burns up the old unrighteous nature or "carnal mind" and makes "all things new," as never before.

This argument from the types, if closely followed, proves to be marvelous in its searching application and absolute fidelity, in every last and least particular; but I have no space here for more than a hint at its outline. But as we apply this key to the church's history we see a perfect parallel.

God chose out or created Israel; but it was hidden away among the nations. Next the church was baptized with fire and with the Holy Ghost, and at once began a work world-wide in its reach. Lastly, the rapture and resurrection will witness the full redemption of the "bride."

Now, just as in Jesus' history, the devil specially opposes and counterfeits God's work, and "the more as he sees the day approaching." Perhaps he is warned by the foreshadowings which may be plainly seen. The great revival of missionary effort is one of the most marked signs of the times, and the gospel is being rapidly preached "for a witness to all nations." And as the Holy Ghost is at work stirring up the most marked and persistent looking for the coming of the Lord that has been known since apostolic times, so the devil is at work with his special agencies to defeat God if he can.

Hence our day witnesses the most extraordinary revival and rehash of exploded errors and ancient sins ever known since the flood. Theosophy, Spiritualism, Esoteric religion, refined Buddhism, Mind Cure, Metaphysics, Christian Science, Polygamy, etc., swarm forth with a spontaneity that is only less astonishing than their ready acceptance by multitudes of people in every land. In the first edition of this book I pointed out the devil's imitating hand in the "mind cure;" but to-day its advances have astounded us all.

The significance of these things lies in the fact that the second advent is specially attended and preceded by the Holy Spirit's work. Therefore the devil appears with all these counterfeits, every one of which exalts spirit or mind (wrongly using the two words synonymously), as the Holy Spirit's office is specially to "guide you unto all truth;" so these various offspring of hell all particularly call attention to the fact that they will show you the truth. Indeed this has become the very watchword among them, and on all sides echoes a meaningless cry, "We want the truth, the truth, the truth."

And finally as the Spirit is to soon reveal a living Christ in His glory, so these miserable snares of the devil are labeled all over *on the outside* with such names as "Christian Science," "The Perfect Way, or the Finding of Christ," "The World's Light," etc.

But as it is always true that the presence of counterfeits proves the co-existence of the real, all these seem to point to *the two great facts* of the day we live in, viz.:

Jesus is coming, and the Holy Ghost is preparing the watchful for the advent.

At His coming the waiting Bride is to be translated, and their physical bodies glorified with those of the resurrected saints. But this great consummation for which the "whole creation groaneth and travaileth in pain until now" has its distinct foreshadowing.

The Spirit has directed the minds and hearts of God's earnest consecrated children to the doctrine and faith of Divine-healing as the necessary preparation for the reception of *translation by faith;* for like Enoch we must have faith for that wonderful transition. How exceedingly reasonable then, and how perfectly in analogy is it that preceding the great change when the life of Christ will be suddenly communicated to the church to such an extent as to cause her to rise triumphant over death; how reasonable it is, I say, that the Holy Ghost should lead us to see the possible reception of that marvelous life *by faith* for the victory over disease as an "earnest of our inheritance."

The temptation which drove man out of paradise, is the last to bar his return. The trump card which won Eden is played again to-day with the same satanic malice. "Yea hath God said?" Are you sure He meant exactly what He said, or was it not a figure of speech? By the thousands on thousands the members of the church of God are falling before this old card of the Serpent; and on every hand the entire list of events attending the second advent are transformed into a series of figures and "spiritual" mysticisms.

It is the purpose of this book to "go through the gates," and to "prepare the way" as much as possible for the coming of the King. "Be ye also ready; for in such an hour *as ye think not*, the Son of man cometh."

1.—SICKNESS FROM THE DEVIL.

THE DEVIL.

Men don't believe in a devil now, as their fathers used to do;
They've forced the door of the broadest creed to let his majesty through.
There isn't a print of his cloven foot or a fiery dart from his bow
To be found in earth or air to-day, for the world has voted so.

But who is it mixing the fatal draught that palsies heart and brain,
And loads the bier of each passing year with ten hundred thousand slain?
Who blights the bloom of the land to-day with the fiery breath of hell,
If the devil isn't and never was? Won't somebody rise and tell?

Who dogs the steps of the toiling saint, and digs the pits for his feet?
Who sows the tares in the field of time wherever God sows His wheat?
The Devil is voted not to be, and of course the thing is true;
But who is doing the kind of work the Devil alone should do?

We are told he does not go about as a roaring lion now;
But whom shall we hold responsible for the everlasting row
To be heard in home, in church and state, to earth's remotest bound,
If the Devil, by a unanimous vote, is nowhere to be found?

Won't somebody step to the front forthwith, and make his bow, and show
How the frauds and the crimes of a single day spring up? We want to know.
The Devil was fairly voted out, and, of course, the Devil's gone;
But simple people would like to know who carries his business on?

REV. A. J. HOUGH.

Rev. Samuel Wakefield in his well-known "Christian Theology," p. 259, says: "We learn from Scripture that they (demons) are permitted to exercise power over the bodies of men." To sustain this he refers to the history of Job and the demoniacs, noticing the fact of the special mention made of the number and language of the demons, and of the manner of their expulsion. Again he says: "They have power to exercise an evil influence over the human mind." In proof of this he cites the cases of Judas, Ananias, and Sapphira, and others. Among other strong statements he uses the following: "It is their constant aim to dishonor God and to injure men, and in prosecuting their wicked designs they submit to no restraint but Almighty power."

Rev. ii. 10. "Behold the devil shall cast some of you into prison, that ye may be tried; and ye shall have tribulation ten days."

Rev. ix. 5, 6, 20. "And to them (the locusts) it was given that they should not kill them (men) but that they should be tormented five months, and their torment was as the torment of a scorpion when he striketh man.

And in those days shall men seek death and shall not find it; and shall desire to die, and death shall flee from them. And the rest of the men which were not killed by these plagues yet repented not."

Rev. xvi. 2, 9, 10, 11. "And there fell a noisome and grievous sore upon the men which had the mark of the beast. And men were scorched with great heat, and blasphemed the name of God, which hath power over these plagues; and they repented not, and blasphemed the God of Heaven, because of their pains and their sores, and repented not of their deeds."

These quotations settle the point that able theologians, with no thought of our doctrine, maintain that the demons have power over the bodies of men, and constantly strive to injure them; and that the Scripture expressly declares that such permission is granted to them for purposes of discipline or judgment.

In spite of the verse "I create evil," Isa. xlv. 7, and the famous account of the lying spirit's mission to Ahab's prophets, 2 Chron. xviii., we all believe that God is not, properly speaking, the author of sin. Of course the coming and existence of sin, and sickness if you please, was included in the divine plan, or else God's foreknowledge has narrow limitations; but when in His wisdom He allows the evil, it only seems, while condemning the voluntary actors, to bring out His glorious redemption. Now sickness is, most unquestionably, an evil. Good may result from it of course, but there is no use in trying to persuade a reasonable man that sickness, in itself, can ever be a good thing. We have already seen how God used it, or allowed it to be used, as a whip to bring the children of Israel back from their sins; and we all know full well that it has often the same use and effect to-day. Most people think Job's case is a mysterious and strange exception; but I long ago determined that it is a regular type of God's dealings with the soul. Job was a good man; so good and honest as to be called "perfect" by God himself. But Job, although perfect in heart, was not *mature;* and God wanted him to grow. This Job evidently failed to see, and therefore strong measures were necessary. Now let us carefully note that Satan was the direct agent who stole Job's sheep and camels, killed his sons and daughters, and at last actually "smote Job with sore boils from the sole of his foot unto his crown." Yes, Satan did it all. Nowadays men would say "the visitation of God," but the inspired writer tells us it was a visitation of the devil. Shall we suppose that the old adversary has lost any of his venom? On the contrary, "he hath great wrath, because he knows that his time is short."

But let us particularly remember that Satan could not and did not make Job sick *till God gave him a distinct permission to do so.* (Why it required the distinct permission of Jesus for the demons to enter the Gadarene swine. Even a hog cannot be touched by Satan except the Lord allow). Here we have a positive statement of the fact that Job had physical health by the keeping power of God alone, and that Job became sick only when that power was relaxed, for the purpose of opening his eyes to the advanced steps God wished him to take. (We all know the story, and remember its significant close; how God restored him to health and strength and possessions, as soon as the desired spiritual experience was received.) O reader! you who are sick in body and have suffered for months and years, does not this wonderful narrative cause you to think that you are halting and hesitating, failing to see God's leading, and just a little unresolved to say with Job to the very uttermost, "I abhor MYSELF?" That absolute death of self, how hard it is!

In Luke xiv. 4, 5, we see a plain inference made by the Lord himself that sickness, like the oxen's fall "into a pit," was a misfortune, which he was glad to heal or remedy when he could.

Again we read in Luke xiii. 11-17, of the "woman which had a spirit of infirmity eighteen years," who was healed on the Sabbath day to the disgust of the Jews. Jesus Himself spoke the words, "ought not this woman, being a daughter of Abraham, *whom Satan hath bound, lo, these eighteen years*, be loosed from this bond on the Sabbath day?" Truly it was a fit work for the Great Physician to break the chains of the prince of darkness, whether forged about the soul or the body.

Yet once more we have a plain statement of inspiration as to the origin of bodily disease. In Acts x. 38, Peter proclaimed *to the Gentiles*, that "God anointed Jesus of Nazareth with the Holy Ghost and with power: who went about doing good, *healing all that were oppressed of the devil;* for God was with him." It would be a very narrow interpretation that would limit this sweeping phrase to the few cases of demoniacal possession recorded in the gospel history. Evidently the entire list of healings is included, by the apostle, in this general statement of the daily work of Jesus. Then those who are sick, are "oppressed by the devil." Most certainly they are; and last but not least, we have Paul's distinct declaration that his "thorn," whatever it may have been, was a "minister of Satan," sent to "buffet" him. Surely nothing could be more conclusive than this.

(It being apparent then that disease is generally from Satan, and that its use, to the Christian sufferer, is purely corrective; it follows undeniably that if the cause or reason for the correction be removed, there is no necessity for the means of correction remaining.) The children of Israel left the task-master's lash in Egypt, and were not obliged to hear it crack in order to keep them humble. I mean by this, that I need not expect to carry a certain form of sickness to my grave, when the leading of the Lord has been seen and accepted. When the Jews turned to God, He received them, and always removed the plagues and bodily diseases which had been used as a means of punishment. And whenever a man came to Jesus, He accepted the faith as far as it went, and never refused to remove the suffering and physical disability.

We are now ready to turn to the Scriptures and read of the intent of the Atonement with reference to the work of Satan. Daniel prophesied that Christ would come after the seventy weeks, "to make an end of sins." Dan. ix. 24. He was to "restrain or finish the transgression," but of sins He would "make an end." What a glorious truth for the fully reconciled child of the King! But this sin is the work of the devil; and we have just seen from the Word that sickness emanates directly from the same baleful source. Why then should not an end be made of that also? If it was done for Israel in the wilderness, shall we, of the dispensation of grace, be less favored? It is admitted that sickness is but the beginning of death, that it is, in fact, death's advance guard and active agent; but Paul tells us that Jesus partook of our flesh and blood, "that through death he might destroy him that had the power of death, *that is the devil;* and deliver them who through fear of death were *all their life time* subject to bondage."—Heb. ii. 14, 15. Here we are distinctly told that the devil has the power of death; and therefore it follows that he has the power of sickness, as the van of death's army. Now Jesus has not yet destroyed death, except in the promise. That "last enemy" still exists and exercises power over us all, "For it is appointed unto men once to die." But here we find a parallel without a flaw. Sin is the disease which leads to the "second death," the death of the soul. Sickness is the disease which leads to bodily death. The Atonement of Christ has fully provided for the soul a salvation which makes an end of sin now, so that we may "serve, Him in righteousness and holiness all the days of our life," "being delivered from the present evil world;" and it has provided that we shall be delivered in the last great day, from the awful death which is the result and consequence of sin. But this latter deliverance is potential, we have it in the promise of God. The actual judicial day has not yet arrived, but we confidently expect it and believe that our names will be found written in the "Lamb's book of life." The advance guard of spiritual death—sin—is thus already destroyed through the work of Christ in our souls, and the main body, the dreadful reality itself is potentially destroyed in God's promise, and will be actually destroyed, so far as we are concerned, after the glorious appearing of our Lord, or at least when the books will be opened, and the names contained therein published to the universe. Now mark the beauty of the parallel. Jesus "took our infirmities and bore our sicknesses," just as He bore sins, and thus He "made an end" of the former, precisely as He did of the latter. His Atonement therefore makes it possible for us to live, as Moses did, and serve Him in health of body, as well as in holiness of heart, "all the days of our life;" and it has provided that we *shall be* deliverd bodily from the physical death which is the natural result of sickness. But just as before, this latter deliverance is potential; we have it in the promise. The actual day of its physical realization has not yet come, although we confidently believe it to be close at hand, when the "Lord himself shall descend from the heavens with a shout, and the dead in Christ shall rise first." "We shall all be changed, in a moment, in the twinkling of an eye." "This corruptible shall put on incorruption, and this mortal put on immortality." Mark the parallel, here clearly and beautifully set forth. The corruptible soul, which still is peccable shall put on incorruption, and be safe forever; while the mortal body which is still liable to the effects of disobedience shall put on immortality, and thereafter laugh at death to all eternity. This sin and this sickness are alike the handiwork of Satan; but the beloved disciple assures us that "For this purpose the Son of God was manifested, that He might destroy the works of the devil."—1 John iii. 8.

Ps. xc. 3, plainly states God's method: "Thou turnest man to destruction (hands him over to the adversary); and sayest, Return ye children of men," when he is humbled by the punishment God holds out mercy).

So also the case of Hymeneas and Alexander, whom Paul "delivered unto Satan *that they might learn not to blaspheme.*" Also the great King of Babylon, who spent seven years as a beast, in order to learn the same lesson.

But an objection arises. There are undoubtedly numerous places where God said, "I send sickness," "I will smite," etc. etc. These verses are many, but a sample of them all may be taken from Deut. xxviii. 58-61. "Then the Lord will make thy plagues wonderful, and the plagues of thy seed, even great plagues and of long continuance, and sore sickness, and of long continuance. Moreover he will bring upon thee all the diseases of Egypt, which thou wast afraid of; and they shall cleave unto thee. Also every sickness, and every plague which is not written in the book of this law, them will the Lord bring upon thee, until thou be destroyed." Or this, from 1 Sam. ii. 6.: "The Lord killeth and maketh alive; he bringeth down to the grave, and bringeth up."

I do not pretend to fathom the entire "mystery of iniquity;" nor to tell how or why the devil and his ministers still are found in heavenly places; (Eph. vi. 12 margin) but I surely know that sin is the primal source of all the "ills that flesh is heir to," and that the devil is the particular father of sin. And I further know that the devil is "he that hath the power of death,"—Heb. ii. 14. Now it is true that the record speaks of God as sending the plagues of Egypt, the plagues in the wilderness, the fiery serpents, and of the "Angel of the Lord" as executing the terrible judgment of the passover night, and as destroying Sennacherib's host, as as well as the Israelites in consequence of David's sin in numbering the people. All this and much more is well known, and I never thought of slighting, much less of denying it. Now let us squarely face the apparent dilemma.

Suppose it be admitted that these afflictions, with many modern ones, issued *directly* from the hand of "the Angel of the Lord," what of it? All that we are required to do is to turn to Ex. xv. 26, xxiii. 25, Deut. v. 38, vii. 15, and the rest of the many references in this book, to see plainly that these things never came except *as a consequence of sin.* And we must also observe that the most positive promises of perfect immunity from sickness were given again and again, contingent upon the good behavior of the people. (If they sinned, sickness came.) If they kept God's law health remained. Nothing can be plainer than this. But we well know that the real source of punishment is the sinful act. If my child disobeys, and I am obliged to whip him, it is perfectly proper to say that disobedience sends the whipping. In very truth Pharaoh's devilish sin sent death flying over Egypt; the great transgression of the Israelites sent the fiery serpents, and Miriam's offence sent the leprosy upon her. But let us remember that faith in the Lord saved the households of the Hebrews in Egypt, faith in the serpent saved the sufferers in the wilderness, and the prayer of faith saved Miriam. Those who contend that we ought to bear sickness with resignation will do well to consider this point. Did not the Lord send the fiery serpents? Yet did He not at the same time provide a means of escape? Ought those bitten Israelites to have patiently endured the bite "because the Lord sent it," or to have quickly looked and lived? Did not the Lord smite Miriam? But did He not heal her in a week in answer to prayer? Did not He smite Abimelech's household? And did He not heal in answer to Abraham's request? Gen. xx. 17. We can well believe that the "Angel of the Lord" did actually carry out the judicial execution of the Egyptians, Assyrians, and others, and that God, in these cases, took the "power of death" into His own hands, just as He twice did in the opposite sense for Enoch and Elijah. But the great fact remains that even if some sickness be admitted to come from God, it is always a punishment, corrective or preventive, and the *Son of Man is always lifted up at the same time* for those who will look and live.

Notwithstanding all these facts, it is entirely possible that the devil always is the direct agent in the coming of sickness. In the case of Ahab's lying prophet, 2 Chron. xviii., we are let into the secret, as we are in the story of Job; and in each of these a demon appears as the direct agent. (God grants His permission of course, for without the distinct permission of the Almighty, Satan cannot even enter a hog.) See Mark v.

(There is not a single case recorded in Scripture of the Lord's directly smiting any one with disease as a chastening or discipline, but that we also read of the entire recovery of the individual as soon as the lesson was learned. And such recovery was always through faith. But we do read of judicial punishments sent from the Lord upon the hopelessly wicked; and in such cases we find no record of repentance or cure.

Frances Ridley Havergal, before her death, wrote a beautiful little book for invalids called, "Starlight Through the Shadows." It contains a short article dated June 2, 1878, written to prove that Satan "is not the usual and normal instrument" in sickness, but that it is generally from God, and consequently is to be endured patiently, and cheerfully "remaimed under." The class of verses quoted by her have already been considered. One however deserves especial notice. Ps. xli. is cited as an instance of God's loving tender care over the sick, and she argues therefore, that the sickness could not be from Satan. The utter absence of all connection between the premises and the conclusion must be apparent to everyone. If we read the psalm in question we will see that David had the right conception of sickness. In verse 8, he says, "An evil disease (thing of Belial, margin) say they cleaveth fast unto him," while in verse 2 he has already declared his belief that the Lord "will not deliver him unto the will of his *enemies.*" No plainer proof could be desired that David considered disease "a thing of Belial," (2 Cor. vi. 15,) and that, to him, being sick was passing under the power or will of his enemies.

Immediately after this sadly deficient bit of reasoning, Miss Havergal sets forth a logical syllogism which is much more plausible. Quoting Ps. cxxi. 7.—"The Lord shall preserve thee from all evil," she says:

(1) What is of Satan must be evil. God's people are preserved from *all evil*. *Therefore*, God's people are preserved from whatever is of Satan.

(2) God's people are preserved from whatever is of Satan. They are not preserved from sickness. *Therefore*, sickness is not of Satan.

Suppose we do a little reasoning in the same fashion. David said, "many are the afflictions of the righteous; but the Lord delivereth him out of them all."—Ps. xxxiv. 19. Then as the Lord delivers the righteous out of *all* their afflictions, and as many righteous are not delivered out of sickness at all, *therefore* sickness is not an affliction.

Now what is the matter with this reasoning? Just this—the premises stated are themselves propositions requiring proof. Or better, the premises stated lead us to attribute perfection in graces to "the righteous" which it is not at all certain they possessed. "What is of Satan must be evil." We will not dispute that. "God's people are preserved from *all evil.*" We will not dispute that in general, but it cannot pass without most rigid explanation. Read the eleventh chapter of Hebrews and then say whether, in the sense assumed by our author, God's people ever were "preserved from all evil." Hear the record, "others were tortured, not accepting deliverance; that they might obtain a better resurrection: And others had trial of *cruel* mockings and scourgings, yea, moreover of bonds and imprisonment. They were stoned, they were sawn asunder, were tempted, were slain with the sword; they wandered about in sheepskins and goatskins; being destitute, *afflicted, tormented;* (of whom the world was not worthy;) they wandered in deserts, and in mountains, and in dens and caves of the earth."

Of course it will be at once admitted that these terrible temptations and sufferings were from the devil and his human agents, yet these righteous men were not delivered from them. Therefore the sense in which our author interprets the words "from all evil" must be radically wrong. This is the whole secret of the defect in all such reasoning. Notice that in this terrible list of afflictions, no mention is ever made of disease. Jesus promised persecutions and tribulations, but sickness never. "Himself took our infirmities and bare our sicknesses." The sickness in Ps. xli. manifestly came upon the writer in consequence of sin, as verse 4 plainly declares; and the sense in which our author uses the words "God's people," implies those who are not sinning, but who are living in perfect and entire conformity to His will.

Just here is a tender point, and one requiring a delicate touch. Many dear people cry out indignantly, "you say sickness is on account of sins and from the devil. I do not believe it, for my dear mother was one of the salt of the earth, and she was an invalid for years. I know she didn't sin." Softly brother! (I say that God alone can testify whether she sinned or not. Love is proverbially blind, and even if it had the eyes of Argus it could not see the "secret faults" which are open to the Lord. For myself I would much rather believe that my loved one had some sin, some failing, some shortcoming, some refusal to follow Christ to the very cross, and to cry, with outstretched hands, "drive the nails! crucify me with him!" than to believe him afflicted with one of sin's consequences and punishments unjustly, he being innocent.)—*It is this kind of reasoning that drives people to doubting God.* God called Job a "perfect man," and Job indignantly denied that his sickness was a punishment for sin. Yet we know that it was from the devil, (with God's permission, and this is always understood in the case of the righteous) and that Job clearly saw the "deeper depths" and "loftier heights" from which he had been holding back, and, so seeing, he "abhorred" himself, and repented in dust and ashes. Whereupon his prayer of faith was answered for his friends, and he was *immediately healed*, and given more abundantly of God's gifts.

Rev. T. DeWitt Talmage, preaching from Isa. vii. 20. said: "God is so kind and loving that when it is necessary for Him to cut, He has to go to others for the sharp-edged weapon. 'In the same day shall the Lord shave with a razor that is hired, namely by them beyond the river, by the king of Assyria, the head, and the hair of the feet; and it shall also consume the beard.' God is love. God is pity. God is help. God is shelter. God is rescue. There are no sharp edges about Him, no thrusting points, no instruments of laceration. If you want balm for wounds, He has that. If you want salve for divine eyesight, He has that. But if there is sharp and cutting work to do which requires a razor, that He hires. God has nothing about Him that hurts, save when dire necessity demands; and then He has to go clear off to some one else to get the instrument."

It *may* be true that God sometimes directly sends a sickness. We will not dispute the point; but it is certain that all such cases in Scripture, (allowing the literalness of language) come under three heads: 1. The judicial execution of sentence upon incorrigible sinners. 2. A sharp and limited punishment of believers. 3. A general plague upon a sinning nation. In the first case there is, of course, no repentance, no hope, no cure. In the second and third, the whip is lifted when the lesson is learned. And in neither of these is there the slightest reason for the "sickness to be remained under because the Lord may have sent it." On the contrary, we ought to pray, with Moses, "Heal her *now*, O Lord, I beseech thee," and, if faith exists, and the conditions can be met, the answer will as certainly come. The serpent is lifted up, brother. Look and live. Praise the Lord!

THE IMPORTANCE OF THE BODY.

We now come to a fundamental truth, which has been most sadly neglected, and has been terribly overgrown with weeds. The marvelous consummation which Paul so eloquently depicts in 1 Cor. xv. will never be brought about, *until* these so-called poor mortal bodies have been completely emancipated from the environment of sin, as well as from its effects. When "this mortal shall have put on immortality," "*then*," and not till then, shall be brought to pass the saying that is written, "Death is swallowed up in victory. O, death, where is thy sting? O, grave, where is thy victory?" Dr. A. J. Gordon, of Boston, has given some attention to this subject, and severely commented on what he calls the "caged eagle theory of the body."* The devil has worked hard and with great success, to persuade men that the body is of no special account. This general belief of the Christian church may be summarized as follows: My body is a great nuisance; it is a regular brake on the wheels of spiritual progress, it is continually forcing me to sin. I could be a tolerably decent Christian if it were not for this miserable body of mine. I make up my mind to act properly and put forth every possible effort of will, but my wretched body gives way and precipitates me into sin and all forms of evil. My soul is all right, it means to do well, but my body continually betrays me. It is a regular cage, with bars of steel, against which my poor soul beats its breast in vain. Heigho! I wish I was out of it. What a glorious thing it will be to see it stuck in a hole in the ground, it is nothing but dirt anyhow, and to soar aloft on spiritual wings, as free as the air of heaven. But as I cannot get rid of it till death sets me free, I suppose it is necessary as a discipline for my spirit. And so the strain runs on.

Now all this is straight from Satan, without any dilution whatever. Your body was made, with your soul, "in the image of God." True it was made out of dust, but please to remember that there was not an atom of sin in the world at that time; God had just made the dust, and "saw that it was good;" there was no evil in it. Now when sin entered, how was it, by an act of the body? Just here we come upon the old fallacy that the actual body of muscle and bone is capable of sin. This is the root of the

---

* See "Ministry of Healing." A book which furnishes the most absolute evidence that faith-healing, without the use of means, except the Scriptural ones of "anointing with oil," and "laying on of hands," has been practised in the church, all along the centuries, from the time of Christ to the present. It can be obtained at the Willard Tract Repositories, and from booksellers generally.

whole thing. My muscle and bone, my hands and feet, my eyes and tongue are merely dead matter, and are no more capable of sin or of sinning than is the marble statue. It is the intelligence within that sins. It is the mind and soul which God breathed into the dead matter and which alone guides that matter and vivifies it, that is capable of a volition, and consequently, of a sin. There are some sins it is true, which, in their commission, necessitate the exercise of some physical appetite or desire but these prove nothing. In fact the mere physical performance of these acts is not, strictly speaking, the sin at all. The gratification of lust is of course an outward sin of commission; but the real sin antedates the physical action. "Whosoever looketh on a woman, to lust after her, hath committed adultery already *in his heart.*" A man steals money from a drawer. The sin lies in the mental or moral act within his soul, and not in the physical motion of his hand. Another commits murder. The sin is in his heart, not in the actual physical extinction of the life *per se.* In no one of these physical acts is there any sin whatever. The relation between the sexes is the most sacred known to man, in its proper place. The movements of the hand properly put forth, are right and necessary; and even the taking of a human life is perfectly sinless when the sheriff touches the drop. My brother, the body which gives you so much trouble is not your physical body at all. It is the "body of sin," the "carnal mind," the "old man," the inbeing of sin. This it is that causes you to do what you hate, and to leave undone the things that you would do. This it is that reddens with anger, flashes with hate, burns with envy, festers with jealousies, puffs up with pride, exults in boasting, and destroys your peace. And this is that "body of sin" which "may be destroyed." Rom. vi. 6. This body was not made by God. It was not formed from the "good" dust. It did not grow in heaven. No, it was manufactured by Satan himself, and was *infused* into the first man in and through his primal act of unbelief. Now, praise the Lord, this cage can be broken open, now and here. You may be "delivered from this present evil world." And you can soar just as high as you please in the atmosphere of perfect love and perfect peace and perfect health of soul and spirit and body. A bird cannot fly higher than the atmosphere; and so we cannot soar into the eternities, for we are yet in time; but we can fly as straight toward the sun as ever flies the strongest eagle, and never strike any cage bars either.

For centuries Satan has been at his old trick of quoting, or misquoting Scripture; and he has systematically drilled Christians to repeat the everlasting excuse, "The spirit is willing, but the flesh is weak." They forget one of the chief names of Jehovah in the old time: "The God of all flesh." He it is who, when Sarah laughed at what she believed to be a physical impossibility, said in tender reproach, "Is anything too hard for the Lord?" Gen. xviii. 14. And He it is who told the weeping prophet, "Behold I am the Lord, the God of all flesh: is there anything too hard for me?"

HEALING OF BODILY DISEASE.

Jer. xxxii. 27. And centuries after the same God said to Paul, "My strength is made perfect in weakness."—2 Cor. xii. 9. This great truth was thoroughly impressed upon the heart of the great apostle to the Gentiles. He never scorned his body. True, he said it was better to be with Christ than to remain in a sinful world, but he never hinted that he desired to get rid of his body. On the contrary no one has ever spoken so earnestly of his desire to retain it. Hear him exclaim: "For we know that the whole creation groaneth and travaileth in pain together until now. And not only they but *ourselves also*, which have the first fruits of the Spirit, even we ourselves, groan within ourselves, waiting for the adopttion, to wit : the redemption of our body."—Rom. viii. 22, 23. The special point that Paul did not wish to lose his body, but only to have it glorified, on account of its circumscribed conditions, is luminously set forth thus: "For we know that if our earthly house of this tabernacle were dissolved, we have a building of God, an house not made with hands, eternal in the heavens. For in this we groan, earnestly desiring to be clothed upon with our house which is from heaven. If so be that being clothed we shall not be found naked. For we that are in this tabernacle do groan, being burdened: *not for that we would be unclothed, but clothed upon,* that mortality might be swallowed up of life."—2 Cor. v. 1–4.

Who but Paul so earnestly entreats us to "present your bodies, a living sacrifice, holy and acceptable unto God; which is your reasonable service?"—Rom. xii. 1. Manifestly he is not speaking of the "body of sin" or the "old man," for to present sin as a holy and acceptable sacrifice to God would certainly be an utterly unreasonable service as well as an everlasting impossibility.* If we read the law of the sacrifices, we are struck with the requisition that everything and every animal which was offered to God, should be absolutely "without blemish;" every sacrifice must be a "perfect sacrifice." I do not intend to arbitrarily distort symbols, and of course this signified and set forth the perfect nature of the Atoning sacrifice of Christ. But who will dare deny that we can also find a plain indication of that truth enunciated by the Saviour, "No man having put his hand to the plow, and looking back, is fit for the kingdom of God?"—Luke ix. 62. "My son, give me thine heart," Prov. xxiii. 26, means the whole of it, of course. God does not ask for a piece of it. Jesus said again, "No man can serve two masters," Matt. vi. 24; and the Psalmist assures us that God will not give his glory to another. All these texts contain the idea of a complete, unreserved, consecration and dedication to God—a "perfect sacrifice." But we may even go farther and say that

---

* I cannot forbear calling the attention of those who believe that the seventh of Romans contains the experience of an "advanced Christian," to this little difficulty. If, in this life, the "body of death," "the old man," "the flesh," etc. etc., are essentially identified with the actual mortal body, how in reason can I present this body, as a "holy and acceptable sacrifice unto God?" And, most absurd of all, how can it be a "perfect sacrifice?" Yet Paul says "I *beseech* you to do so."

there is another suggestion after all this. Is it going too far to imagine that a perfect body presented perfectly to God, and able to run upon His errands of mercy in all directions, is more "acceptable" to Him than a poor, dilapidated, sickly weakling, whose every moment is necessarily absorbed with self? You may answer that an invalid may truly serve God, and may manifest His sustaining grace. Very true. Israel in Egypt, toiling under the taskmaster's lash could, and to a certain extent, did do the same; but Israel on the other side of the Red Sea, and Israel in Canaan, served Him much better, and spoke so powerfully of His sustaining grace, and of His *conquering power*, that the world rings with the song of praise to-day. Miriam could never have sung her triumphal hymn while she was making bricks without straw, but she could have worshiped the God of the promises.

But we have not done with Paul. In 1 Cor. vi. 13, we read: "Now the body is not for fornication, but *for the Lord;* and the *Lord for the body*." If my body then is "for the Lord," is it not reasonable to suppose that a whole body is better and more pleasing to Him than a mere wreck? "Know ye not that your bodies are the members of Christ."—v. 15. Here the apostle, beyond any possible question, speaks of our physical bodies. But, he says, they are "members of Christ." How dreadfully incongruous to think of Christ possessing "members" deformed and defaced by every kind of disease; especially when we remember that disease generally is of the devil! We can readily look upon the scar of an old wound, but it is hard to tolerate the presence of a gaping, running sore. *It is a sign of corruption in the blood.* "What, know ye not that your body is the temple of the Holy Ghost, which is in you?" The tabernacle was not only entirely consecrated to God, and anointed in every part, but it was built of perfect materials. In such a temple the overpowering glory of God could dwell. But how can I (*if I have the light on the subject*) retain in my body a portion of the devil's work, and then look for the new Shekinah, the glory of the Holy Ghost to dwell within? "For ye are bought with a price; therefore glorify God in your body, and in your spirit, which are God's"—v. 20. Here the apostle distinctly and undeniably stretches the infinite folds of the Atonement over the body as well as the spirit: for one, as well as the other, is "bought with a price."

Yet again, Paul says, "know ye not that ye are the temple of God, and that the Spirit of God dwelleth in you? If any man defile the temple of God, him shall God destroy; for the temple of God is holy, which temple ye are."—1 Cor. iii. 16, 17. "In whom ye are also builded together for an habitation of God through the Spirit."—Eph. ii. 22. "But Christ is a Son over his own house; whose house are we."—Heb. iii. 6. And thus Peter speaks, "Ye also, as lively stones, are built up a spiritual house, on holy priesthood, to offer up a spiritual sacrifice, acceptable to God by Jesus Christ."—1 Pet. ii. 5. And Paul insists, "So now also Christ shall be magnified in my body, whether it be by life, or by death."

Phil. i. 20. "But the body is of Christ."—Col. ii. 17. Surely, in view of these marvelous texts, I should strive to welcome my Lord and Master into a clean house, a house free from any corruption of sin, or any of the remains or effects of sin. In this very line we find Paul offering his famous prayer, "I pray God your *whole spirit and soul and body* be preserved blameless unto the coming of our Lord Jesus Christ."—1 Thess. v. 23. And then follows the glorious assurance, "Faithful is he that calleth you, who also will do it." Here again we see the great yearning of Paul's heart for the day of complete redemption when the entire man shall, in perfect unity of being, stand before God. But we see with renewed force that Paul considered his body as absolutely necessary to that glorious consummation, and so he prays for the body in precisely the same language that he uses for the soul and spirit. Each must be preserved "blameless."

Jude 9 testifies to the importance of the body *before* the resurrection day, in a way that is as remarkable as it is strange. There we read that the great Archangel Michael disputed *with the devil* about the body, of Moses. Here we have unimpeachable testimony to the practical fact that the devil has the power of death. Further than this, it seems as if this strange power of Satan over the body endures after death; at least if the idea be correct that the occasion of the dispute was when Moses needed his body for the scene upon the Mount of Transfiguration. As is well known, it has been remarked that Elijah had never laid aside his body, but that the body of the great lawgiver had passed under the power of death; and hence it is imagined that Satan opposed even the temporary use of the body upon that wondrous occasion. Moses could not appear with a resurrection body, else Christ would not have been "the first fruits of them that slept."

The thought suggested itself to my mind that the dispute may have taken place at the time of Moses' death. We know that Moses went up to the top of Pisgah, and that the Lord was there with him, and showed him all the land of Canaan. And then we are told Moses died, and the Lord buried him in a valley over against Beth-peor. There is an old tradition which has come down from the earliest times, amongst the Jews and Arabians, that when the moment for dissolution arrived, the Lord kissed him, and that the supreme ecstasy of that crowning manifestation of the divine love separated the soul from the body. Now, before the idea contained in this tradition is utterly condemned, let us consider a few facts. We are positively assured that Moses was not sick, but that up to his death he possessed perfect health and strength. Though one hundred and twenty years old, "his eye was not dim, nor his natural force abated."— Deut. xxxiv. 7. It is therefore clear that he did not die from disease. But in all our experience death has never been known to result from any cause except sickness, decay or accident. The word of inspiration settles all question as to each of these. There was no decay, no disease, and no accident. How then did Moses come to die! We might ask, how could a man be claimed by death in whom was no disease and whose vitality was unimpaired? This will prove an interesting problem for scientific thought. We have just seen that the devil has the power of death, and hence it follows that when the body comes to die, it must pass, in that sense, under the hand of Satan. Now death in Scripture is always spoken of as an enemy; and in this light we see Satan standing, with scythe in hand, ready to cut down the body, even if the soul escapes his power. Unquestionably, therefore, the devil appeared on the top of Pisgah to claim his dominion over the body of the greatest of the prophets. But at this point a wondrous vision rises before us. We see Mount Sinai "altogether on a smoke," and a terrible glory flashing from the thick darkness upon its summit. Moses has interceded for the great sin of the people, in the matter of the golden calf, and God has pardoned, at his word. Hungering and thirsting after God, Moses presses his request, "I beseech thee, show me thy glory." No honest prayer, from such a heart, goes unanswered; and God said, "I will make all my goodness pass before thee, and I will proclaim the name of the Lord before thee. And he said, *Thou canst not see my face: for there shall no man see me and live.* And it shall come to pass that, while my glory passeth by, that I will put thee in a cleft of the rock, and will cover thee with my hand while I pass by: And I will take away mine hand and thou shalt see my back parts: but my face shall not be seen."—Ex. xxxiii. 18–23. And all this was wondrously fulfilled. "And the Lord passed by before him, and proclaimed, the Lord, The Lord God, merciful and gracious, long-suffering, and abundant in goodness and truth."—Ex. xxxiv. 6.

God had nearly forty years of work for Moses then, and so He could not answer him any further. But the prayer remained before the throne, calling for the full response; just as thousands of God's servants have waited a score of years or more for the reply from heaven to their prevailing petitions. And now the scene changes to another mountain, and again God and Moses stand together looking out upon the promised land. The great prophet's words have all been uttered, the mighty leader's work is done, and his time on earth is over. "He who has the power of death" exultingly draws near to claim what he can as his prey, and the fatal dart is drawn. But now, after forty years, the urgent prayer of the thirsting soul makes itself heard,—"I beseech thee show me thy glory," and before death can discharge his shaft, God's mighty hand, that once covered Moses in the "cleft of the rock," is tenderly and lovingly withdrawn, and *God's face is seen at last.* Such ineffable glory is too much for a mortal body, and in an instant the spirit bursts all bounds of flesh and bone, and death is despoiled of a victim. Satan may "dispute," but the great Archangel replies, "The Lord rebuke thee," and Moses' body is laid to rest by heavenly ministers. The prayer offered upon Sinai is answered, after so many years, upon Nebo; and Moses sees God's face. The prayer for the flesh, that his feet might tread the promised land, was denied, and he was told to forbear asking; but the greater request was finally granted. He looked upon the land and it delighted his eyes, he looked upon God, and it ravished away his life. Only the pure in heart shall see God, and none but the pure in heart will ever dare to pray, "I beseech thee show me thy glory."

3. "To the Law and to the Testimony."

A powerful argument to show that God intended the Atonement to make provision for the body, as well as for the soul, can be found in the book of Leviticus. Beginning with the eleventh chapter, and running to the end of the fifteenth, we have clear and specific directions for bodily diseases. In the eleventh chapter is laid down the distinction between clean and unclean beasts, with the corresponding laws of diet.

A SANCTIFIED DIET.

Is the eleventh chapter of Leviticus binding upon us to-day? Let us look at this question, for it is a very important one and has vital reference to the next chapter.

People foolishly imagine that the Jews were permitted to eat the ox, and were forbidden to eat swine, hare, shell-fish, etc., etc., purely for arbitrary reasons known to the Almighty; or that at best a mere symbol was desired in order to teach a spiritual truth.

We know that in Eden man was permitted to eat of every tree, and told that each one was good for food, but that he was restricted from the tree of knowledge. And while this command had all the moral significance desired, it also involved injurious physical consequences in its disobedience, even death. Now Moses expressly explained to the Hebrews that all God's laws and statutes had a perfectly reasonable basis. "And the Lord commanded us to do *all* these statutes, to fear the Lord our God, *for our good always, that he might preserve us alive!*— Deut. vi. 24. These dietary laws were included in "all these statutes," and they were "for their good always," that the "Lord might preserve them alive!" There is a very important thought here for Christians who profess absolute and entire consecration to God. The latest modern science thoroughly agrees with Moses that the list of "unclean beasts" are without exception unhealthy, and actually injurious to the human system. *If, therefore, I have comprehended this light* upon the word, and deliberately eat that which God told my fellow men not to eat "for their good always," I may expect to be brought under condemnation for committed sin, and possibly may experience physical punishment also. But before we go any farther let us meet and permanently settle the few objections which are sometimes made to this view.

I. Peter's Vision.—In Acts x. 15, God said to Peter, "What I have cleansed, that call not thou unclean." The sheet contained all manner of beasts of the earth, and Peter objected to eating them when ordered to do so. Surely any man of common sense will admit, after a moment's thought, that the whole thing bears the indelible impress of purely typical teaching. 1. It was a vision, and not an actual occurrence. 2. Peter did not proceed to kill anything, much less to eat it. 3. Peter evidently did not attach any physical significance along the line of diet, but was wondering what it could mean. 4. While he was thus wondering the messengers of Cornelius arrived, and in verse 28 he distinctly announces the purport of the vision, saying "God hath shewed me that I should not call any man common or unclean." Rom. xiv. 14, is so obviously explained by the context that it needs no remark, except to say that a man's "esteem" for a poison will make no possible difference in the time of his funeral.

II. PAUL TO THE CORINTHIANS.—In 1 Cor. x. 25-27, occurs the injunction to eat "whatsoever is sold in the shambles," and "whatsoever is set before you, asking no questions for conscience sake." It ought not to be necessary here to say that the apostle simply referred to the one point of meat which had been offered to idols, only this and nothing more. He is plainly advising conscientious Christians to buy meat without asking whether it had been in a heathen temple or not, giving as a reason that "the earth is the Lord's and the fullness thereof," and consequently, as the meat was created by the Lord and really belonged to him, it did not put any moral taint upon it if a heathen offered it to his idol. This is rather an unfortunate place from which to raise an objection to the Scripture law of diet, for the apostle adds "whether therefore ye eat, or drink, or whatsoever ye do, do all to the glory of God." We can honor God most by simple obedience, and the *commands* of Leviticus and Deuteronomy as to diet stand without the shadow of a repeal.

III. PAUL TO TIMOTHY.—But, some one will say, "What are you going to do with the plain declaration of the apostle, in 1 Tim. iv. 4., "Every creature of God is good, and nothing to be refused,' etc?" We respond by asking, What are *you* going to do with it? We await your reflection on this. Read the whole passage. If you cut these words out and hold to them literally, fully, and alone, where will you be? Set your table and invite your friends. Lay out your bill of fare. "Every creature is good" remember; so pile them on: Cats, dogs, rats, mice, vultures, wolves, vampires, snails, worms, insects, snakes, spiders, the poisonous herbs like deadly nightshade, and all the list of vegetable poisons, and every repulsive and unwholesome creature under the sun, for they are all "good." And when you sit down to eat remember "nothing is to be refused." Brother, if you will carry out your faith and eat the meal, we will promise you a sensational funeral, and will endeavor to put up a stone bearing the epitaph, "*Here lies the victim of the* "*letter which killeth.*"

To be serious, is it not perfectly plain that the apostle's thought contained a certain limitation on the words "every creature." But did his language give any such intimation? It did. He is predicting that certain seducers will arise in the last times who will forbid to marry and command to abstain from meats.* What meats? He plainly says, "which God hath *created to be received with thanksgiving*," etc. Now please institute the simple inquiry, What meats or creatures has God created to be received with thanksgiving? Even your marginal reference here will send you to Gen. i. 29, where the herbs were given. But, as we have seen, many herbs are absolutely deadly, and have been so back before the days of Moses. Therefore, passing over the permission to eat flesh given to Noah, we come to Moses and his plain and detailed directions on this point. Here we find a list which agrees with the *best* scientific opinion everywhere, and which has never been repealed. While some scientists differ as to certain creatures therein described, as, for example, the oyster, yet the great mass of modern testimony is summed up in the words used some time ago by Hall's Journal of Health, when it declared, "It takes the world three thousand years to find out that Moses's laws of health cannot be surpassed." (These word are not exact, but the sense is).

There is a very general tendency in our day to study health laws, and a more moderate tendency to practise them. God is getting his people gradually ready for the coming of His Son, who, when He comes, will desire to find us fit physical temples for the Holy Ghost, and clean in every particular. What a revolution it would make in the health of a generation of Christians if they could join in Peter's magnificent testimony, "*I have never eaten anything common or unclean.*"

Dr. Adam Clark's witty grace at table, was meant in earnest, and hits the nail on the head; "Lord bless these vegetables, and this fruit and bread; and if thou canst bless under the gospel, what thou didst curse under the law, bless this swine's flesh also."†

If a man so much as touched one of these unclean beasts he was ordered to wash himself and to be "unclean unto the even." And God said that if a man ate of any of these he "defiled himself," whereas God commanded, "Ye shall be holy, for I am holy."—Lev. xi. 44.

When a woman bore a child, we read that she was to be purified during several weeks; and that she should then bring a lamb, and a young pigeon or a turtle-dove to the priest, "Who shall offer it before the Lord, and make an *atonement* for her; and she shall be cleansed."—Lev. xii. 6, 7. As if this were not strong enough, the eighth verse adds, in case of her inability to bring a lamb, that she shall bring two doves, "*the one for a burnt offering, and the other for a sin offering:* and the priest shall make an *atonement* for her, and she shall be clean." Here we have the idea of sin in an unavoidable bodily sickness or weakness, made specially

---

* See Appendix C, for Theosophy and "Esoteric" Devilism.
† The name of swine in the Latin is *scrofula*.

emphatic; and our thoughts turn back to the primal curse on account of sin, "in sorrow thou shalt bring forth children."—Gen. iii. 16.

In the thirteenth and fourteenth chapters we find the law of leprosy. Always considered to be a special type of sin, its method of treatment is very important. From first to last we find that the leper has to do with the priest and God. The rite for cleansing is minutely described, and was very elaborate. Two birds were taken; one killed in "an earthen vessel over running water," the living bird dipped in the blood of the slain and then set free; while the leper was sprinkled seven times with the blood, after which he must shave and wash. Again after seven days, he must shave off all his hair even to his eyebrows, and after washing on the eighth day, he must bring "two lambs *without blemish*," one ewe lamb, with flour and oil. These the priests took and offered before the Lord. The lamb was slain "in the place where he shall kill the *sin offering*." The blood was to be touched upon the tip of the right ear, the thumb of the right hand, and the great toe of the right foot; and the oil was used in a similar manner. Then the priests offered the *sin offering*, and made "*an atonement for him that is to be cleansed from his uncleanness.*" Now let us specially note that all this was to be done *after* the healing of the disease; or in other words, when the patient possessed in his body only the consequences or stigma of sickness. Then follow the strange directions as to the plague of leprosy in the walls of a house, and the visible appearance of it is described, with the same provision of bird's blood and sacrifice for its cleansing.

In chapter xv. we read of a general class of bodily disorders, which in all ages have been very wide-spread, and which afflicts an enormous percentage of the human race, in one form or another, sapping vitality and impairing the life-forces of the entire system. Yet for these also we read that the same general line of treatment should be followed. The individual went to the priest, who offered "a sin-offering and a burnt-offering," and after certain washings he was made whole and clean.

In these cases, and in some others, the Jews were distinctly ordered, as we have seen, to go to the priest and have him offer a sacrifice, and make an atonement for them. Beyond a doubt this indicated the necessity of the blood to cleanse even from *sins of accident and ignorance*; but there is strong ground afforded also for the Atoning Sacrifice for disease.

But another valuable argument is found in The Law of the Priesthood. Reading carefully Lev. xxi. we find that no man was allowed to perform the functions of the office who was not perfect physically. He must be very careful of his body, so much so that he could not even touch the dead body of a dear relative; and he could not even marry a widow. But of his own personal physique we find the most explicit command. "Speak unto Aaron saying, Whosoever he be of thy seed in their generations that *hath any blemish*, let him not approach to offer the bread of his God. For

HEALING OF BODILY DISEASE.

whatsoever man he be that hath a blemish, he shall not approach a blind man, or a lame, or he that hath a flat nose, or anything superfluous, or a man that is broken-footed or broken-handed, or crook-backed or a dwarf, or that hath a blemish in his eye, or be scurvy, or scabbed, or hath his stones broken. No man that hath a blemish of the seed of Aaron the priest shall come nigh to offer the offerings of the Lord made by fire; he hath a blemish; he shall not come nigh to offer the bread of his God. He shall eat the bread of his God, both of the most holy, and of the holy. Only he shall not *go in unto the vail*, nor come nigh unto the altar, because he hath a blemish; *that he profane not my sanctuaries;* for I the Lord do sanctify them." In close connection with this we see that a man afflicted with a certain infirmity which absolutely interfered with the exercise of full manhood's powers, "should not enter into the congregation of the Lord."—Deut. xxiii. 1.

We have already considered the New Testament argument from Rom. xii. 1. In Heb. ix. 22, Paul tells us that "almost all things are by the law purged with blood;" and in Heb. x. 22, he speaks of "having our bodies washed with pure water." Peter calls the church " a royal priesthood," 1 Pet. ix. 9, evidently referring to Ex. xix. 5, 6, where God said, "Ye shall be a peculiar treasure unto me above all people; for all the earth is mine; And ye shall be unto me a *kingdom of priests* and an holy nation." John declares, in Rev. i. 6, that God "hath made us kings and priests unto God," and the "new song" of the elders and the redeemed before the throne bore the same glad refrain. Rev. v. 10 and xx. 6. And Paul also assures us that we have "boldness to enter into the holiest by the blood of Jesus, by a new and living way, which he hath consecrated for us through the veil, that is to say, his flesh."—Heb. x. 19-22. Manifestly all these latter references are primarily to the soul's experience, but there is certainly much food for thought in these close parallels between the body and the spirit. If God was so pleased to see a whole body, in the person of His ministering priest under the old covenant, is He any the less pleased under the new and better way?

A single reference will show that able commentators have seen the fact, that an atonement was required for bodily disease, under the Mosaic economy. The Rev. Samuel Wakefield, in his Theology, while discussing the Atonement, says, page 351: "But in proof that the life of animal sacrifices was accepted *in place of the life of man*, we observe, *that the law required a sacrificial atonement even for bodily disorders.* All such unclean persons were liable to death, and were exempted from it only by animal sacrifices. This appears from the conclusion of the Levitical directions concerning the ceremonial which was to be followed in all cases. 'Thus shall ye separate the children of Israel from their uncleanness, when they defile my tabernacle that is among you.'—Lev. xv. 31. So, then, by virtue of sin-offerings the children of Israel were saved from a *death* which they would otherwise have suffered for their uncleanness (bodily), and that by substituting the life of the animal for that of the offerer." This is certainly strong enough for the preceding argument. It is then clear that, under the Mosaic dispensation, God was the only physician, and He ordained that disease should be healed and its consequences removed, through the Atonement of blood.

4.—Who may be Healed.

Having established the great truths that sickness is from the devil; that the body is not a mere cage for the soul, but is destined to be united with it always; and that disease was formerly healed, and may now be removed, through the merits of the Atonement of our Lord, we are naturally led to inquire into the extent of this gift of God in Christ Jesus. After every objection has been met and vanquished, the last stand has always been made upon the ground, "It may not be God's will to heal me." I have previously considered this objection in a little tract, "If it be Thy Will,"* but it needs some treatment here. The chief way to know God's will is to read His word. Let us therefore look for any directions to the sick which it may contain. G. W. McCalla recently compiled a valuable little book of Scripture texts, called, "The Word of the Lord Concerning Sickness," which is of inestimable value to any soul seeking light on this point. Now we have already seen that in the earlier dispensations God was the Great Physician. Abraham prayed for Abimelech's household, Gen. xx. 17. Moses prayed for Miriam, Num. xii. 13. We have seen that Moses prayed for the people repeatedly. Solomon prayed for the nation; 1 Kings viii. 37-39, and 2 Chron. vi. 28-30. Elisha healed Naaman; 2 Kings v., Hezekiah prayed for himself and again for the people; 2 Kings xx. 5, and 2 Chron. xxx. 20. David prayed for himself; Psalm vi. 2, and expressed his faith in the healing power of God, Ps. xxvii. 1; xxx. 2, 3; xli. 3; xci. 3-7; ciii. 2-5; cvii. 20; cxviii. 17. Jeremiah does the same, Jer. xvii. 14; xxxiii. 6. Ezekiel xxxiv. 2, 4, 16, and Mal. iv. 2, all testify of the same glorious truth. Besides these unmistakable texts, there is a large class of promises which can just as well be taken for bodily healing as for anything else. "Cast thy burden upon the Lord and he shall sustain thee," Ps. lv. 22, and "Give us help from trouble, for vain is the help of man," Ps. lx. 11, are good examples of these. Any trouble, surely, is meant; and who will say that severe illness is not a trouble or a burden? The entire list of these promises, in Old and New Testaments, can therefore be readily cited to show God's will in the matter.

But, outside of these and of the Mosaic economy, is there no direction whatever to the sick. Let us see. The word

PHYSICIAN

only occurs eleven times in Scripture. In Gen. l. 2, we read of the physicians who embalmed the body of Jacob at the command of Joseph.

---

*G. W. McCalla, 813 Arch St. Philadelphia.

HEALING OF BODILY DISEASE.

2 Chr. xvi. 12, speaks in gentle sarcasm of Asa's great mistake in seeking the physicians instead of the Lord; and of his death in consequence. Job. xiii. 4, gives the idea that physicians might or might not be of use. Jer. viii. 22, intimates that no physician could heal the disorder of the chosen people. Matt. ix. 12, Mark ii. 17, and Luke v. 31, each quote a Jewish proverb, and apply it spiritually. *Mark v. 26, and Luke viii. 43, speak of the woman who had suffered many things of many physicians, spent all her living upon them and only grew worse. And finally, Col. iv. 14, mentions the former profession of Luke. The word MEDICINE is found only (four) times. Prov. xvii. 22, uses the word in a comparison, and Ezek. xlvii. 12, speaks of it in a figure. While Jeremiah declares, xxx. 13, that there is no healing medicine for his people, but that God can heal; and in xlvi. 11, he similarly uses the words, "In vain shalt thou use many medicines." We read however a great deal about Him whom we love to call the Great Physician; how He healed every sickness and every manner of disease among the people, and *never turned away a single one*. "He healed all that were sick." The plain fact stares us in the face that the only human physicians mentioned in the Bible, are those who embalmed a dead body, those who killed King Asa, those of whom the poor woman suffered many things, and Luke, who changed his profession for the ministry, and, with the others, healed the sick by using the Lord's means. Matt. x. 1., Luke x. 9-17. And again, there is not a single command or intimation in the whole Bible which directs the use of medicine. Certainly this is very singular, to say the least.

But the singularity of this total neglect of the subject of doctors and remedies is fully explained, when we remember the very large number of references to the healing power of God. We have seen that this extends throughout the sacred books, from Genesis to Revelation. *The tree of life was left in Eden, and God is its sole owner and dispenser.* And " he giveth life to whomsoever he will." Thus we find miracles of healing everywhere, and *always* by the "mighty power of God."

If, then, God is the Healer, we only need to read His directions to the sick in order to know His will. Jesus Christ gave the first commission to the apostles thus: "He sent them to preach the kingdom of God and to heal the sick. And they departed and went through the towns, preaching the gospel of the kingdom, and healing everywhere," Luke ix. 1, 2-6. In Matt. x. we read: "He gave them power against unclean spirits, to cast them out, and to heal *all manner* of sicknesses and *all manner* of diseases," and He commanded them, "As ye go preach saying, The kingdom of heaven is at hand, heal the sick, cleanse the lepers, raise the dead,

---

* Luke iv. 23: "Physician heal thyself" may have been a proverb of sarcasm Possibly it was customary to quote this saying at that time because of the general failure of physicians to heal anybody. It seems to suggest the idea that the profession were not ready to take their own remedies. In sober earnest, it was certainly a sarcastic saying, and the Word says it was a "proverb" in the days of Christ.

cast out devils; freely ye have received, freely give": vs. 7, 8. When He commissioned the seventy disciples, He commanded them to preach, and "into whatsoever city ye enter heal the sick that are therein," Luke x. 8, 9. This was certainly a free command to heal every one who came to them and asked for healing. Just before Christ ascended He said to His apostles and disciples: "And these signs shall follow *them that believe:* in My name shall they cast out devils; they shall speak with new tongues; they shall take up serpents; and if they drink any deadly thing it shall not hurt them; they shall lay hands on the sick, and they shall recover," Mark xvi. 17, 18. And then He said, "All power is given unto Me in heaven and earth," Matt. xxviii. 18: "And lo, I am with you alway, even unto the end of the age"; vs. 20. But "Jesus Christ is the same yesterday, to-day and forever," Heb. xiii. 8; and if He is with us, and is the same, why should it not be His will to heal to-day just as much as it was yesterday, when "He healed all that were sick?" Again, we are told that "God hath dealt to every man the measure of faith," Rom. xii. 3. "Faith should not stand in the wisdom of men, but in the power of God," 1 Cor. ii. 5, and "all the promises of God in Him are yea, and in him Amen, unto the glory of God by us," 2 Cor. i. 20. This plainly means that it is for the glory of God to fulfill His promises in and to us, at all times.

In the twelfth chapter of First Corinthians we read of the existence in the church of "gifts of healing," in conjunction with others, all bestowed "by the same Spirit," upon various members in the church of that day. This follows as a natural consequence of Christ's parting words as recorded by Mark. The early Christian Fathers, for several centuries, assure us that "miracles" and "gifts of healing" prevailed in the church and were known to them as of frequent manifestation until the church mounted the throne in the person of Constantine. But all along the centuries we find record of simple faith in God's word being honored in the healing of the sick and in other ways. The testimony on this point is simply unanswerable, and convincing to any honest mind.* I do not adduce this evidence here, but mention it as of collateral importance. We are now simply searching the Word of God. It is well however to know that many of the children of the Kingdom have so understood the Word.

The case of Epaphroditus, recorded in Phil. ii 25–27, plainly indicates that he had recourse to God and not to the physicians, for "God had mercy on him." Now we well know that "without faith it is impossible to please God."—Heb. xi. 6. Hence faith must always please Him. God therefore must always be glad to see trust in His power alone manifested by the sons of men. Again James tells us that "faith without works is dead," ii. 17. But what could be more

---

*See Dr. Gordon's Ministry of Healing.

tangible to ourselves and to others, than to show our faith in the promise by our works, in actually relying on God the Unseen, for the visible healing of our bodies? "That men may *see* your good works and glorify your Father which is in heaven." Then again James says, "Is any among you afflicted? Let him pray."—v. 13. Now notice that the apostle does not promise that the affliction shall be removed. This point is of the greatest importance. Prayer here is recommended as a comfort, and as a means of obtaining grace from on high, but no assurance is given that the trouble shall be removed. The apostle remembered that Jesus said "In the world ye shall have tribulation," and "If they persecute me, they will also persecute you." And the various epistles are full of allusions to the real discomfort, trouble and unjust treatment which may be expected by the true child of God. Those who sang so joyfully around the throne in John's vision, were "they who had washed their robes in the blood of the Lamb, and had come through great tribulation." Now with this fact sharply outlined before us, that Jesus not only does not propose to save us *from* trouble and affliction, but rather to save *through* or *in* tribulation, we are ready for the vivid contrast afforded by the next verses.

"*Is any sick among you? let him call for the elders of the church; and let them pray over him, anointing him with oil in the name of the Lord. And the prayer of faith shall save the sick, and the Lord shall raise him up; and if he have committed sins, they shall be forgiven him.*"—Jas. v. 14, 15.

Now no sane man can deliberately read these words without admitting that they plainly direct "any sick," to call for the elders, and be anointed with oil in the name of the Lord; whereupon he is assured that God will certainly heal him, through the prayer of *faith*, and that if he has committed sin, as an exciting cause of the sickness, it shall be forgiven him. For those who hold authority as truth, I advise a careful reading of Dean Alford's comment on this passage. See Introduction, p. 17. That this command was not given to the immediate apostolic family is proved by the opening words of the epistle: "James, a servant of God and of the Lord Jesus Christ, to the twelve tribes which are scattered abroad." Surely this is sufficiently comprehensive. Now it is certainly remarkable that the apostle should open his letter with the caution "count it all joy when ye fall into divers temptations, knowing this, that the trying of your faith worketh patience," and should close it with a plain direction to "any sick," to be cured by the Lord alone, if he considered sickness of the body to be in any sense *essential* to growth in grace. He makes no exceptions whatever, no limitations, but gives the broad promise to "any sick among you."* And then, as is to amplify it, he adds, "Confess your faults one to another, and pray one for another, that ye may be healed.

---

*Undoubtedly we are to understand this now, among you who love the Lord in sincerity and truth. Manifestly it would be almost blasphemous for a rebellious soul, refusing allegiance to Jesus, to come and ask a favor at His hands purely for selfish reasons.

The effectual fervent prayer of a righteous man availeth much,"—vs. 16. Are we to confess our faults in this year of grace? If half the promise is dead, we have no business to use the other half, but should bury it also in the tomb of the apostles.

But James goes further still. As if pursuing the doubts that might arise, about these visible physical things, he recalls the fact that "Elias, a man *subject to like passions as we are,* prayed earnestly that it might not rain: and it rained not on the earth by the space of three years and six months. And he prayed again and the earth brought forth her fruit." vs. 17, 18. Of course he did not mean to teach that every believer could pray *at will* for physical things, but to support faith in God's power to answer prayer in the domain of matter as well as of spirit. As to God's will in sickness, verses fourteen and fifteen absolutely settle that. Let the reader ask himself, if God had meant to give a promise of physical healing, through faith in Jesus Christ, could it have been given in any plainer language than we find in these verses of James' epistle? What could God say? What could be asked of Him? Should He have said, Let any sick man call upon me and I will certainly cure him by my power alone; would it be sufficient? Yet this is just what we do find in that word which shall never pass away, though the heavens and the earth be moved. God says, let any sick call for the elders; let them pray; let them anoint the sick with oil in the name of the Lord; whereupon the prayer of faith shall save; the Lord shall raise him up, and forgive his sins. Now, in sober earnest, what more could be asked? If this is not clear, specific, and conclusive, what is? Let some one try to improve it, if he can. He will fail more signally than the man who attempted to improve on the parables of Jesus.*

5.—THE SIN UNTO DEATH.

I ask the most earnest attention to this section. If it be read with care, and remembered, much adverse criticism of Divine healing will be forestalled.

"The number of thy days I will fulfill,"—Ex. xxiii. 26. "The days of our years are three-score years and ten."—Ps. xc. 10. "Bloody and deceitful men shall not live out half their days."—Ps. lv. 23. "To deliver such an one unto Satan for the destruction of the flesh, that the spirit may be saved in the day of the Lord Jesus."—1 Cor. v. 5. "Of whom is Hymeneus and Alexander, whom I have delivered unto Satan, that they may learn not to blaspheme."—1 Tim. i. 20.

These verses bring before us the possibility of a forfeiture of the benefits held out in a certain class of promises. While the full number of days is unquestionably assured, yet by wickedness this may be-

---

*Let those who say that faith-healing is "only a privilege and not a command," recall the oft-repeated words of John Wesley, "Every command of God implies a promise," and then consider whether the converse is not good also, every promise implies a command.

come null; while we see clearly that it is often necessary for men to sicken, suffer and even to die in order that the "spirit may be saved." But it is equally clear that such a dire necessity only exists because of their offenses, and persistence in disobedience. Had they turned to God earlier, it might have been different. Manifestly then these people cannot be healed in answer to prayer; but we must be very careful how we sit in judgment on such cases.

But there is another side to this. It is entirely possible for some offense to bar out the holiest saints from these benefits. Our friends who recoil from the imputation of persistent disobedience upon their invalid loved-ones may take comfort here, and at the same time see nothing against the doctrine of Divine Healing. I repeat the thought, one of the holiest Christians *may* be unable to find healing through faith, not because of persistence in unbelief or disobedience, but because of some single past offense *long since forgiven*.

We are well aware that Moses, "the man of God," was guilty of an offense in the wilderness, for which he was forbidden to enter the land of promise. His heart yearned to cross over Jordan, and he, who was never unheard, prayed for premission to go. But God said "Let it suffice thee; speak no more unto me of this matter."—Deut. iii. 26. Moses did not lose his spiritual standing, he did not get "under a cloud;" he continued to be the friend of God, and God spake to him face to face; yet this offense was "unto death." Even when God told him "thou shalt not go over Jordan," He gave him the unasked privilege of standing on the summit of Pisgah, and seeing the whole land. In no sense then was Moses' sin unforgiven; but it was "unto death."

With this clear example before us we may understand two passages in the New Testament. In 1 John v. 14–17, we read: "And this is the confidence that we have in him, that, if we ask anything according to his will he heareth us; And if we know that he hear us, whatever we ask, we know that we have the petitions that we desired of him." This is as unlimited a statement as could well be framed. But one thing John thought necessary to guard against, and that was the very point of physical healing. "If any man see his brother sin a sin which is not unto death, he shall ask, and he shall give him life for them that sin not unto death. There is a sin unto death; I do not say that he shall pray for it. All unrighteousness is sin: and *there is a sin not unto death*."

Now the merest beginner in the Scripture knows well that "the wages of sin is death," and we are absolutely certain that no sin, however insignificant, can ever be said not to clearly merit its wages. What then could John mean? He distinctly affirms that "there is a sin not unto death." This sin we are told to pray for, and we are assured that God will give life. Job was directed to pray for his friends, and God said "lest I deal with you after your folly."—Job xlii. 8. Was this entirely spiritual punishment that was remitted in answer to Job's prayer? The men who hunted out the marginal reference certainly did not work to support faith-healing, yet I find them connecting this verse in John with the one in Job, just quoted, and with Jas. v. 14, 15. Evidently they saw clearly that physical life is meant. To say that "there is a sin not unto death," means that some sins do not necessarily require eternal death or damnation, is to falsify all Scripture. Physical death is then the only possible interpretation. Some attempt to explain that the sin "unto death," for which we are told not to pray, means the "unpardonable sin." But what is or was the unpardonable sin? Simply and solely persistent unbelief. The ascription of the miracles of Jesus to Beelzebub was nothing but the expression of stubborn unbelief. Now it is absolutely evident that the prayer of faith cannot be offered for a persistent infidel or skeptic; hence the "sin unto death" of our text cannot be the "unpardonable sin." Jesus set this point beyond dispute when He said so often "Thy faith hath saved thee." He only healed those who believed enough to seek Him.

We have additional light upon this point in 1 Cor. xi. Paul severely rebukes the converts for turning the Lord's supper into an occasion of feasting, and tells them, "For he that eateth and drinketh unworthily, eateth and drinketh condemnation to himself, not discerning the Lord's body." And immediately he adds, "*For this cause many are weak and sickly among you, and many sleep.*" Plainly he declares that many of these Corinthian Christians were sick because of their offense, and that many had died, for the same reason. Their sin was not unpardonable, but it was "unto death."

There can be no doubt in any reasonable mind that these things are repeated in our day. Many good people, who are most undoubtedly saved, fall into sin through a variety of causes, and in consequence, while forgiven, are taken from the world or prostrated beneath chronic diseases. Their case is analagous to that of one who has sinned away his day of grace. The sickness cannot be removed, and the apostle says, "I do not say that he shall pray for it." Many a chronic disease has been brought on by persistent, careless violations of a known law. The man does not seem to wake up to the importance of the matter, and at last, after repeated warnings, he is stricken down; and like the Israelites, turned back from Kadesh-barnea, he cannot pass over Jordan. He may remain a child of God, he may worship in the tabernacle under the shadow of the cloud, but he must tramp and die in the wilderness.* His sin is "unto death." It may seem uncharitable to some, but the truth must be spoken. There is strong reason to believe that if the true inwardness of the early death of so many active, earnest Christians could be laid bare, we would find some sin at the root of the matter, yes, even a sin "unto death." Satan hates a Christian, and is always on the alert for a chance to speed

---

*His *body*, so to speak, is justified, but not sanctified wholly; hence the seeds of sin (disease) remain, and cannot be exterminated.

the fatal arrow. I do not mean to say that is always the case; but I believe it to be true in the great majority of instances. It is almost incredible how many "good Christians" are persistent, habitual gluttons, stuffing their stomachs with unhealthy food at all sorts of hours; and you cannot make them feel that is a *real sin*. They will admit that "it is not exactly right," but that is all.

Paul declared that he "believed all things that are written in the law and the prophets."—Acts xxiv. 14. And Peter, as already quoted, testified that he had "never eaten anything that is common or unclean." But how many can join in these two utterances to-day? Thousands of Christians, indeed the overwhelming majority, in all lands, fill themselves with almost every animal *expressly forbidden* in "the law." Unlike Paul, they do not believe "all" they read therein; and are much inclined to laugh at any one who rises up to warn them that only evil consequences can be expected when swine's flesh and other food which are directly declared to be "an abomination" unto God, are freely indulged in. True! the attention of the vast multitude may not have been called to these facts; but a man's ignorance of or inattention to the injurious character of a food will not prevent the evil results. As old Dr. Jewett, the famous temperance worker so frequently observed: "Most men dig their graves with their teeth."

Many earnest working Christians of full habit sin frightfully through intemperance in the marriage relation, and yet are ready to laugh at any remonstrance, even when it comes from their own physician.*

People say, How sad the death of such a useful man! I wonder why God took him away in the midst of his usefulness, etc., etc. There it is again! Just like Job, laying it on the Lord. The devil took Job's children away, and it is extremely probable that he had also something to do with the departure of the "useful man." George O. Barnes, in his sharp way, says: "If I die before I am seventy years of age you may say the devil killed him." I would rather not say that in any case, for I cannot tell all that has been done or left undone; but I feel very sure that, in the great majority of cases, with adults at least, some sin has been "unto death."

The words of the Psalmist are singularly apt. "Let their tables become a snare before them; and that which should have been for their welfare let it become a trap."—Ps. lxii. 22. Truly it is a trap that catches

---

*The extent of this evil, amongst the best people in the churches, is simply appalling. Men are paralyzed, and women die of consumption. The family physician can give the reason,—intemperance in the conjugal relation. The devil takes advantage of Christians on this point, because it cannot be publicly discussed in mixed assemblies. But every Christian, seeking to be entirely conformed to the will of God, should remember that bodily appetites are not to be exterminated, but sanctified, as much as any thing else. Every bodily appetite is right *in its place;* but the body must "be kept under" and not allowed to rule all sense and judgment. Should I write facts which have come to my knowledge, the reader would be horrified beyond measure. I recommend on this subject," Princely Manhood," S. H. Platt, Southampton, N. Y.

vast multitudes of people. There is "death in the pot" (2 K. iv. 40) to those who "feed themselves without fear." Jude 12. Solomon asked the question, "Why shouldest thou die before thy time?" Eccles. vii. 17, which clearly intimates that the wise man knew of no *neccessity* for an early death.

It may be asked how are we to tell when any one has sinned unto death? It is extremely unlikely that such a man will be able to summon real active faith in the promise. For instance, a man is seeking sanctification, or the cleansing from heart depravity. He is addicted to the use of tobacco, and will not give it up, although it rises between him and God every time he asks for a clean heart. Of course he will never receive the cleansing, nor *ever feel he has faith to grasp it*, while the filthy habit remains. A cripple told me that she was fully persuaded that healing by faith was not for her. There was no use arguing the case: she was convinced. Manifestly no prayer of faith could be offered for her; nor would she request it. Yet she was an earnest, happy Christian. These questions answer themselves when they arise. "There is a sin unto death." Therefore, there are people who cannot be healed of sickness, but no man can point them out unless specially directed by the Spirit. It is ours to hold up the promises; to lift up Jesus Christ as a whole Saviour, and, sure as the Eternal Himself, he who looks in faith, will live.

6.—The Perfect Means.

It is in very truth a perfect recipe. But then all God's commands and statutes are perfect, and perfectly adapted to all men. Examining these directions to the sick, we see, first of all, that *perfect humility* is necessary. Many a man will cry to God in secret, who will never let others know of his desire; but here he must first "call for the elders of the church." In order to do this he must feel that others are of more importance before God than himself, and also that he is willing publicly to confess his desire, his helplessness, and his faith in God. Ah! confession is ever necessary. We must honor Jesus before men. Just here Hezekiah failed. The King of Babylon sent to inquire concerning the "wonder that was done," but he displayed his riches instead of testifying to God's power.

Having thus prostrated self and confessed his belief, he is to be "anointed with oil in the name of the Lord." The old, old symbol and sign of perfect and entire consecration to God is here used, speaking of the fact that he who would receive from God, must belong to God, and that God knows no divided worship.

Again, this rite, enforces the truth, that "God's ways are not our ways." Man seeks health through the medicaments of science, but God heals through simple faith, or if you please, blind belief in a power that is absolutely unknown and incomprehensible. And with this comes the thought, we must take God's gifts in God's way. Jordan is no better than Abana and Pharpar, nor so good to the eyes of man, but Naaman will never get rid of his leprosy till he goes and dips seven times in the muddy stream.

Just here we come upon the idea of absolute, unquestioning obedience: the first law of the universe. "To obey is better than sacrifice." How many will gladly sacrifice time and money in pursuit of health, who will not travel the path to Jordan's lowly bank. The great Assyrian general has a vast army still living.

So far, direction for human action and obedience. Now we have the promises of God. "The prayer of faith shall save the sick." A great deal is implied in these words. It is not said that the prayer offered shall be efficacious, but "the prayer *of faith*." In the days of Christ's earthly ministry it is highly probable that the individuals who came to Him for healing, had real faith, not only in His power, but in his willingness to heal. In modern times, experience teaches that the faith required must be found, not only in the "elder," but in the patient. No elder or collection of elders can bear up, by their own faith, a patient who, in *the possession of his faculties*, withholds his own personal confidence and trust in God, as being both able and willing. Again, the "prayer of faith" cannot thus be jointly offered if *anything whatever* stands between the patient and God. Examples of this have been frequently observed by all who pray with the sick. It is apparent that the patient is not in the proper condition of mind and attitude of soul; he is not "on believing ground," and hence we cannot feel any confidence in praying for him. In other words, true, realizing faith in God cannot and does not exist in a soul which, in any way whatever, holds back "part of the price." Many of the "best people in the world," when brought face to face with God in dire extremity, evince an unwillingness to give up some special appetite, or passion improperly indulged, or refuse to become absolutely nothing in God's hands. (They are not willing *to be, to do, and to suffer*, to the very uttermost application of these verbs.) Some action, some confession, some fear of people's opinions, and of what men will say of them; an unreadiness to devote every moment and every ability entirely to God; a desire to retain some small portion at least of this world's goods, social standing, amusements, and employments; some liking for tobacco or other sensual indulgence, or a desire to be healed simply to be rid of discomfort and not solely for the glory of God: one or more of these things stands between the soul and God. In all such cases "the prayer of faith" is simply impossible. The elder may be pure in motive and strong in trust, but it will avail nothing for the ultimate end in view, until the way is clear. There is only room upon the bridge of faith for Jesus *and the naked soul*. Now if this complete "prayer of faith" be offered, if all these conditions be fully met, God is pleased, and, more certainly than that the heavens and the earth exist, "the prayer of faith *shall save the sick*." Jesus himself said, more than once, "thy faith hath saved thee." I mean what He meant. Faith is the hand with which I reach out and take the benefits of the Atonement.

"And the Lord *shall raise him up*." The excellency of the power is of God and not of us. "We must believe that God is, and that he is the rewarder of them that diligently seek him;" but He alone does the work. A man, alone in a boat, without sail or oar, throws a rope to the steamer, and is drawn along with speed and safety. So we throw out the rope of faith, and Jesus draws us into the harbor, while we sit and sing praises to the "mighty power of God." The promise is just as absolute as any in Scripture, and God always fulfills His word. We must notice here that nothing is said about the precise manner, nor the time of the raising up. It may be instantly; it may be gradually. Cases have been known where the patient has been directed to certain special remedies, in such a way as to leave no doubt as to God's will in the matter. I am not at all prepared to take the extreme position that God does not sometime use visible means. He employed the east wind to open the passage through the Red Sea, but used no such manifest agent at the Jordan. God is not to be circumscribed. He is not to be shut up behind a cast-iron barrier. He sometimes makes apparent exceptions, and perhaps real ones, to his ordinary methods and rules.

But that the whole tenor of the Scripture is unfavorable to the use of drugs, is unquestionable. The *general* doctrine is certainly "I make alive —and I heal."—Deut. xxxii. 39.

"And if he have committed sins, they shall be forgiven him." Here we see the wondrous liberality of God's grace. Not only healed in body, but cleansed in soul. There is, however, a very clear inference here that is extremely important. It appears, from these words, that the apostle, and the Holy Ghost who directed him, fully appreciated the close connection between sickness and sin. First, it is plain that the sickness is a result of sin (*probably* in the patient, but certainly somewhere); and secondly, that God will not heal without also forgiving. In nine cases out of ten sickness is caused by some personal sin; *in which I include all violations of the strict Biblical laws of health, diet, etc.* Of course the Sin-Bearer will not remove the effect and leave the cause; so the sin must be forgiven. This is strong testimony to the truth of the idea, previously advanced, that, even in miracle, God does not actually break His laws, but uses other laws to remove the cause as well as the effect. I take it that God's law, if law at all, is a truth; and, of course, God cannot break a truth, for that would be destroying Himself, who *is truth*. The word law is here used in the sense of a *principle*. But God has "statutes" which may be changed when He sees that is best. This He has done. He has "blotted out the handwriting of ordinances that was against us"—Col. ii. 14. But where has He annulled the provisions for health? In healing the disease, Jesus forgives the sin; and thus the glorious Atonement is used, in its fullness. Many a sufferer is compelled to exclaim, I suffer justly, I brought it on myself.) True, but the Great Physician will forgive the sin, and bear the sickness for you. Truly this way of physical life in Christ Jesus, like all the ways of God, is a perfect way.

How beautiful and helpful it is to thus trace out God's teachings. What could be more complete, or more satisfying to the Christian than this *Scriptural means of Healing?* (We have seen that it requires humility, confession of faith, absolute consecration and surrender, implicit obedience and living faith in God's word; and it promises and sets forth salvation from sickness, this to be by the hand of God alone, and complete cleansing from sin in the soul. What child of God can ask a better way? And finally, in these acts of consecration and faith, we find the suggestion of the great underlying principle, that (*God is always ready to give life to man, if only man will devote the life to God.*) God's salvation for the soul requires that the "new heart" be entirely given to Jesus; and God's salvation for the body stipulates that the new physical energy be devoted to His service. Praise the Lord!

CHAPTER IV.

KEPT FROM SICKNESS.

"Himself bore our sickness."—Matt. viii. 17.
"I will take sickness away from the midst of thee." — Ex. xxxiii. 25.

IF, when I read, "Who his own self bare our sins in his own body on the tree, that we, being dead to sins, should live unto righteousness" (1 Pet. ii. 24), I am authorized to believe that the words mean just what they say, and indicate that Jesus has actually borne all my sin of commission and of principle, of act and of depravity; surely when I read that "himself bore our sicknesses," that he lifted them up as a load, etc., I must infer that it is not at all necessary for me to bear sickness, any more than sin. (If this is not true, there is an end to all sense in language, and nothing can be predicated upon God's word.)

This chapter need not be greatly extended. When we have acknowledged that Jesus came to save us from all sin in "this present evil world;" and that sickness is a work of the devil, and allowed by God as a corrective, not merely as a judicial punishment; we cannot possibly hesitate long to admit that Jesus will keep us from disease as well as from sin, if *His conditions are met.*

This is the clear, general, logical, conclusion from the Scriptures. And yet it will not do to let this pass as the absolute truth without a more searching study. We will be led astray, in our present limited condition, if we take any isolated text, or even a group of texts, and carry them to the extreme. Stockmayer says, "If the word is to remain the Sword of the Spirit in our hands, we must practise the Master's '*Again* it is written.'

"We read in Romans viii. 23–25, that the redemption of the body remains an object of hope, even to these who have the first fruits of the Spirit. Granted that the primary meaning of this redemption of our body be exemption from physical death, still we cannot claim at all times and *unconditionally* to be exempt from all pain and disease, so long as we have to wait with patience for the redemption of the body.

" Assured as we are that the Lord bore our sicknesses as well as our sins on the cross, we yet cannot place then both on a level. In the domain of our physical life we still groan with a groaning creation.

"With regard to sickness our position is more difficult (than as regards sin). Yet even there the example of Elijah shall serve us. Let us begin by rooting out of our hearts and homes all Baal-worship; let us put to death our own will and our own notions; let us no longer ask whether it suits us or not to be ill, but simply, 'what does God expect of us, what position are we to take in this present case of sickness in order that God may be glorified?' And then if God does not interpose His 'my grace is sufficient for thee,' we take God at His word and remember that sickness is not his chosen and final will for His children. As long as the Holy Ghost gives us liberty, we ask for and expect our healing with renewed assurance, however long and severe may be the trial to which it may please God to subject our faith."*

Dr. Arthur Pierson, of Philadelphia, says, "I have never seen my way clear to say that no true saint should ever be ill. But I am clear that if our relation to Christ and the Spirit were really felt as a fact, our prayers would be with a faith and a power now unknown, and so far as disease is connected with Satan's power over our bodies, it must come to an end."

No sin is absolutely necessary to humility, yet all holy men make mistakes, and err in judgment; while most saints at least occasionally feel slightly condemned for some failure to be as careful as they should. So sickness is not intrinsically necessary to a good discipline, and yet the mistakes and errors, and ignorances of life often affect the body, and bring some disturbance of the physical equilibrium.

The presence of sickness cannot always be taken as a proof that the Spirit's possession of the man is only partial; but it may indicate the desire of the Spirit to teach a lesson which has been unseen through other means. I am not attacking the character of sick saints; but am trying to prove all the possibilities of grace for mortal man.

But the general promise stands unchallenged. "I will take sickness away from the midst of thee." The *conditions* must not be forgotten for a moment. They are exceedingly particular and exacting. But here is the possibility. Is there any ground for believing that this promise and other

---

* Sickness and The Gospel, new edition.

similar ones have been repealed? Not the least. These promises were specifically in "the law." Now Paul tells us that the covenant made with Abraham could not be disannulled by the law although it came after. Gal. iii. 17. If then the law did not disannul the Abrahamic covenant, while it took its place, may we not infer that the new covenant of the Gospel, while replacing the law, has not disannulled it?

But we have positive testimony on this point, for "God keepeth covenant to a thousand generations."—Deut vii. 9. And this is followed in vs. 14 by the promise under consideration, " I will take away all sickness from the midst of thee." Since God has joined these together I venture to say that since one thousand generations, at thirty years to each, equals thirty thousand years, it is plain that this covenant is still for us, for only three thousand three hundred years have elapsed since it was given. This argument may be novel, but in the light of other Scriptures it cannot be gainsaid

Jesus Christ expressly declared that He did not come to destroy the law and the prophets, but to fulfil them in every jot and tittle, and Paul's affirmation that "all the promises of God in him are yea and in him Amen, unto the glory of God by us," logically settles all debate upon this point. The apostle does not declare that all the ordinances and all the ceremonial laws are yea and amen in Jesus; but that "all the promises" are to be so taken Admit if you please that we are on a higher plane of faith, and hence must believe harder, so to speak; yet this is only emphasizing the conditions, not vitiating the promise.

David tells us that the promise was realized in the desert, "for there was not one feeble (sick) person among their tribes."—Ps. cv. 37. Before this time we have no recorded death through disease in all the long line of patriarchs till we come to Jacob; and he went down to live in Egypt, the land of diseases. Elisha's "sickness" admits of the rendering "weakness;" and only when the kingdom became filled with worldliness and sin do we read of Asa seeking the physicians, and Ahaziah sending to other than the "God of Israel." The fate of these, however, is not encouraging.

If there is any inspiration in John's letter to the "elect lady," we must give great weight to the words "Beloved, 1 wish above all things, that thou mayest prosper and be in health, even as thy soul prospereth."—3 Jno. i, 2. The connection and parallel between the soul and body are here too distinctly established to be avoided by any effort whatever, short of open illogical unbelief, or reckless disregard.

If the soul is wholly the Lord's, without any possible reservation, He will keep it from sickness. But in the physical parallel, there is the point of stumbling. It is so hard to see the necessity for sanctification in the body, and even harder "to present the body, a living sacrifice," when the duty is seen. There is a text of Scripture that should be written in living light over the daily pathway of every sanctified Christian.

DIVINE HEALING.

"Who hath despised the day of small things?"—Zech. iv. 10.

It is the "little foxes" that spoil the *vines;* they don't waste their time gnawing at *weeds*, they nibble the vines that are bearing "tender grapes." To be plain, a weed requires strong measures to kill it, but a very little thing will spoil and destroy a fruitful plant. It is when we are bearing fruit for the Master that very little, little things stand in the way of our obeying the command, "come up higher." Christians who have consecrated every power and disposition of the soul to God, often fail signally to see the necessity or the method for consecrating the body also, *except in service.* They are alive to the necessity of working for Jesus with the body, but the consecration of natural appetites, desires and affections is strangely wanting. We see some, who profess, and no doubt enjoy, perfect love and purity of heart, using tobacco, over-eating or drinking, rashly neglectful of proper sleep, working eighteen or twenty hours a day, or habitually violating established sanitary laws. Often this is done in ignorance; they have not seen the light on these points. But God says "come up higher;" and the bodily illness consequent upon these offences operates slowly and surely to open the eyes to the truth.* Well is it for them if with David they are at last able to exclaim, "It is good for me that I have been afflicted; that I might learn thy statutes."—Ps. cxix. 71. Statutes are the *little* laws; the small things; the apparently unimportant details of the law. Peter exhorts us to be "mindful of the words which were spoken before by the holy prophets, and of the commandment of the apostles of the Lord and Saviour."—2 Pet. iii. 2.—If we will simply read and obey without any hesitation the *conditions* laid down by the prophets and apostles we will receive the fulfillment of the promises. But this *statutory* obedience is so hard; it seems so small, and insignficant, that the devil persuades the very best Christians too often to neglect some little detail; and thus he frequently secures the entering wedge for a sickness. Read Jeremiah xi. 1-10, and see how God represents Himself as "rising early and protesting, saying, obey my voice." Oh! this obedience! this obedience! how hard it is for us all!

The context in Peter warns us that "scoffers" always begin by ridiculing some—to them—unimportant word of Scripture, and that their ridicule always first takes the form of a comparison with human experience. Hence we need not be surprised to see so able a scholar as Dr. Buckley basing his whole argument against Divine healing upon the observed "phenomena" of human experience, instead of upon the "Scriptures of truth." "Scoffers" are always alike, whether in or out of the church.

---

* People are often criminally ignorant. They could easily know so much better. Some professors of holiness are so grievously mistaken as to suppose that the marriage relation gives unlimited license for sexual indulgence. A few minutes reading in any good medical work would convict scores of such people of *real sin in this matter.* But they must learn by the slow method of sickness and experience.

A recent writer has said: "The day is dawning when men will make the distinction of Christian and unchristian health. Serious and intelligent people begin to perceive that it is possible to be free from sickness. Multitudes already realize that good health is something for which they are responsible. They already begin to feel that sickness which is contracted by defective, low-down and self-indulgent living is a reproach to Christian profession. (The true people of God are waking up to the fact that there are right ways and wrong ways of living.) They see that feebleness, languor, disease, decay and premature death may be avoided, and with this comes the sense of moral obligation in this matter. Realizing that God in nature and grace intends and provides that His people shall have health, they will deal with sickness as an enemy and consider that in a sense it is a shame to them, when they fall under its cursed power, and a discredit to the name of Christ.

(When the saints of God fully realize that health is preserved and restored in obedience to nature's laws and through the recuperating power of the Spirit of God, and that the system of drug-cure, so-called, is for the most part a practice harmful and deadly, founded on conjecture, speculation and experiment, that drug-doctors confess their arts inadequate to the recovery of the sick;* then, to forsake the word of God and prayer, and the great Physician, and put the case completely into control of Christless quacks, and meekly swallow mysterious and horrible doses of which they do not even know the name or nature, will be considered a deep disgrace.

Beloved, let us not dishoner God, and shroud the whole world in the gloom of deeper doubt. Defeat disease and premature death by faith and prayer.

> "Grow old along with me!
> The best is yet to be,
> The last of life for which the first was made;
> Our lives are in His hand
> Who saith, 'A whole I planned,'
> Youth shows but half; trust God,
> See all, nor be afraid."

"'Glory to God. Every thing shall live whither the river cometh.' —Ezk. 47; 9."

The above language is rather vigorous, but the main points are well put. (The necessity and use of *physical obedience* to God's statutes has not been taught. It is not taught to-day, except in rare instances. I mean it has had no place in the modern pulpit.) Yet it is a vital truth, and deserves better care at the hands of the "shepherds." Perhaps a more careful reading of Ezek. xxxiv, and the woe pronounced upon the shepherds for not healing the sick, would be conducive to a better understanding of God's complete salvation.

The case of Paul is exceedingly pertinent here. In Phil. iii. 6, we find a bold statement made by the apostle. Speaking of his former life, under

---

* See their admission on page 126

the Hebrew faith, he emphatically declares that he was, "touching the righteousness which is in the law, BLAMELESS." Hereupon I declare, with equal emphasis, that this necessarily included or implied the testimony of *exemption from all sickness.* Either this, or God's promises were untrue. Paul was "an Hebrew of the Hebrews;" and the God of the Hebrews had given him a number of promises like this: "If thou shalt obey his voice, and do all that I speak .... I will take sickness away from the midst of thee" (Ex. xxiii. 22, 25). "And the Lord will take away from thee all sickness"—if ye hearken to these judgments, and keep and do them"—(Deut. vii. 12, 15). Standing on these promises of Jehovah, I declare that, when the great apostle unhesitatingly claims a "blameless" keeping of the law, I must make God out untrue if I do not fully accept the practical fulfillment, in his case, of the promises contained in that law. It is simply this, my brother. God said, keep my law, and I will take all sickness away from you. Paul says he perfectly kept it. Therefore, Paul experienced the deliverance from disease.* Now this will stand as many turnings as a kaleidoscope, but it will never vary a hair's breadth. Paul here places himself on record in the same class with Zacharias and Elizabeth, as those who, walking "in all the ordinances of the law blameless," must have realized the promised deliverance from disease so distinctly and repeatedly promised in that law. Yet he did not plume himself on any of these things. All his gain he counted loss for Christ. All things must take rank *after* the one great consuming thought of Jesus and His will. This will explain why so little is said about the body; the spiritual was vastly more important. But what was said is clear and conclusive.

The whole thing turns upon that glorious promise "If we walk in the light as He is in the light." (Ah! here is the condition, *we must walk in the light*, or there will be no "fellowship" and no "cleansing from all sin." The "cleansing from all sin" is only promised to those whose spirits obey God in every little thing; and exemption from sickness can only (through faith) be his *whose body obeys in all things*. Reiterate this again and again.

As in my own case, the great fear in this matter is that we may get sick, in which event others must know it, and the profession apparently fall into disgrace. I thank God for a revelation on this point. I saw that if I hesitated for this reason, it was clear that I was not delivered entirely from that Spirit that "loved the praise of men more than the praise of God." The temptation was to refrain from taking so radical a ground for fear that, if I failed, men would know it; whereas I might profess Scriptural holiness, and be conscious of sins, without any man being aware of my fall. Ah! God knows. As soon as this became clear to my mind, I resolved, in the strength of Jesus, to confess His glorious work *to the uttermost*, and not to allow a single thought of the future to enter my

---

*For the "thorn in the flesh," see page 102.

mind for a moment. Any one can see that, professing to trust Christ for exemption from sickness, while you are contemplating the possibility of speedily falling ill, *is not trusting Him at all.* As well might a man say, "I am trusting Jesus this moment for cleansing from all sin, but I rather expect to sin before night." Such professions are only an insult to God, and are miserable travesties on true faith.

I sometimes fear that the teachings on holiness have not always shown that "boldness to enter into the holiest" which they should have manifested. Far be it from man to boast; and undoubtedly the less said about the future the better. But when man or devil suggests the question, "Now do you really expect to live one year, one month, one week, even one day, without sin?" we should answer in faith, I do not expect "to continue in sin," but I expect the Lord to perform His word.

The "walk with God" is the most delicately balanced union in the world. There is only room for Jesus and me. Everything must be put away, and every leading of divine love must be instantly followed. Temptation to sin is useful and beneficial in keeping constantly before our souls the great truth, spoken by Jesus, "without me ye can do nothing;" and temptation to sickness is not wanting to remind the trusting Christian that Jesus alone is the "Saviour of the body."

If I am asked what I mean by "temptation to sickness," I reply that Satan produces frequently upon me the preliminary symptoms of cold, headache, or other sickness. Instantly I look to the Great Physician and say, Dear Lord, thou hast taken my infirmities and borne my sicknesses. These symptoms are a temptation of the devil, deliver me. And lo! the indications vanish, and I am not sick at all. For five years I have known *temptation to be sick*, just as distinctly and unquestionably as any temptation to sin. But the dear Lord always keeps His word, and "with the temptation provides a way of escape, that I may be able to bear it." Glory be to His name alone! In this way the "keeping power" against sickness is made just as much to depend upon, or to work through faith, as in the case of sin. I cannot rest upon past pardon; I must trust to be kept in the cleansing fountain to-day. And just so, I dare not rest upon yesterday's healing, but am constrained to actively trust, as I breathe, moment by moment.

The life of faith, in any path, is a life supported by only one breath at a time.

Unless Christ came to destroy the law and the prophets, it is then clear that perfect physical obedience to-day, secures the right to expect health of body as well as perfect spiritual obedience secures soul-health. Or perhaps it would be better to say that complete obedience to all God's statutes, warrants the expectation of health of soul and body together. I have no thought of writing this chapter to prove that the most saintly Christian who carelessly or even ignorantly abuses his stomach, exposes himself to draughts and dampness, keeps all sorts of hours, or in any other way breaks God's nealth laws, has any right to expect this immunity. He *may* continue well in spite of these offenses. Some do; but that proves nothing. In fact, we may inquire, are such as healthy as they would be if more careful? And we know that God is "long suffering."

On the other hand, the case of Job undeniably establishes the fact that God *may* see fit, *for disciplinary and educational effects on the individual, and for the display of the strength of His grace*, to allow a man whom He pronounces "perfect," to pass under the power of the adversary for a time, and to be diseased, although by reason of his obedience he has the right to expect health. Such a trial is a severe one to pass through, for the soul, like Job, feeling sure of its integrity, is tempted to wonder if God has forgotten His promises. Job was certain he held God's note; but he marveled that the bank of providential circumstances refused to discount it immediately.

But he never seems to have thought of taking it anywhere else. He endured to the end—the butt and ridicule of all his friends—and was saved. May God multiply his seed in these days, and help them to cry, "I desire to reason with God—ye are all physicians of no value," (xiii. 3, 4). "The breath of the Almighty hath given me life" (xxxiii. 4).

Finally, when we pray the Lord's prayer from the heart, we ask for God's will to be done on earth, now and here, even as it is done in heaven. And again we ask to be delivered from evil of every possible kind and description. Jesus Himself indited this prayer. Now in comparison with His own express promise of tribulation, persecution and fiery trial, we can see that deliverance from them must mean from all moral injury as a result of their presence and power. But He never gave us any hint that we shall necessarily have sickness; and as this is unquestionably "evil," deliverance from it must mean from all physical injury as a result of its presence and power. But as already stated, the deferment of the "redemption of the body" till the second Advent, and the express declarations of Scripture concerning death, make this parallel not quite so rigorous. When all these allowances have been made, however, we see clearly in the light of the overwhelming promises of the law and the overwhelming examples of the gospel that, in general, sickness is an "evil," and the Lord's final will is to put His own divine life in us and cause our "health to spring forth speedily." Isa. lviii. 8. Let us pray "Thy will be done," not merely in the sense of reluctant and difficult resignation to disagreeable inevitables, but with the definite purpose of reaching and obtaining all the high and holy purposes of our God in our being. Then we will be kept by "Him who is able to keep you from falling, and to present you *faultless* before the presence of his glory with EXCEEDING JOY."—Jude 24.

CHAPTER V.

OBJECTIONS AND QUESTIONS.

"Be ready always to give an answer to every man that asketh you a reason of the hope that is in you." 1 Pet. 3, 15.

1.—IF PAUL THOUGHT SO MUCH OF HIS BODY, WHY DID HE CALL IT HIS "VILE BODY?"—(Phil. iii. 21.)

The apostle, as I have shown, was always looking towards the great day when Jesus shall come and bring about the full reunion of the soul and body in the glorified state. In this case he was expressing the same thought. He says, "For our conversation is in heaven; from whence also we look for the Saviour, the Lord Jesus Christ; who shall change our vile body, that it may be fashioned like unto his glorious body, according to the working whereby he is able even to subdue all things unto himself." The word translated vile is *tapeinosis*, and means *low estate, humiliation, abasement*. That is, the apostle spoke of his body being in a low estate, not the highest possible condition; as being abased, not exalted; humiliated, not glorified. It is plain, therefore, that this verse does not bear against our position in the slightest. On the contrary, it serves to enforce the idea that a body destined for such a marvelous "change," cannot for a moment be called "vile" in the sense of worthless or repulsive. Paul cherished his body, though it was in a "low estate," and ardently longed for the time when it should be glorified. In the same epistle he declares that "Christ shall be magnified in my body."—i. 20. Not the faintest shadow of an argument in favor of sickness can be deduced from this reference.

2.—TROPHIMUS.

The case of Trophimus, whom Paul says he left behind him "at Miletum sick" (2 Tim. iv. 20), is of some importance. Why did not Paul pray over him, raise him up and take him along? This question naturally occurs to the mind of an honest inquirer; but the case can readily be shown to be in perfect accord with the Scriptural doctrine of healing. For two years, at Ephesus, and for three months, at Miletum, Paul had healed the sick continually, and not one single case of failure or incomplete restoration is even hinted. Now was Trophimus affected with a disaster that defied the power of God? Did Paul fail to pray with him? Or was it the Lord's will for him to be sick?

Dr. Boardman, in the "Great Physician," has treated this point with ability. He presents the idea that Paul was on his way to Rome, a prisoner. Trophimus was not obliged to go, and very probably the Lord wanted him to stay behind. So, just on the eve of the vessel's departure, Trophimus was taken sick. Of course he and Paul prayed for healing, but in this case it was delayed. Paul went on to Rome, and Trophimus was left to work for the Lord in a different sphere. Paul was not a stranger to gradual healing, for he had seen Epaphroditus sicken, and though he prayed, yet the patient drew "nigh unto death" before the turn came and the Lord raised him up.—Phil. ii. 25-29. This accords most fully with the timeless nature of the promise in James. "The Lord shall raise him up," gives no time, but the fact is as true as God's inviolable word.

But there is another thought about this case. We have not any record of Trophimus' personal experience. We know he was a Christian, a companion of Paul's, an Ephesian, and a worker in the new cause. But we do not know his precise inward experience, as in the case of Paul. Now it is perfectly possible that Trophimus made a mistake, or that he did not absolutely follow the leading of the Holy Ghost. He loved Paul, and desired above all to keep his company. We will suppose that God desired him to enter another sphere of labor, and that, very possibly, certain delicate indications of the divine call had reached him. But his affection for the great apostle, and his own soul-joy in his company, persuaded him to close his eyes to anything else, and he determined to go to Rome. Then sickness fell upon him. He could not go; but he could pray. Yet though he prayed, and Paul himself doubtless interceded, he could not be raised up till he had seen and accepted God's will. This he did not do until the ship had gone and the thought of Rome had been banished from his mind. With the bias removed, there is no doubt that God's leading became plain, and that Trophimus arose and went to work where God called him. Again God may have made of him a case like that of Job. Of course, all this is theoretical and inferential, but it is entirely possible. Finally, there is nothing at all in this case to shake for a moment the belief in God's plain promise.

3.—PAUL'S THORN.*

In the case of the apostle, we are confronted by the fact that he repeatedly relates his experience; and protests that God "always caused him to triumph in Christ." He furthermore distinctly avers that he "fought a good fight," and even set himself up as an example for others. See 1 Cor. xi. 1, 4, 16., Phil. iii. 17., 1 Thes. i. 6, 7., 2 Thes. iii. 9., 1 Thes. ii. 10. In other words, Paul made the most unhesitating profession of personal cleansing from all sin. Now if Paul became sick, is not the whole doctrine of this book overthrown at once? Let us see.

Paul had a "thorn in the flesh." Like most other matters concerning

---

* Dr. Adam Clarke stoutly maintained that the "thorn" was an evil-minded person who was stirring up trouble in the church. He scouts the idea that it was any sickness at all. See Clarke's Commentary.

him, this fact comes from his own mouth, in open confession. He was wonderfully fond of "confession with the mouth." In the first place no one can deny that this "thorn" never clouded Paul's faith in God's willingness to heal everybody else, of any possible affection. The record of his work absolutely establishes this. Dr. Boardman pertinently asks, "Why then should it cause *us* to doubt?" Further, we see that he himself had no doubt about it, but took it straight to the Lord. Three times he prayed, and the trouble still lingered. Why was this! Had Paul reached a plane upon which temptation was impossible? Did his faith not need exercise? Did he forget Abraham, and Elijah, and the widow before the unjust judge? No. He exercised faith, and it grew so strong that God answered him, and distinctly explained the whole matter to him. The "abundance of the revelations" made to him had been so great and so unspeakable, that this "thorn" came to "buffet him," "lest he should be exalted" by the marvelous favors shown him. The whole aim of the thing was to establish, as never before, in the apostle's heart, that even he, with all his revelations, was absolutely nothing apart from Jesus. It was not what he had been forgiven, not what he had received, not the measure of blessings he felt and experienced, but the personal abiding presence of Jesus, excluding and exterminating any possible form of self in the inmost soul. This was the lesson, *and Paul learned it*, and exulted in the knowledge, glorifying God, —2 Cor. xii. 7–10. See also xi. 30.

In Gal. iv. 13, 14, Paul says: "Ye know how through infirmity of the flesh I preached the Gospel unto you *at the first*. And my *temptation which was in my flesh* ye despised not." It is likely that this refers to a different affliction from the "thorn," but whether referring to that or not, two things are plain. 1. Paul recovered from this, for it was only "at the first." 2. It was a "temptation in the flesh." Now God "tempteth no man;" hence this sickness was not from God direct, but probably from Satan, as the "thorn" certainly was. The opponents of Divine healing will find cold comfort in Paul's experience.

There are several points in this case that are important. First, the word translated "infirmities," is *astheneia*, meaning literally *weakness*. It is the same word rendered in vs. 9, "weakness," and in vs. 10," weak ;" also in xi. 30, "infirmities," and xi. 29, "weak." I am not stickling for a shade, but it is plain that anything like virulent disease is not indicated in the text. This is amply sustained by the personal history of the apostle. One thing is certain, that the "thorn" never prevented him from working "more abundantly than all" the rest of his brethren; and he distinctly affirms that he "ceased not to warn every one night and day with tears" for a "space of three years."—Acts xx. 31. He must have enjoyed very good health during that long ministry; and when he died, it was not from any sickness, or even a "thorn in the flesh." It is then clear that Paul's "thorn" was in no sense a disabling affection. The Lord did not allow it to stop Paul's work, but *to make him more fruitful.* You, therefore, who are seeking consolation in utter prostration under permanent disease, will not find any reason for continued inaction in this record. Paul said, "Christ shall be magnified in my body, whether it be by life or by death,"—Phil. i. 20; but he emphasized the fact that, if he lived, it was to "labor," vs. 22, not to lie idle upon a sick bed.

We may assume from the facts that there is no *necessity* for a "thorn in the flesh," *such* as tormented Paul, unless, like him, we have been "caught up into the third heaven." Also, that if a "thorn" has made its appearance, we have Paul's example for steadfastly praying *in faith* for its removal, until we get an answer from the Lord, about which there can be no mistake.

But further, we are led to inquire as to the nature of the "thorn." If it was not active disease, what was it? There are two well known suppositions on this point. One is that his eyes never entirely recovered from the blinding effect of the light on the Damascus road. The other is that his "bodily presence was weak, and his speech contemptible."—2 Cor. x. 10; and these physical deficiencies constituted the "thorn." Now nothing could be more absurd. His eyes were good enough to enable him to write, "with his own hand," those closely covered parchment rolls, the transcribing of which taxes good eyesight to-day. But his own words absolutely settle both these points. If the "thorn" had been in his eyes, it would have dated from the day of his conversion; and the supposed defect in appearance would have been much older. But his express language is that this "thorn" was given him to keep him from being exalted by the wonderful revelations vouchsafed to him, *long subsequent* to his conversion. Again in 2 Cor. x. 11, Paul sharply declares that the talk about his insignificant presence and contemptible speech was utterly false, and avers that his word of mouth will be found fully equal to his pen. He as plainly declares as language can express it, that this was a miserable slander, originating among his enemies. "For his letters *say they* are weighty and powerful; but his bodily presence is weak, and his speech contemptible." Note that "they" say this; but the apostle denies it point blank, and declares that they will find him to be exactly what they read him. (There is not a particle of real evidence to show that Paul was little, or thin, or crooked, or weak of speech; but a great deal to the contrary. His own denial, quoted above, should be sufficient; and the fact that at Lyconia the people called Paul Mercury, who was the very personification of eloquence, sufficiently attests the power of his speech. And then let us remember his address before King Agrippa, and forevermore give up this absurd tradition of the Middle Ages that Paul was a sort of mumbling dwarf. Still further, he specially informs us that the "thorn" was "the messenger of Satan." What frightful blasphemy it would be to assume that a partial blindness, caused by the visible manifestation of Jesus Christ, could by any figure of speech, be called "the messenger of Satan!" And almost equally abominable would be the application of these words, to the natural stature and appearance of the body, which owes its very existence to the creative power of God.

It is noteworthy that Paul speaks of his trials in detail, but does not mention sickness. In 2 Cor. vi. 4, 5, he writes, "In much patience, in affliction, in necessities, in distress, in stripes, in imprisonment, in tumults, in labors, in watchings, in fastings." And in the eleventh chapter he enumerates again his persecutions and troubles. "In labors more abundant, in stripes above measure, in prisons more frequent, in deaths oft "(see 1 Cor. xv. 30, 31, 32 ; 2 Cor. iv. 8–11, vi. 9). "Of the Jews five times received I forty stripes save one. Thrice was I beaten with rods, once was I stoned, thrice I suffered shipwreck, a night and a day I have been in the deep; in journeyings often, in perils of waters, in perils of robbers, in perils of mine own country men, in perils by the heathen, in perils in the city, in perils in the wilderness, in perils in the sea, in perils among false brethren. In weariness and painfulness (*mochthos*—labor, toil), in watchings often, in cold and nakedness." The "thorn" is mentioned in the following chapter, so that we have here the strongest reasons for believing that Paul had no sickness or disease, properly so called, in all this previous experience, for no word of such a trouble is found in the terrible catalogue of his afflictions and persecutions.* After all the "thorn" may not have been a real disease, as Dr. Adam Clark maintains.

It is perfectly clear then that the "thorn" was a special affliction sent upon Paul after his marvellous experience, for the special purpose of causing him to rely, not upon the gifts of God, but solely upon the giver Himself. And even this affliction or sickness is expressly stated to have emanated from Satan. But it will be urged that after all has been said does not this case disprove the provision in the Atonement for all sickness? This brings us to a very special question under the subject of the thorn.

Did Paul Recover?

Do not be startled. Let us carefully and prayerfully examine the record. "To the law and to the testimony." Without question there is no ground in Paul's case for any doubt as to God's willingness to heal all disease. This has been abundantly shown already. But I do not feel it right to relinquish the matter at this point. Is it true that Paul prayed three times, but that God refused to grant his request, while promising him grace to bear up under the affliction? I unhesitatingly affirm that

The Thorn in the Flesh was Healed.†

The only case in Scripture similar to this is that of Moses, when he

---

* Unless we except 2 Cor. i, 8–11. But this distinctly states that he did not trust in man, but "in God who raiseth the dead." And God delivered him.

† Even after all these years I believe I am the only writer who has advanced this thought. But after a great deal of added light, I see no reason to alter my opinion.

besought God to let him pass over Jordan, and the Lord told him not to speak any more concerning the matter. But the two cases are not at all analogous. Moses had sinned, and God's word *had gone forth*, "because ye believed me not to sanctify me in the eyes of the children of Israel, therefore ye *shall not* bring this congregation into the land."—Num. xx. 12.

When, therefore, Moses asked to go over Jordan, he asked God to break His word. It could not be; but, as we have seen, the Lord bore him over a better Jordan, into a fairer land. But Paul's thorn was not punitive; it was a preventive. So he distinctly states. And when he prayed for its removal, he asked God not to break His word, but to destroy one of the works of the devil; the very thing Jesus Christ came to do.

If it be argued that the apostle continued to need the thorn, and therefore God could not, in wisdom, grant this request; I reply that, if this be true, it follows that Paul did not learn the lesson which the thorn was sent to teach. God would certainly not allow a "messenger of Satan to buffet" his chosen apostle, except for a purpose. That purpose was to teach Paul that he was nothing but weakness, apart from Jesus. This we are distinctly told. Now, if the thorn remained, it was solely because Paul did not learn the lesson. But he did learn it; nothing can be more positively certain than this. To suppose that Paul felt the thorn, realized what it was for, had God's word for it; and then, cherished the thorn, refusing to accept and apply its teaching, is to suppose that the apostle was openly rebellious, and willfully sinful, even when he said, " I always triumph in Christ." If any Christian can accept this dilemma, let him do so.

But it may be answered, look at the language used ; does it not say that the Lord told Paul he should have grace to endure? No, it does not. The facts are these. Paul prayed. No answer. Paul prayed the second time. No answer. With undaunted faith, Paul prayed the third time. And unless he had less faith than Elijah he would have kept on seven times, if necessary. But at the third request, God answered. He said, " My grace is sufficient for thee. " The word translated sufficient means suffice, satisfy. When we remember that we are " saved by grace, " Eph. ii. 5–8, it is easily seen that the word " grace, " in the text, may well have the element of salvation in it. In fact the idea of salvation is inseparably linked with the word in all the Scripture. Now God told him "My grace is sufficient, or satisfying. " This would surely accord with all Scriptural analogy, if we understand the reply to be an assent and not a denial. Suppose I should go to God with a besetting sin, a regular and genuine "messenger of Satan, " and cry for deliverance ; only to be met with the assurance that I should receive grace to bear it? *What! to bear a sin!* To retain that which is hateful to God! *Grace to sin, and to bear up under it!* What a thought ! Yet here we are plainly told that a "messenger of Satan," having accomplished the end for which it was allowed, is to be retained and *endured by grace*. Could anything be more awfully absurd?*

Again, Paul remarks at once; "Most gladly therefore will I rather glory in my infirmities, that the power of Christ may rest upon me." What, Paul! do you mean to say that you will deliberately glory in "messengers of Satan," even if it be that "the power of Christ" may be shown? If so, how did you come to write that famous sentence, "Shall we continue in sin, *that grace may abound?* God forbid!" Shall we cherish or retain any "messenger of Satan," merely that Christ's power may be manifested in continued deliverance? Is that the meaning of the apostle? God forbid; indeed. How plain it is that he gloried, not that these things came, nor that they remained, nor yet that he was enabled to bear them; but rather in that he *was delivered from them*. See the very context itself, for proof of this. He "took pleasure in infirmities, in reproaches, in necessities, in persecutions, in distresses." Did he take pleasure in these things *within himself*, or externally? Did he not take pleasure and glory in the fact that, in the midst of the burning, fiery furnace, he walked absolutely unscorched, because one, like to the Son of God, walked with him, saying, Courage Paul, "My grace is sufficient for thee?" Paul had no belief in "imputed holiness," nor in imputed health either. He does not say, I am weak, but I am called strong on account of Christ's strength, imputed to me. But he declares, "When I am weak, then I am strong." How? By the "power of Christ," in which alone "I glory."

With special emphasis, he refers, in the twelfth verse, to his miraculous gifts. He says, " Truly the signs of an apostle were wrought among you in all patience, in signs, and wonders, and mighty deeds." This serves to prove that he had no doubt as to the power and willingness of God to heal, for "they shall lay hands on the sick, and they shall recover," was one of the "signs" mentioned by our Saviour himself, as following "them that believe."

The rational and Scriptural view of this case then is this. The thorn was sent as a precautionary measure, or a warning. It had a lesson. This Paul learned, and asked for healing. *After a trial of his faith*, his request was graciously granted. Whereupon he praises God that in all things, in infirmities, persecutions, reproaches, necessities or distresses, God's grace is sufficient and satisfying, and gives him complete deliverance from all the "messengers of Satan." And in confessing this he confesses that he is so "weak" that he cannot save himself in the least degree, but Christ is so "strong," that He can and does save to the very "uttermost."

Ah! God is a personal God, Jesus Christ a personal Redeemer, the Holy Ghost a personal Sanctifier, and the salvation of the Cross is a *per-*

---

* Note the force of the word "And." It is not written, I asked for it, *but* God said, etc. It is, I prayed, *and* God said. A very great difference.

sonal salvation " in this present world." It saves the individual through and through. It saves him *from*, and not *in* or *under*.*

4.—THE MAN BORN BLIND.

In the ninth chapter of John we read of a remarkable case. The query of the disciples, "Master, who did sin, this man, or his parents, that he was born blind?" and Jesus' reply, "Neither has this man sinned, nor his parents; but that the works of God should be made manifest in him," may be cited to disprove the idea that sickness is the result of sin. The Lord give us light to examine it!

In the first place I am struck with the plain fact that the apostles all thought the presence of such a calamity a sure evidence of sin, either in the man or his parents. They considered the affliction to be a punishment for actual transgression; which proves that they, as Hebrews, remembered the physical promises and warnings of the covenant. But in this case they were mistaken, precisely as were the three friends of Job. The Patriarch of Uz was ill in body, not as a punishment, but in order to lead him to a depth of surrender of which he had not dreamed. Paul's thorn was purely precautionary, and intended to warn him against self-conceit. And Jesus said that this man was blind, not because of special offence, but that the works of God might be manifested in him. Now, when we remember that Job's boils and Paul's thorn came straight from the hand of Satan, and when we read that "for this purpose was the Son of God manifested, that he might destroy the works of the devil," it becomes plain that the blind man's case was of precisely similar nature.

What are the "works of God" in a mortal man? Are they not essentially to overthrow and cast out Satan and sin, with all the corruption and taint of evil? But it may be said that the words mean that God's power might be shown. Indeed! Is this all? Why select a man? Would not the "power" of God have been much more plainly manifested by some unquestionably miraculous work in nature. Suppose Christ had actually done what he told his disciples was possible to faith—plucked up a mountain and cast it headlong into the sea—would not the mere question of power have been settled much more positively than in healing the sick? A thousand other wonders would have displayed power; but Jesus "*came to seek and save the lost.*" Who can dare say that this man would ever have been saved, if he had been born with eyes? Had he not known such desperate privation, would he have ever believed in the Son of God?

Beyond question, he stands as an example of God's love and grace. Bound by Satan, not merely for eighteen years, but all his life; deprived

---

* I would say that this idea of the "thorn" was first given me by Dr. Cullis, five years ago. He simply stated it as his belief that Paul was cured. Since then the Lord has opened to my mind the beautiful unfoldings of the truth, and **I give Him** all the glory.

of the precious boon of sight, and feeling his helplessness, as only the blind can; he meets the Great Physican. The beautifully significant words, "as long as I am in the world, I am the light of the world," sounded in his ears; the divine hand touched his eyes, and the command followed, "go, wash in the pool of Siloam." He went, he washed, he saw. A trial of faith followed, and then his spiritual eyes were also opened, and he exclaimed, in adoring confidence, "Lord, I believe." To the man this sickness was saving. To God it was glory.

A significant thought is here presented. Modern experience confirms the record in the fact, that *a wondrous spiritual blessing invariably accompanies the healing faith.* In the long years of the faith work at Mänedorf, at Bad Boll, under Dr. Cullis, and with many others, this has proved the universal rule. (No one ever trusts God for anything without being blessed in spirit.) And this is what we might expect, for is not faith laid down in Scripture as the express channel of communication between God and man?

We see, therefore, that, while the blindness was not a punishment for any special offence, it most certainly was no exception to the rule, that sickness emanates from the devil, and exists on account of sin. It saved man from his sins, just as the thorn saved Paul from falling into pride, and the boils brought Job to the actual death of self. And thus, in each case, the works of God were manifested, in *destroying the works of the devil.*

5.—LAZARUS.

In the eleventh chapter of John we have a very similar case. Christ loved Lazarus. Is it possible that God allows the works of the devil to afflict those whom He loves? It is written, "Whom the Lord loveth he chasteneth, and scourgeth every son whom he receiveth." Some one will say, "You have quoted a verse that weighs directly against you this time." Have I? On the contrary the Lord gives me to see in it a mighty argument in my favor. I ask, how does the Lord chasten his children? We know that it is by trial, tribulations, sorrows, and sickness if you please. But whence come these? Do not trials come from the opposition of sinners? My patience is tried by somebody's impatience. My love is tested by another's ugliness and hatred. My faith is used in repelling the doubts which Satan interjects. Is it not perfectly plain that the things which give us by far the greater portion of our "chastening," unquestionably emanate from sin and Satan? Why, how could we be "chastened" if we lived in an angelic community, where Satan's cloven foot could not tread? Will anybody try to explain? And are we to conclude that sickness is to be arbitrarily separated from all the other ills that flesh is heir to, and ascribed to the direct agency of "Him who hath loved us and bought us with His blood?" We all believe that whatever the punishments of perdition may be, they will be directly under the hand of the prince of darkness. Then how horrible it is to imagine that He, who is love, actually swings the scourges of hell in order to punish His own children.

If you say you do not believe God does that, then our position is granted at once. These things are all unquestionable evils. Now they do not send themselves. And if God does not send them, the devil must do so. The whole difficulty is cleared by simply regarding the double character of God. He is justice, but He also is love. "We have all sinned, and come short of the glory of God." Therefore we are all under judicial sentence. This is our present condition. But love intervenes, and temporarily suspends execution. Meanwhile the "roaring lion" is raging around the "hedge"* which God "hath set about" us; and claiming us as his own. He is constantly striving to break through and slay us forever. But God withholds him by His mighty hand. Now we are either outbreaking sinners, or, like Job, we do not "follow on to *know* the Lord" as He would have us. In this state of affairs Love asks the aid of wisdom and God, apparently listening to Satan's taunt of unfair protection, withdraws the hedge, and says, "Behold he is in thine hand, *but save his life.*" At once the darts fall thick and fast. It may be the loss of family and of fortune, or it may be bitter personal pain. The arch-enemy has not learned backward since he displayed his ingenuity in the land of Uz. He has the "power of death," and he uses it *just as far as God will let him*. If the "hedge" is not withdrawn from the body, he must be content with spoiling the goods, blowing down the house, and sending fire upon the sheep. Men were ready to ascribe Satan's work to God three thousand years ago, for Job's servants said, "The fire of God is fallen from heaven;" when the fact is it was the *fire of hell*, sent by Satan himself. I have not a shadow of a doubt that if God would only withdraw the "hedge" about the human race, the devil would kill every single soul upon earth in an hour. He would kill the saints out of pure malignity, and to prevent their serving God: and he would kill the sinners to make sure of their damnation.

An ancient tradition says that when man was created "in the image of God," all angels and created beings were called upon to do him honor, as the most remarkable work of God. But Eblis, or Satan, revolted at the command, became a prey to envy and hatred, and rebelling against God, was cast down from his high estate, carrying his followers with him. Certain it is, that the old legend holds an important truth. It is the undying hatred, and venomous, sleepless animosity which Satan has ever displayed towards our race.

Job's case was not on exception, but rather, almost, if not quite, the rule. In this view of the matter, how plain does the case of Lazarus become!

---

* This hedge is made of Angels, for "The Angel of the Lord encampeth round about them that fear him and delivereth them."—Ps. xxxiv. 7.

HEALING OF BODILY DISEASE. 111

Jesus loved him; therefore he needed chastening. For some reason sickness was allowed. Satan had full swing, and the dart was dipped in deadly venom. Lazarus died, and hell rejoiced that a friend of the Nazarene was slain. Satan has no foreknowledge, he is but a creature, and cannot read God's purpose in advance. But "this sickness was not unto death, but for the glory of God, that the Son of God might be glorified thereby." The word went forth, the works of the devil were destroyed, and Lazarus came back to life. Note especially, that Jesus said, "I am glad for your sakes that I was not there, to the intent ye may believe." What did this mean, but that, if He had been with the afflicted one, His presence would have necessarily banished sickness from one who loved Him, and whom He loved; and mark, how great spiritual blessings came to them who stood by. "Then many of the Jews which came to Mary, and had seen the things which Jesus did, believed on him."

And finally we see again, permanently displayed in this chapter, the great truth that God maketh "the wrath of man (or devils) to praise him."—Ps. lxxvi. 10. It is in this light that we can read of Pharaoh, of whom it is said that God especially raised him up. Rom. ix. 17. The reason of the raising up was that God might show forth His power, and declare His name through all the earth. But was not Pharaoh a fearful sinner, given over to the entire power of Satan? And how did God show forth His power? Was it not by destroying the reign of Pharaoh over His people, and by drowning Pharaoh himself in the midst of the sea? The more we look into the Scriptures, the more we become convinced that the way God gets to Himself glory, is by saving and delivering His children *from* evil, and not merely by giving grace to remain under bondage *to* evil. Jesus Christ came " *To save His people from their sins.*"

The method by which God *sends* evil, and disease and trial, and tribulation, and distress, and peril, and sword, is outlined or suggested in the words of the Prophet, " Ephraim is joined to idols, *let him alone.*"—Hos. iv. 17. And we see the same thought in the dying words of Joseph, "But as for you, ye thought evil against me: but God meant it unto good, to bring to pass, as it is this day, to save much people alive."—Gen. l. 20. But most conclusive of all, is it not manifest that God saw fit to give us salvation through sin? *In the proper sense*, this is most tremendously true. It was sin that rejected Jesus of Narazeth; it was sin that nailed Him to the cross; it was sin and death and hell that rejoiced in the darkness of Calvary. (But God "meant it for good, to bring to pass as it is to-day, *to save much people alive.*)" Of course if there had been no sin, Jesus would not have given Himself for us; but sin there was, and beyond all controversy Christ could not have died, except by the works of the devil, the great representative of sin. But Jesus did not triumph by *remaining* under the power of sickness or sin. He conquered death and hell by destroying their power over Him, and living in health and strength until the time for His departure drew nigh. And he wants us to "walk, even as He walked."—Heb. ii. 14, 15.

6.—DEATH APPOINTED TO ALL.

People often say, "Well if all this is true, nobody will ever die." There are several answers to this thoughtless and really ignorant remark. First we are told "that all men have not faith." Christ himself asked, "When the Son of Man cometh, shall He find faith on the earth?" "O ye of little faith, wherefore did ye doubt?" is the query that finds very wide application to-day. When it is apparent that a mere handful in the world can manage to trust God for healing, and clear from Scripture that only a few will be ready to meet him "at his appearing," it is at once seen that the objection is inconsequential. But the real thought goes deeper than words. The idea is, how will a man, who does exercise faith for healing, ever manage to die? A moment's reflection makes this clear. *The very essence of healing, as of holiness, through faith, is God's will.* When Jesus so wonderfully cured my heart disease, it was done *after* I had resigned all to the will of God. I said, if God wants me to die, then I *desire* to die. If He wants me to live and suffer, I desire to do so. But if he wants me to recover and praise Him, I desire that. But I only desire the glory of God. In this attitude before God I was led to see His will in my recovery, and God alone is glorified thereby. But to-day how is it? I am living for His glory, and am ready by His grace without a moment's notice to depart and be with Jesus. With Paul I can say "to be with Christ is far better." The man whose whole being is given to Jesus, will not seek to live, when God's time has come to carry him over the river. The heart that is all the Lord's has its treasure in heaven, and waits, almost impatiently, for the Lord's appearing. Such a man is fully satisfied with life on earth, and like Paul, it is only by God's grace that he is content to stay there. His whole conversation is in heaven, from whence also he looks for the Lord Jesus. The very sweetest sound in all this wide universe, to a heart full of the love of the Master, is the welcome call, "Behold the bridegroom cometh, go ye out to meet him." Lord hasten the day when Jesus shall come and "we which are alive and remain be caught up to meet him in the air." "Amen! even so come Lord Jesus." Of course I do not expect the world to comprehend this, for these things are spiritually discerned. But all God's children ought to understand.

"It is appointed unto men once to die, and after that the judgment." —Heb. ix. 27. No one seeks to evade this Scripture. But we know that God will give deliverance in death itself. The story of Esther beautifully sets forth this deliverance. The laws of the Medes and Persians cannot alter, but the King authorizes the Jews to stand for their lives; and by this permission, as well as for the fear of Mordecai, who stood before the King in the place of his people, the day of the edict brings victory, although the law is not repealed. So Jesus stands for us, making intercession for us. The law of death cannot be changed: but even in that dark hour, He gives strength to cry, "O grave, where is thy victory? O death, where is thy sting?"

But there is no Scripture which even hints at the *necessity* of sickness coming upon God's children, who are walking in the light. If then it be finally asked, "Will you not have to be sick, in order to die," I answer, look about you. Is it true that all men die from illness? Go back to the apostles. Were they ill? Eleven died by violence, even as their Master; and of John the beloved, who will dare to say that he wasted away under the hand of a "messenger of Satan"? To-day, how many leave the world from violence, from accident, and from that sudden taking off without a day's suffering which is so common? How many old persons simply fail? The sands of life run out almost imperceptibly; they are not sick; but suddenly the golden cord is loosed, and the spirit departs to God who gave it. Surely this question is abundantly answered already.

7.—For the Apostolic Age.

We are told, with much confidence, that these miracles of healing were only for the Apostolic Age. This idea is of a piece with the theory that all the miracles of Christ were wrought simply to establish a belief in His divinity. But it is no new idea that Christ performed these miracles out of His overflowing love and goodness. Dr. Nast, in his "Introduction to the Gospel Records," advances the thought that Jesus did not have to exert Himself to work miracles, but rather was obliged to restrain the outflow of life from His loving heart. As we have already seen, the Master could well have established His superhuman character by astounding miracles in nature; but His love for man, so to speak, compelled Him to heal and bless wherever He went.

The only attempt at a real argument on Scriptural grounds ever yet made has as a necessity advanced the dogma that the promises of the law are now inoperative—that the old has passed away. On this point I quote from Stockmayer's "Sickness and the Gospel."

"We often hear that these promises no longer hold good under the New Covenant; but the Lord said, 'Think not that I am come to destroy the law or the prophets. I am not come to destroy, but to fulfill!' (Matt. v. 17). Only under the New Covenant God's claims upon us, and with them the conditions upon which we obtain the promises, are higher. Six times the Lord reiterates, 'Ye have heard that it was said by them of old time . . . . but I say unto you.' The distinctive character, then, of the New Covenant, is that now all is summed up in the person of Christ; He is the end of the promises as well as of the law. To him who seeks first the Kingdom of God, and his righteousness, all other things shall be added; the present things, or the things to come—the world, life, death—

all belong unto those who are Christ's. (1 Cor. iii, 22–23). Now all that was promised to the faithful and obedient Israelite, besides health and fertility, may be summed up in the words, "daily bread." Do we not still ask God every day for our daily bread, and has not that been secured to us by the Lord himself (Mark viii. 14–21); not only for the body, but also for the soul (Jas. i. 5; 1 Cor. x. 13; compare Heb. xiii. 6). The promise of long life is also expressly renewed under the New Covenant" (Eph. vi. 3).

It becomes the man who claims that the Old Covenant has passed away to show us how he manages to rescue the ten commandments from the wreck. And it also is reasonable to require him to show why he clings to the thousands of spiritual promises contained in the law and the prophets, while throwing away those of a physical import. Every sober thinker will admit in a moment that only the ceremonial or ritual was abolished when the great Antitype was offered on Calvary. The moral law, the spiritual law, the physical law remain intact.

If I be asked to account for the fact of the general disappearance of the miraculous gifts from the church, nothing is easier. Picture the apostolic church "full of faith and the Holy Ghost." By degrees the church began to lose faith and grow spiritually weaker. Where and how would this appear? Would it not be first in the failure of the momentary walk with God, so essential to the highest experience?

This momentary, personal trust failing, faith became more figurative and less literal; more general, and less particular, more theoretical, and less practical. But what more practical than the visible, tangible effects of faith upon the body? Hence men while managing to still trust God for eternity, became unable to trust him for time, and thaumaturgy disappeared from the general view. (The mustard-seed-faith—the faith that lays hold upon the impossible, that sees the great tree in the tiny seed, and reaches out in confidence in order to produce it—this kind was not found among the apostles themselves until after Pentecost.)

But we are not left to theory and analogy; Scripture is not silent upon this subject. The last words of Jesus, according to St. Mark, were, "and these signs shall follow *them that believe;* in my name shall they cast out devils; they shall speak with new tongues; they shall take up serpents; and if they drink any deadly thing, it shall not hurt them; they shall lay hands on the sick, and they shall recover."—Mark xvi. 17, 18. Now, "them that believe" is a pretty broad promise. If men and women rise up to-day and say, "We believe, and these signs do follow us," who will undertake to disprove the fulfillment of the Lord's words? Again, Paul, in 1 Cor. xii., speaks at length of the "gifts of the spirit." He says, "God hath set some *in the church*, first, apostles; secondarily, prophets; thirdly, teachers, after that miracles, then gifts of healings, helps, governments, diversities of tongues." Now we all believe that "teachers" exist in the church to-day; but if any of these gifts were restricted to the

Corinthians of the first century, we cannot consistently claim a single one. Moreover Paul enjoins the church to " covet earnestly" these very gifts. Does that look like a special apostolic privilege?

But James settles the matter beyond any successful dispute. He writes "to the twelve tribes scattered abroad," that is surely general enough. And he gives a direction to the sick *which, for clear cut specific detail, is not surpassed by any promise in the Bible.* "Is any sick among you (Is that sufficiently comprehensive?) let him call for the elders of the church, and let them pray over him, anointing him with oil in the name of the Lord; and the prayer of faith shall save the sick, and the Lord shall raise him up, and if he have committed sins, they shall be forgiven him."—Jas. v. 14, 15. Now, if any man can point to a plainer and more positive promise in the Bible than this to the sick, let him produce it.

I make the positive assertion that the following cannot be denied by any man living:

1. There is no law in the Old Testament laid down with more distinctness and positiveness than the law of physical health through the healing power of Jehovah Rophi.—Ex. xv. 26.

2. There is no command with attached promise more absolute than the commission to the apostles.—Matt. x. 1, 7, 8. To the seventy disciples. —Luke x. 1-9. And to the entire church.—Mark xvi. 17, 18.

3. There is no command and no promise more general in its application, nor more unqualified in its terms, than the direction to the sick.— Jas. v. 14, 15.

4. There is not a sentence, a word, or even a hint, anywhere in Scripture, that either of these were confined to any special age, or to be limited by any special conditions. Each expresses its own conditions.

I am fully persuaded that any Christian, who prayerfully considers these four points, will speedily be convinced that God's promises are not outlawed by time. Let us not forget the curse pronounced against him who shall add to, or take from, the words of Scripture.—Rev. xxii. 18, 19.

8.—THE DAYS OF MIRACLES HAVE PASSED.*

(This proverb was coined in hell, and bears the most unmistakable signs of the devil's imprint.) The Bible covers a period of four thousand years of actual history. During all that time God wrought special miracles. Looking forward into the future, the seer of Patmos pictures miracle on miracle, wonder upon wonder, until the mind can scarcely follow the letter, much less the sense. These are to come. We are now trembling on the very verge of the glorious appearing of our Lord and King—a miracle more stupendous in its effects than any that the world has known. (Who says that the days of miracles are no more? Who

---

* "I do not know but that the chief advance of the Church is to be in that direction (Faith Cure). Marvellous things come to me day by day which make me think if the age of miracles is past, it is because the faith of miracles is past."—T. DE WITT TALMAGE.

will dare to say it? Is it written? Is there the least intimation in the Word? Does not Paul say "Covet earnestly the best gifts," after naming the gift of miracles fourth in order? I could bring modern evidence of the weightiest kind, but we are dealing with God's Word alone.* Is it not plain that a sleeping church has "made the Word of God of none effect through your tradition, which ye have delivered?"—Mark vii. 13. Jesus Christ is "the same yesterday, to-day, and forever."—Heb. xiii. 8.

But let us look at the objection critically and logically. In his wonderful and delightfully witty answer to Ingersoll, Rev. Father Lambert takes the ground that the only way to really reply to an infidel is to show his false assumptions, false logic, and false statements. Upon this principle, let us examine the saying, "The age of miracles has passed."

1. It is a bold and positive statement. Now, an unalterable rule in all argument is, that a mere statement has not one atom of weight unless it be proven. The opposite party has only to say, "I deny it," in order to force from the assumer the grounds for his assumption. Of course, this is not always necessary. For example, the blatant type of infidels make a practice of denying matters which have been abundantly established by the most complete proofs hundreds of times before they were born. In such cases the mere denial has no force. But, in the statement under discussion, this cannot be said. Who has ever proved, or undertaken to demonstrate, that the "age of miracles has passed?" I do not wish to unnecessarily enlarge this article, and, therefore, simply assert that no such undertaking is on record. If it is, let it be produced. It therefore becomes necessary for the objector to bring forward evidence to establish his claim. Can he do it? Let him remember that we are standing upon an established condition of things. Miracles have frequently occurred, as he himself admits, and we hold that they still continue.

2. We can now properly see that the attempt to prove "the age of miracles past" involves the proof of a negative proposition, viz., there have been no miracles for a number of centuries. Either this, or else the words mean that the decree of God has gone forth announcing the end of miracles. Which horn of the dilemma will you fall on? The logician well knows that a negative cannot be demonstrated; but this must be attempted, unless the Divine decree can be produced. I therefore invite the quoters of this saying to search the Scriptures for the decree, or else go to work on the proof of a negative proposition. A negative *statement*, however, may be established by personal evidence; and I here make the assertion that from cover to cover, not one word can be found in God's word which hints at such a decree as the abolition of miracles or any other "gift of the Spirit." On the contrary, I read of this gift as in

---

* Let the reader examine the evidence in "*Supernatural gifts of the Spirit*," Pastor Blumhardt, Dr. Cullis's "*Faith Cures*," etc., etc.

the Church, and read also the injunction to "covet earnestly" these good things which come from above. And in the early records of the Church I find abundance of testimony to the continuance of these gifts for several centuries.

There is, therefore, only one way possible for our objector to attempt the substantiation of his "proverb," and that is by seriously examining the evidence in the case of each cure through faith; and then to obtain the decision of his audience, acting as a jury, whether they deem it sufficient to establish the claim of the Divine interposition. This kind of judicial trial has been going or for the last ten years most actively (although going on all along church history), and a rapidly increasing number of devout Christians, and many worldly people, are becoming convinced that the "proverb" is a lie.

3. "*The age* of miracles has passed." My next point is that the above words assume another thing which calls for the most rigid demonstration. The conception of a certain period specially set apart during which miracles should occur is forced wholesale on the mind. But wait a minute! Who says anything of the kind? Does the Scripture? Did God ever say so? How are you going to prove this? Positively I will not assume anything, except it be based on Scripture.

Dr. Marvin Vincent, in his criticism on Dr. Stanton's book, takes the ground that miracles always cluster about great epochs, and that in the interim they cease to occur; but even he never ventured to say that God declared their "age" to have passed. Now we are perfectly ready to admit the general statement—miracles have seemed to cluster around great epochs; but we deny emphatically that they were ever *limited* to such periods. Was there any special "epoch" like the Exodus, or the time of Elijah, when the Lord miraculously saved Hagar and Ishmael? Was there any "epoch" when the Lord healed Abimelech's household, or answered Isaac's prayer for his wife? What particular "epoch" called forth the marvelous miracle of the "dial of Ahaz," or even the slaughter of Sennacherib's host? And in any case Dr. Vincent's shaft turns squarely against himself, for it must be evident that his "epochs" were times when no one on earth believed in present miracles except the few prophets and workers. When Moses faced the King of Egypt he stood alone, and the cry was, "Bring forth the magicians; there is no miracle here." Truly if Dr. Vincent and his fellow-unbelievers are as numerous as they claim, this may be another "epoch" and he be found on the wrong side.

But, again, will the doubter answer the inquiry whether those who lived just before an "epoch" likely believed that miracles were coming? Was there any remotely antecedent prophecy of the great wonders that "clustered around" the Exodus? We know that there was none. Then we must admit that the succession of most startling miracles the world has ever known came on without any previous warning. The prophecy and the fulfillment were only separated by a few hours. Has God ever wrought miracles in the past without previous announcement? Was the great miracle of Jonah and the whale described in prophecy? Verily, these modern Christian doubters would brand a Jonah of to-day as the biggest liar of the ages, even if a thousand men saw him come dripping from the water. Did they ever consider the total lack of corroborative testimony concerning that most wonderful event? Not one soul among men is reported as having seen Jonah swallowed by the whale, or cast upon the shore. It all rests upon Jonah's word and its place in the Scriptures. Of course the latter alone gives it acceptance. *Would that as much weight were allowed to Scripture when we seek to prove a point not handed down by tradition.* But when the Bible says, "Himself took our infirmities and bare our sicknesses," the Church exclaims almost with one voice, "We can't believe that means what it says; bring out Jonah and let's hear his account." We bring the witnesses, but of course those who turn from God's word, and seek to spy out human indorsement are unbelieving still, and pronounce the whole thing "a big fish story."

4. "The age of miracles *has passed*." These words are easily understood, but not so easily demonstrated. We have seen the negative proposition which is involved; here is another weak point: Suppose "the age" has gone by, do our friends mean to assert that there can never be and will never be another such "age"? Now hold still a minute, brethren, and think this over. Do not answer rashly. There are weighty reasons for great care and consideration. But I propose to push this to the wall. What do you mean by "has passed"? I will give you another pair of horns. Either the age of miracles, or rather *an* age of miracles, may and will occur again or there will never be such another. Which horn will you accept? If the latter, read the awful descriptions given by the prophets Daniel, Isaiah, and Jeremiah, and by Jesus Christ and his Apostles of the stupendous miracles that will precede and attend the period of the second advent. The Exodus, Elijah's life, and even the deluge itself, will sink into insignificance beside the overwhelming manifestations of Omnipotence that are to pour upon this earth and its inhabitants. Then you will admit that *an* age of miracles is coming. Evidently, therefore, you must fall back on the first horn and decide that one age has passed, while we are now living in the interval between "epochs."

Well, suppose we are, are you going to prove that the interim is indefinite in length? Had you better not move slowly in your condemnation, lest the angel messengers of another day have perchance appeared to some who are more wakeful than yourself? The Lord comes in miracles always, and the great condition is "watching."

If you are not watching for the miraculous you are not watching for the Lord.

In the total absence of certain limits set in the Scripture for this "age" in which we live, be careful to watch for a miraculous Saviour in ways that are not clearly mapped out in your limited brain, or you may be looking for a mountain to fall on you after a while.

Finally, I hope that all my brethren in Christ will be enabled to look on these "lying spirits" who flock around us in the "traditions of men" in the light of God's truth and by the power of Jesus' name cast them out whenever we meet them. Jesus said "These signs shall follow them that believe." Do you my brother, believe these words? If you arbitrarily relegate them to a past "age" of course the "signs" will not follow you, but do not be so blind as to refuse the evidence of those who solemnly declare, "I believe," "I expect," and the signs do follow. Be not unbelieving when God's word is so plain. The only sign given to a "stiff-necked generation" is the "sign of the prophet Jonas." Jonah preached only three days in Nineveh, and foretold the most absurdly improbable catastrophe ever voiced among men. But the heathen city believed. Either this was the most terribly arbitrary piece of distorted Calvinism—the city being absolutely forced to believe—or else those old heathens, living when "the age of miracles had passed" for centuries, had a faith in the miraculous that may well put to shame the Christianity of this year of grace, eighteen hundred and eighty-eight.

A miraculous God made this world. By a succession of miracles He has made himself known through the ages. Miraculously He saved and cleansed my soul. Miraculously (in the sense that men utterly failed) He healed my body eight years ago. He is coming soon and coming in a storm of miracles. I can understand a God who can work only through the natural causes known to man, and, with Daniel Webster, I find that a God I can understand is no God at all. I look for His miraculous footsteps and I find them; and the promise is, "He that believeth shall never be confounded." Praise the Lord!

9.—The Use of Means.

Has not God provided physicians, medicine, and means for healing the sick? These questions need but little thought, though they may require some space. I am writing to Christians, as to those who believe God's Word. Hence, the great question is What does the Word say? That is enough. But let us look at this question of means.

We have already seen how exceedingly uncomplimentary the Bible is to physicians. The word medicine occurs only four times in Scripture. One is "Thou hast no healing medicines."—Jer. xxx. 13. Another, "In vain shalt thou use many medicines."—Jer. xlvi. 11. Another, where Ezekiel speaks in his vision of the tree of life whose leaf should be "for medicine."—Ezek. xlvii. 12. And the fourth, "a merry heart doeth good (like) a medicine."—Prov. xvii. 22. The margin has it "to a medicine." Of course these are largely figurative; and I admit freely that these brief words plainly indicate that remedies were known and used at

DIVINE HEALING.

the time they were written. But it is certainly strange that not one single case is even *mentioned* in the Bible, where any man was healed of disease; solely by the use of medicines. This is not surprising however to the soul that has learned to literally believe, "It is better to trust in the Lord than to put confidence in man." Certainly a wonderful change has taken place in our day when there are 190,000 physicians in the world, and medicines without number. *Scripture never advises us to trust in anybody or anything but God.* There are several cases in the Bible where something of the nature of physical means seem to have been employed.

1. TIMOTHY. Paul wrote, "Drink no longer water, but use a little wine for thy stomach's sake and thine often infirmities." The word is *oinos, grape juice.* Dr. Boardman presents the argument that this was no more advising medicine, than would be the counsel to eat rare beefsteak, since wine was regarded as a provision for nourishment.* This is undoubtedly true of the sweet unfermented wines, which, like the famous Lesbian variety, were according to Pliny, more highly esteemed than any other, except by those who drank to get drunk.

Paul reminds Timothy twice of the "gift" which he had received.† From all analogy we must conclude that Timothy, in common with the seventy, the deacons, and "them that believed," healed the sick, while he preached the gospel; for this was the distinct commission. But if he was seriously and permanently ill, would not the proverb which Jesus quoted, have been flung in his teeth, "Physician heal thyself?" Again Paul says, "Thou, therefore, my son, be strong in the grace that is in Christ Jesus."—2 Tim. ii. 1. And he charged him to "Preach the word; be instant in season, out of season," etc. Surely the apostle did not count on any interference from sickness. If we can imagine Paul and Peter, after their day's work in preaching and healing, soaking their feet in mustard and hot water, and swallowing black draughts or liver pills, we can then easily conceive of Timothy's taking medicine in any proper sense of the word. Why didn't Paul send him a "handkerchief" or an "apron," if he was sick and needed healing? See Acts xix. 11, 12. This case gives no more argument against faith-healing, than it does against total abstinence.

2. HEZEKIAH. The good king was "sick unto death."—2 Kings, 20. Isaiah came and told him he must die. But Hezekiah wept and prayed, and before Isaiah had crossed the court yard, the word of the Lord came to return, and promise the King fifteen years of life, in spite of the previous positive announcement—"Thou shalt die."‡ "And Isaiah said,

---

[* *Great Physicians*, p. 107.

† 1 Tim. iv. 14. 2 Tim. i. 6.

‡ Rev. Samuel Wakefield, Theology, p. 238, says of this: "When God said to the Jewish King, 'Thou shalt die and not live!' it was only the announcement of what must have been the inevitable consequence of this sickness had it not been divinely prevented. But as Heze-

take a lump of figs. And they took and laid it on the boil, and he recovered."—vs. 7. Without any discussion whatever, as to the possible medicinal properties of figs, when used as a "plaster," I note the following telling points. In vs. 5. God said, "I have heard thy prayer. *I will heal thee.*" Then the Lord gave a most miraculous sign to confirm faith in the promise that the third day the King should go up to the house of the Lord. The shadow went backward on the dial of Ahaz ten degrees. Hezekiah prayed. God answered. God said He would do the healing, and add fifteen years of life. The fig medicine (?) would not have been used, but for the mandate of the prophet. Hezekiah evidently put no confidence in the plaster, but asked for a miraculous sign from God. God gave this also, and raised him up according to the promise. I consider it a perfectly fair suggestion to physicians, who really believe that the figs cured Hezekiah, that they apply similar plasters to every fatal carbuncle they encounter. I do not dream of sneering at any man's profession, or any man's faith, in making this suggestion; but if figs cured carbuncles in the days of Isaiah, they will do the same to-day. But let us remember that Hezekiah was cured in three days.

3. THE BLIND MAN. "Jesus spat on the ground and made clay of the spittle and anointed his eyes." Here again was a semblance of means. But does any one seriously suppose that the clay had any part whatever in restoring sight to man who was "*born blind?*" Spittle and earth are plenty and cheap. Have they ever healed anybody else? If we look rightly, we see here but another example of those tests of humility and of obedience, which God so often sees fit to send. The common dirt, and the almost repulsive saliva, sharply teach the great lesson that he who would be healed by God, must be content to accept God's way, *no matter how humiliating that way may seem to the natural heart.* Cæsar's famous letter is far outdone in the simple, humble, obedient testimony, "I went, I washed, I saw." This case is very similar to that of the great Syrian General.

4. NAAMAN. We all know the story of his healing. How he heard of the "Prophet in Israel," went to the King, was sent to Elisha, terribly offended at the humiliating treatment he received, and wrathfully refused to bathe in Jordan. He expected Elisha to come out and make passes "up and down" (Heb.) over the places, in the manner of the mesmerizing sorcerers of Assyria. Did the prophet think him a fool? Were not Abana and Pharphar better than Jordan? Now any one can see that the water of Jordan had no possible virtue as a medicine; that Naaman thought he

---

kiah did not believe the sentence to be unconditional, he 'prayed unto the Lord,' and 'wept sore,' and God regarded the supplication, removed his disease, and added to his days 'fifteen years.' So also in the case of the Ninevites the threatening was conditional, as the event clearly proves; consequently, when they 'turned from their evil way' they escaped the threatened judgment,"

knew better than Elisha what should be done; that he was haughty, proud and *unbelieving.* But to apply the story to ourselves to-day, is not so easy for the natural heart. Yet no better illustration can be found.

I boldly assert that the real trouble with those Christians who refuse to accept faith-healing, is that the characteristics of the old general of Syria are literally reproduced in them. 1. They think they are wiser than the Word of God. 2. They are too proud to give up every trace of self, and obey without a question. 3. Most important of all, *they will not believe.* As soon as Naaman made up his mind to give up his pride and obey, he was healed. The same road is open to-day. Note especially that spiritual blessings attended the bodily healing, and Naaman became a worshipper of the true God. Nor should we forget that Jesus himself referred to this very case and said, in so many words, that the only reason why other lepers were not healed was because of their unbelief. Is this the reason why so many languish to-day?

The case of Paul and Silas, when they had their stripes washed by the jailer of Philippi (Acts xvi. 33), and that of Paul when he was stoned and left for dead at Lystra (Acts xiv. 21, 22), show that in cases of accident or other mechanical, physical injury, God may allow a gradual, natural recovery, or send a quick supernatural healing, as He sees fit. But we are not warranted in expecting the latter unconditionally. Hence hygienic, and even surgical appliances should be used unless there is the most positive leading of the Spirit to the contrary.

I believe this covers every case of healing in the Bible where anything approaching the nature of medicine was used, except those whom the disciples "anointed with oil."—Mark vi. 13. This brings us fairly to the question.

5. WAS OIL IN ANY SENSE A MEDICINE? Notwithstanding the opinion of the learned Dr. Adam Clarke, it is with difficulty that I can seriously debate this point. We can easily find refuge aginst Dr. Clarke in the decided stand taken by John Wesley in opposition to the great commentator on this point. In the matter of authority, I will simply place Wesley against Clarke. The latter thought the oil was used as a medicine; the former utterly rejected the idea.*

But no authority to-day stands higher than the late Dean Alford, whose conclusive comments on the passage in James† settles forever the foolish notion that the oil had any medicinal character. This argument is about as marked by ignorance and absurdity as that of an editor who recently wrote that the word "sick" in Jas. v. 15 (Greek *kamno*) never means bodily sickness at all, but merely "weariness," etc., concerning which remarkable exegesis Dr. Daniel Steele, the learned Greek scholar and teacher,

---

* For the benefit of the curious, and particularly of the inquiring Methodist, read the extracts from Wesley's Journal in the note on page 174.

† See Introduction, p. 17.

wrote to me, "the author of this is either an ignoramus in Greek or an intentional deceiver." Unfortunately such ignoramuses often come to the front in theology.

But we do not have to ask either of these men. Our eyes are open; we can read for ourselves. What does God say? We find eight or nine Hebrew, and half a dozen Greek words translated by *anoint, anointed, anointing*. This word, in its three English forms, occurs 137 times in Scripture. It is sufficient to note that all but four or five of these clearly and directly refer to the sacred or ritualistic anointing, or consecrating to God in some manner. A large number refer to the "anointing oil" of the Mosaic law. Many others speak of the anointing of kings, and others of prophets. Yet it is noticeable that several of these words mean literally, *to smear or to rub on*. The particular word which is used in James v. 14, is precisely the same as in Mark vi. 13. It is *aleipho*, and means distinctly, *to anoint*. Three other Greek words, *engchrio, chrio*, and *epichrio*, have more the sense of *to rub on*. Yet the latter are used in such texts as "God anointed (chrio) Jesus of Nazareth with the Holy Ghost and with power."—Acts x. 38. See also 1 John ii. 27. The word *chrisma* is here used. It is perfectly plain, therefore, that there is not the faintest Scriptural ground for making even the conjecture that the oil was used for its supposed medical properties. On the contrary the evidence against such an idea is absolutely unbroken, and stands 137 to 1. We do know that every one or everything that was specially set apart or consecrated to the Lord's service was anointed with oil. Was this to cure the disease of sin? And when we find Jesus himself commanding his disciples to preach the gospel, for the saving of souls by faith alone, and to heal the sick by the laying on of hands and anointing with oil, and find that an inspired apostle connects this healing with the forgiveness of sin, what can we believe or suppose as to the use of the oil? Besides James most distinctly says, "The Lord shall raise him up." In short, there is not the faintest hint in Scripture that oil was ever considered in any other light than the symbol of consecration. For the benefit of those who ask for human authority we will now turn to history.

I lately read an article by a minister of the gospel in which it was stated that oil was about the only medicine the physicians used in the time of Christ, or at least that it was exceedingly prominent. Such a statement can only proceed from inexcusable ignorance in the writer.

From a book called "Gleanings," by C. C. Bombaugh, M. D., under the head "Nothing New under the Sun," is taken the following:

"Harvey discovered the circulation of the blood in 1619; but from a passage in Longinus (chapter xxii), which the "Father of Critics" obtained from the "Timæus" of Plato, we learn that this fact was known at least two thousand years before; or in the fourth century before Christ. Dr. Bombaugh further shows, that the use of anæsthetics to deaden pain in surgical operations was well known in the time of Christ. Dr. Morton, of Boston, in 1846, first practically adopted the vapor of sulphuric ether in surgery, while Dr. Simpson of Edinburgh, in 1847, first applied chloroform; but, he adds, the idea of thus deadening the pain and torture under the knife, etc., by the use of the juices of poppy, henbane, mandragora, and other narcotic preparations, disappears in the darkness of a remote antiquity. Herodotus, in the fifth century B. C., describes the Scythians as using the vapor of hemp-seed to produce stupefaction. From the account of our blessed Lord's crucifixion we know that "vinegar mingled with gall"—(Matt. xxvii. 34), was one, at least, of the mixtures administered to alleviate the horrors of such a death.

Pliny, the naturalist, Dioscorides, a Greek physician of Cilicia, Apuleius of Madaura, all of whom lived in the first and second centuries of our era, describe the use of mandragora, rocket, and a stone called Memphitis, which, when powdered and mixed with vinegar, was applied to those about to have a "member mutilated, burned, or sawed."

The doctor also cites the Chinese, saying, "they understood, ages before they were introduced into Christendom, the use of substances containing iodine for the cure of goitre, and employed spurred rye (ergot) to shorten dangerously prolonged labor in difficult accouchements."

"They used moxa, and gave a preparation of hemp, when incisions or amputations were necessary, and he quotes from one of their famous medical works, in the library at Paris, the following sentence: After a certain number of days, the patient recovered, without having experienced the slightest pain during the operation."

Rev. Arthur Sloan, in an able article on "Medical Knowledge in Ancient Times," says:

"I will now mention a fact that came under my own observation. In the winter of 1870, I met a physician, in the city of New York, who said, 'To show you that there is "no new thing under the sun," as Solomon says, I will give you a bit of my experience.' He then related how he had been for a long time perfecting a surgical instrument of complicated structure, and when just upon the point of patenting it, at Washington, he was going down town one day, and being attracted by some photographs in a store window, he turned aside to look at them. To his complete astonishment he saw his own instrument part for part, pictured among these 'antiquities,' dug out of Herculaneum and Pompeii. It will be remembered that these cities were destroyed in the first century after Christ. Eighteen centuries ago, therefore, the practice of surgery had reached a point where as complicated an instrument was required as in the same practice in 1870. When we consider the length of time, experience and knowledge needed to produce such an instrument we can see to what a state of perfection surgery had been brought at that time. This is a fact of great importance in such an inquiry as the present."

In this connection I quote Ezekiel xxx. 21: "I have broken the arm of Pharaoh king of Egypt; and lo, it shall not be bound up to be healed, to put a roller to bind it, to make it strong to hold the sword." The word translated "roller" means more literally *bandage;* and we at once see the figure to be an exact description of the *rolls* of linen used as bandages for a broken limb. Truly in the light of all these facts, and those set forth in the Introduction on this point, the man who has foolishly striven to show that "oil" in James means a "medicine," will appear to the well informed if not as an "intentional deceiver," at best as an "ignoramus" in history. A rather caustic writer has the following on this point:

"Holiness literature seems to some extent to be tainted with rationalism. The *Free Methodist* is so far gone in materialism that it construes the anointing with oil in the name of the Lord, James v. 14, to be a medical prescription. It discusses the virtue of oil as a medicine and concludes that the 'Elders' were called in to give the patient an oil bath!"

"Dr. McDonald, the editor of the *Christian Witness*, sustains the same puerile opinion. He says, 'The remedy James prescribed was OIL —a very common prescription among the Jews.' He shows how it was taken, 'inwardly and outwardly,' and says, 'with a similar intention, no doubt, its use was enjoined by St. James!' There is nothing remarkable about all this but its extreme stupidity. These brethren ought to issue a treatise on all-healing oil. They consider it a cure-all, a grand catholicon, a universal restorative, exterminating every disease, for does not St. James say 'is any sick among you?' No matter what the disorder is, call in the 'elders' and let them smear the invalid with oil from head to foot, and the malady, whether acute or chronic, cutaneous or intestine, will at once disappear! The effect is complete and instantaneous! They should state how their wonderful panacea should be applied and how long a patient must remain in an oil-pack. They might explain why this all-healing specific is never applied but once, and why this medicine must never be administered by a nurse, or drug-doctor, but by the 'elders.' Beloved, you had better both go into the oil business."

But let us look at it in the light of common sense. Suppose it true that the oil was to be well rubbed on as an actual remedy. Are we not confronted with the absurdity that an inspired Apostle and Jesus himself ordered a medicine to be universally used, which in many cases would prove only an aggravation? Imagine rubbing oil upon an open sore or an inflamed eye! Of what use to rub oil upon the skin in order to cure the vast array of deep-seated internal disorders which cannot be possibly reached in that way? And why should the Apostle ignore the hundreds of remedies known and used all around him? Why did he not say—*use appropriate medicines,* then lay on hands and pray, and the Lord shall raise him up? These questions answer themselves.

The laying on of hands was also eminently ritualistic and symbolical. Beyond doubt, physical manipulation and rubbing were used as remedies, but the evidence is wholly against any such sense in the case of healing. Why did the Apostles "lay hands" on the disciples at Samaria? Acts viii. 17, and at Ephesus? Acts xix. 6. See also Acts vi. 6, ix. 17, xiii. 3; 1 Tim. iv. 14, v. 22; 2 Tim. i. 6. The whole tenor of Scripture establishes beyond controversy that this was a sacred rite, intended to convey the idea of a distinct impartation from a divine source.

But has not God allowed medicines to be discovered for a good purpose? Undoubtedly. Medicines and physicians are the signs of God's love. Foreseeing that "all men have not faith," and that only a small percentage of the sick will exercise trust in Him, He has provided these means in nature for stemming the tide of disease, and thereby alleviating sufferings, while also extending the day of probation to millions, and he has allowed man in his restless effort to find an alleviation of "the curse of the law" to discover them. Notwithstanding God's first plan is an inward impartation of divine life, rather than an outward improvement of fallen humanity. Man seeks for means by which to restore himself. Hence medicines. Medicine for the body is much like "works" for the soul. Cain's descendants early began the long line of discoveries, inventions and sciences, which fill the world to-day with their praises*—the great army of doctors who in all ages are striving to reconstruct fallen man by natural means.

But is it not true that "faith without works is dead?" And ought I not try to help myself,† while at the same time trusting in God as the real fountain of power? I reply that "Providence is on the side of the heaviest artillery" may do for a Napoleon, but not for a Christian; and when the latter quotes "God helps those who help themselves" in matters of faith, he is treading dangerously near to the great Frenchman's maxim.

"Faith without works is dead." True. But the kind of works God calls for is best expressed in this—*acting precisely as if you believed every word of God's promise. It is a great deal more* WORK *to go to Jordan without a question, than to essay "some great thing."*

But do you not believe in any means at all, under any circumstances?

---

* Gen. iv. 21, 22.

† Let modern physicians speak as to the reliability of their "means."
Dr. Valentine Mott—"Our remedies are unreliable."
Dr. Rush, of Philadelphia—"We have multiplied disease."
Dr. Frank—"Thousands are slaughtered in the sick room."
Sir Astley Cooper, M. D.—"The science of medicine is founded on conjectures, improved by murder."
Dr. Evans, Edinburgh, Scotland—"The medical practice of the present day is neither philosophical nor common sense."
In Wood's great work on Therapeutics, he says of the fifty remedies prescribed for dysentery—"We are ignorant as to whether the patient recovers by their aid, without them, or in spite of them."

Yes. At all times, and under all circumstances, go to the best and most successful physician ever known—Jesus of Nazareth, and use the *Scriptural means for healing the sick.*

1. LAYING ON OF HANDS.
2. ANOINTING WITH OIL.
3. PRAYER OF FAITH.

In the LAYING ON THE HAND of power, I see suggested the Almighty Father, the fountain and source of life. In the ANOINTING I find set forth the blessed influences of the Holy Spirit, drawing, regenerating, cleansing and applying all the benefits of grace to soul and body. And in the PRAYER OF FAITH, I discover the living Word, the glorious Son of God, my Lord and Master Jesus Christ, through whose name, by faith in his name, we are enabled to stand before the world and before God as monuments of Redeeming Love. Praise the Lord!

10.—WHO ARE THE ELDERS.

This question often takes the form of an objection. Some one says, Why cannot I pray for myself? You can; and if God lays it on your heart, do so, by all means. Cases have greatly multiplied, in the last few years, where different people have been led to trust God for physical healing, and have been raised up through faith. Some of these have been circulated far and wide by the secular press. But there can be no doubt that these are exceptions, so to speak. The great mass of cures have come in the literal obedience of the plain command, " Is any sick . . . let him call," etc.

Several years ago, I talked long and earnestly on this subject with a gentleman, who was afflicted with chronic disease. He believed in my healing, accepted the fact of God's power working in these matters, and desired to throw himself on the promises. But he seemed doubtful on this point of the " Elders." He said, " Why can't I call for any of the good brethren here to pray with me? There is Brother C—— and Brother P——, and others ; why not call on them? They have faith in God, and are about the best men I know." I replied, " My dear friend, they have not the special kind of faith required, and they do not feel at all called to pray in this way. Dr. Cullis does feel called, and the Lord has honored his prayers." I strongly advised him to go on to Boston and claim the promise in humble obedience. He seemed much impressed, and I hoped he would go. But he lingered and hesitated. Three or four years passed away in this manner; and then, in a moment, he was summoned away from earth. I do not pretend to assert that he died because he would not go to Boston, but I do certainly know that he was decidedly averse to straightforward, simple obedience to the command, " Let them call for the elders of the church," etc.

There can be no reasonable doubt that "the elders" are those whom God has called to this special work. (And just as a man should not enter the ministry without a distinct call from God, so no one should undertake to act as an "elder" in this matter of healing, unless he is perfectly sure that the Lord has called him to the work. At the same time I most emphatically believe in any one who has faith, acting in emergencies. For a man to lay on hands and anoint with oil in the name of the Lord, without faith, would be a mockery. Is then every minister of the gospel called upon to pray with the sick? Yes, *if he has faith;* faith for that special work. He has no business to preach the gospel if he has not positive faith for results, seen or unseen. And he has no right to pray with the sick, without expectant faith. Nor has any one. As a matter of plain fact, there are hundreds of men and women in Christendom to-day, whose prayers, according to James v. 14, have been repeatedly answered in the healing of all manner of diseases. I am personally acquainted with a large number of these earnest servants of God, and know of the results of their work.

11.—Gifts of Healing.

But do you believe that anybody has such a thing as a special gift of healing in these days? Most certainly I do. This point was lately held up to ridicule by a prominent clergyman, in a well-known religious paper. I wrote him a letter privately, and gave him some real information concerning well-attested facts. He responded with a short letter, which I here transcribe, as the best possible presentation of the real reasons for the rejection of faith healing by so many good Christian people. I do not feel that I am violating any confidence in so doing, as the writer had already publicly attacked the doctrine, in very similar language. He says:

"*Oct.* 1883.

"My Dear Brother :—

"Thanks for your frank and friendly letter. All sane Christians believe that God hears prayer and, when it pleases Him, can and does restore the sick to health. What I utterly *disbelieve* is that He confers this miraculous gift of healing on the 'Brother P—s' and other special wonder-workers at Boston, Old Orchard, and elsewhere. The best proof that Brother P. really did nothing for Mrs. M. is that he, if he really *could* do all she asserts, he would have become the most celebrated and *sought-after* of men; whereas, he only remains an obscure 'Evangelist.' The woman's idea of sending for 'Bro. P.' in order to 'do God's way,' is ridiculous. If *he* (or any man) can by 'anointing' and prayer, raise the sick—then God has given him special Apostolic powers, and it is absurd to suppose that 'Bro. P.' would *fail* to exercise that miracle-working power upon thousands. The trouble is that your theory builds an *immense* presumption on a few sporadic cases. Bro. Gordon is an admirable man, but his devout volume* fails to convince me, or nine-tenths of the intelligent ministers of the land. The *special* gifts of those special servants of God, the Apostles, *ceased* with them. The legitimate function of believing, submissive prayer, is almost caricatured in such cases as the preposterous little pamphlet you sent me. If Mrs. M. *can* do what she describes, *why*

---

* *Ministry of Healing.* Dr. A. J. Gordon of Boston.

does she not do it *oftener*, and in cases of eminent and specially valuable lives? The immense number of *failures* go for nothing with good people of your 'school.'

"In haste and with cordial respect,
"Yours in Christ Jesus,
THEODORE CUYLER."

It answers itself, to a devout and truly humble Christian. May the dear Jesus mercifully spare this servant the "woe to the shepherds of Israel," who teach not the truth! But let us look at his letter. He specially disbelieves in "gifts." And the "proof" is that, if Bro. P. could do what is claimed, he would be famous, "sought-after," and not an "obscure 'evangelist.'" These gifts perished "with the Apostles." Our brother should read and ponder upon 1 Cor. xii. He will find that all these "gifts" were broadcast "in the church." He should read history. He will find that they were *common* in the church for four centuries after Christ. As to the point of fame, etc., he should remember that "not many mighty men" are called, but that God hath used the weak things of the world to put to nought the great. He should remember that while Jesus and the Apostles were "sought-after," it was only by the "common people," and by the sick who "had need of healing." Nine-tenths of the intelligent ministers" of the day would not have anything to do with Christ, or any of His Apostles. "Have any of the rulers or of the Pharisees believed on him?"—Jno. vii. 48. If this dear brother would take a pilgrimage to Boston he would find Dr. Cullis besieged by the sick for two hours, five days in the week. In Connecticut he would find a humble colored woman "sought-after" continually.* Crossing the ocean, he would find dear old Dr. Boardman's wife and Mrs. Baxter with a full household of sick, seeking healing. At Bad Boll, near Stuttgardt, he would find Pastor Blumhardt's son, at the head of a vast establishment, which, for more than thirty years, has been crowded with guests from all portions of the world, all looking for the miraculous healing power of God. And at Mänedorf in Switzerland he would see Samuel Zeller, in charge of the great faith work, established by the simple-hearted Dorothea Trudel. Perhaps the "obscure evangelists" are more "sought-after" than our brother imagines.

Again he asserts that for the lady to send for Bro. P. "in order to do God's way is ridiculous." To this awful statement I reply: "*It is written*, is any sick among you, let him call for the elders of the church, and let them pray over him, anointing him with oil in the name of the Lord."

"It is absurd to suppose that 'Bro. P.' would *fail* to exercise that miracle-working power upon thousands." It seems to me I read in the Book of the fact that the prophet Elisha, gifted with a "double portion" of his master's spirit, only healed one leper out of the "many that were

---

* She has now departed to be with the Lord.

in Israel." And of many widows, who, when the heavens were shut up, failed to receive a visit from the "man of God." Where shall Bro. P. find the "thousands" upon whom to exercise his "miracle-working power"? If the thousands are all as skeptical as our brother, it is plain that Bro. P. would not and could not be sent. And just here we see another special failure to apprehend the word "sent." Does our brother suppose that Paul or Peter healed the sick, right and left, without any guidance at all from God? Does he suppose that anybody to-day claims a power as *his own*, that is, as his own possession or property, to be used according to his discretion? The very nature of the promise used limits the exercise to those who "call for the elders." And does he suppose that any very large percentage of the sick are willing to do anything of the kind? If he does, a little practical inquiry will soon undeceive him. If our brother should be taken sick, could any "elder" cure him? Would he "call?"

"Your theory builds an immense presumption on a few sporadic cases." My theory (I can say "my," even as Paul said "my gospel," for it is mine; my Jesus gave it to me) *does not build on any case at all.* It did, at first, because faith was very weak. But long ago I built not on the sand of human testimony, but on the Rock. The only foundation I lay for the doctrine and practice of faith-healing is, "*It is written*," and I joyfully affirm, that if every case of cure, with which I am familiar, were to be wiped out of existence, I would cry out, Lord, I believe Thy word. That grandly intelligent man, Thomas Erskine, found it possible to do this, without any human evidence.* "Blessed are they who have not seen and yet have believed."—Jno. xx. 29.

"Why does she not do it oftener, and in cases of eminent and specially valuable lives?" This has already been partly answered. As to the "valuable" and "eminent" lives; I ask, who says they are eminent and valuable? God, or man? If they are valuable enough to God to have them raised up, depend upon it, it will be done. The ten spies were eminent men in Israel, and the entire nation considered them valuable men, but God thought only Caleb and Joshua, the most unpopular men out of three millions, were "valuable" enough to live. The ten died because they "brought up a slander on the land," which God had told them to possess.

"The immense number of *failures* go for nothing with good people of your 'school.'" Well, praise the Lord! they should count for nothing. We should not be discouraged if we prayed with a thousand and every one died. I am not dodging in the least. I have already shown that the foundation of the doctrine is God's Word, *and not results*. He has said, "My word shall not return unto me void." That is enough for me. Our brother has preached more sermons from which he has seen no posi-

---

* See "The Brazen Serpent."

tive results, than those which have been *visibly* instrumental in healing souls. Do these "failures go for nothing" with him? Was the trouble with God, or with him, or with the sinners? Did he ever labor with a number of inquirers, and see some emerge into the light, while many others slid back into darkness? Yet did these "failures" cause him to doubt the doctrine of soul-healing?

The dear Lord knows that there is in my heart only the kindest and most loving feelings toward this brother, and toward all Christians, in this matter. But I mean to be as severe with *error* as I can find words, means and grace. It is the *error* solely, and not the man that, by the grace of God, I strive to strip of its plausible dress, and reveal in all its naked hideousness and deformity.

Here I must make another personal confession. After my own healing and sanctification, the thought of praying with others occasionally presented itself to me. I left it with the Lord and bided His time. The day came when my own darling wife lay in puerperal fever, with a pulse running to *one hundred and eighty* in a minute. I ventured to lay hands on her in the name of the Lord, and to claim the promise in Mark xvi. 18. In an hour the fever had gone, the pulse was nearly normal, and the skin moist. Shall not Jesus have the praise? After this, for some time, I had no call; but the matter lay upon my heart. Once I was asked to pray with a lady, and felt that I dared not refuse. God honored faith this time, also. At length I felt a constant pressure or call upon the subject, and prayed long and earnestly for light and guidance. Walking alone one day in the open country, the burden of my heart was, Lord, use me, if thou canst, in this work. I have been healed, and the words keep ringing in my ears, "Freely ye have received, freely give." Lord send me. But then the words rose in my heart, as they had often done before, and I exclaimed aloud, "I am a man of unclean lips, and in the midst of a people of unclean lips; how can I be fit for such a work?" Suddenly I stopped short, and said aloud, "See here; the blood of Jesus Christ cleanseth from *all* sin; now, do you believe it, or don't you believe it? Which?" For a moment I hesitated, and then, raising my eyes to heaven, I replied, "Lord, I believe; Thou knowest that I do." "Then what are you talking about your unclean lips for?" How sharp and clear the question came! The heart works quickly under such pressure, and I answered steadily, "Master, I will never do so again. I do not understand it. It is a complete mystery how such a soul as mine can be *fit* for Thy service, but I will take Thy word for it, and believe it. Yes, I will even believe that my heart and my body are actually fit to be a temple of the Holy Ghost, and to receive the 'gifts' of the Spirit. Made so by the blood that cleanseth; how, I cannot comprehend, but fit for Thy service. Here I am Lord, send me."

In a few days I received a note from a lady, unknown to me, asking me to call on her for prayer for healing. I prayed earnestly that if the

Lord had really given me what *He means* by "gifts of healing," that I might have a certain specific sign while praying over this case. And in the event of this sign being given I solemnly promised never to doubt that God had really bestowed these "gifts" upon me. Suffice it to say that the sign asked for was distinctly given. From that day to this I have never entertained a doubt of God's "gifts." Praise the Lord! I have not been "called," very frequently, but that is a matter I leave with Jesus entirely. A single case will be all I can give here.

A man came to me, suffering intensely from a strange and complicated disease, which had absolutely baffled the combined skill of the physicians at the Jefferson hospital in Philadelphia. He had shortly before sought and obtained the blessing of a clean heart, and was rejoicing in the peace of God. After some conversation, I prayed with him, with anointing and laying on of hands. He had come to my house with difficulty, pale and covered with a clammy perspiration. As soon as the prayer was ended, he arose from his knees, grasped his hat, shook my hand and abruptly departed; going off with a vigorous step. He at once began to tell of his healing; and from that day to this, has not had a symptom of the disease. After six months of health, he got into spiritual trouble, and became dangerously ill with another complaint—heart disease. So serious was this that his physician left word at the church for special prayer in his behalf. When I visited him, he was lying on a lounge, gasping for breath. His pain had been so severe that he could not bear the weight of a sheet upon his chest. His spiritual difficulties had been all removed, and his simple faith took hold of Jesus again as the Healer. After prayer he sat up at once, and shortly amazed his physician and family beyond description by rising and going about his business. The next day he walked upward of six or seven miles; and has been perfectly well ever since.* According to his faith it has been unto him. Let Jesus have all the praise. Amen!

But how about the failures? I do not "count" either failures or healings. God keeps the books. It is my business to run his errands. He will take care of all results. "My Word shall not return unto Me void, but shall accomplish that whereunto it is sent." That is sufficient for me. We should never forget that the oxen may stumble without the least danger to the ark of testimony. If there was not a single recorded case of healing in history, I would stand on the promises of God, and declare them true.

12.—Casting Out Devils.

Another objection urged is, that if we take part of Mark xvi. 17, 18,

---

* In the years that have elapsed this man has proved the doctrine again and again. A lapse into sin is followed by an attack of disease (different in kind). When he repents he is healed.

we must take all; and in this case what will we say for the casting out of devils, drinking deadly things, etc., etc.?

The best reply to this is of course the Scriptural one. We can afford to lose those verses from Mark and throw ourselves upon that wonderful verse, which no man would ever have dared to imagine had Jesus omitted to utter it; "Verily, verily I say unto you, *He that believeth on me*, the works that I do shall he do also, and greater works than these shall he do, because I go unto my Father."—Jno. xiv. 12. Notice this declaration is of "him that believeth on me." But do you mean to say that devils actually possess people to-day? Most certainly I do. Any doubter is referred to "Pastor Blumhardt"* or to "Supernatural gifts of the Spirit"* for modern evidence on this point.

The distinguished English physician, "Dr. Forbes Winslow, expressed his conviction that a large proportion of the patients in our lunatic asylums are cases of possession, and not of madness." He distinguished the demoniac by a strange duality, and by the fact that, when temporarily released from the oppression of the demon, he is often able to describe the force which seizes upon his limbs, and compels him to acts or words of shame against his will."†

I myself have known such cases in Philadelphia. The prophecy of Paul in 1 Tim. iv. 1–3, cannot be avoided. The "last times" are upon us and the number of those who are listening to these "seducing spirits," and giving themselves up to the "doctrines of demons" is appalling. Truly we need "casting out," if it was ever needed.

Let me ask, who originated the idea that in these "practical times," the personal devil no longer takes possession of the bodies of men? Who suggested the thought that even the "possession" of Christ's day may have been only a form of insanity? I answer the personal devil himself is the author of both. What more natural for him than to use his best endeavors to divert men's attention from himself and his works? He well knows the first law of legerdemain—while doing one thing, talk about another, and thus fasten the spectators' eyes upon a false issue. Don't read Genesis; it records the original curse upon the serpent. If you do read it, make it all figurative. Don't read Revelation; it describes the final doom and punishment of Satan and his legions. It is all figure anyhow and you cannot understand it. Skip Ezekiel altogether; it deals in the next age of the world, and presupposes the curtailing of the devil's power. Read diligently of the "lying spirit in the mouth of Ahab's prophets," and never forget the original question of "free thought." "Yea, *hath* God said?" Is it not plain that this is all of a piece with the lying influence which to-day preaches the gospel of materialism, and laughs at the supernatural in any form or dress? Satan is

---

* Willard's Tract Repository.
† "Earth's Earliest Ages." Rev. G. H. Pember.

not dead. He is not tired. "He hath great wrath, knowing that his time is short." There are hundreds of men and women to-day, just as thoroughly and literally "possessed of a devil" as was the boy who was brought to Jesus, or the man in the tombs of Gadara. But, glory to God! "they that believe," shall and do cast them out, in the name of the living Jesus, who hath "all power in heaven and earth." I really believe that the real secret of many diseases which baffle the skill of physicians lies in this unnatural "possession." Medicine of course is worse than useless, and God's power is not invoked in simple faith. But the light is breaking through the clouds of doubt again, and God's power is being shown. Praise the Lord!

13.—MODERN THORNS.

It may be pertinently asked whether the experience of those who believe for faith-healing ever coincides with the theory? Are there any modern "thorns in the flesh?" I suggest this question intentionally, as I wish to open every possible point to the light of God's truth.

Yes, there are many instances of "thorns." This serves to show that cases like Paul, and other Bible characters, are not rare exceptions, but rather types of a pretty general experience. Dorothea Trüdel herself carried a personal deformity ; something of the nature of a crooked back; Samuel Zeller, who succeeded her at Mänedorf, is healthy and strong, but his brother, who has great faith for others, is himself troubled with some ailment. Dr. Cullis is somewhat near-sighted. George O. Barnes has, or had a short time ago, defective sight. Mrs. Edward Mix was more or less threatened with throat affection. Mrs. Baxter (of the *Christian Herald*) is near-sighted, but otherwise healthy and strong. I am acquainted with a great many others, some of whom have symptoms more or less frequent, from which they would like to be relieved.

I have thus frankly stated what may be considered to argue strongly against the doctrine set forth in this book; but I do not fear it. As I said long ago : this thing depends upon God's Word, not the testimony of man. God kept Moses to one hundred and twenty, without any other thorn than his real or imaginary slowness of speech; and the same God is alive to-day. Now be it noticed, that in none of these modern cases has the "thorn" been of such a nature as to prevent incessant work for Jesus. These people were, or are, doing a prodigious amount of work; laboring in the most varied ways to spread the glad tidings of salvation. What then can be argued from the existence of these "thorns?" Certainly nothing against faith-healing in general, for every one of them has testified to the healing power in them. Dr. Cullis' eyes were seriously affected. He prayed about it, trusted Jesus for them, and has not been *troubled* since. Mrs. Mix was dying of consumption, and George O. Barnes was very delicate, but both were healed. In fact, for me to mention one who has a "thorn," is to mention one who has been wondrously raised up through the "prayer of faith." The only point, therefore, which may seem to be affected by these experiences, is the one of exemption from sickness. Before discussing this I must speak of my own case. In Miracles of Healing, I related how I was led to trust God for my eye. Well, all these years He has kept me. I have used the eye constantly; teaching, reading and writing, and have never taken my glass out of the case to this day. Praise the Lord! But whenever I close my normal eye, I find the old defect or dimness in the sight still there. This indicates that the astigmatism remains. But at the same time it wonderfully speaks of God's power; for my physician said that unless relieved by the glass, my eye would always be unfit for use, and give me great pain. Since I trusted the matter to Jesus, however, I have used it as much as I pleased, and yet have not suffered any serious pain. Thus the Lord's power is constantly manifested in the continued miracle of healing, by which the natural consequences of using an astigmatized eye are entirely prevented. When both eyes are open my sight is very good, and I am conscious of no defect whatever. So this "thorn" cannot be said to cause me any inconvenience at all. Nevertheless I have prayed for its removal, many times. I have earnestly besought God to give me some indications, from the Word, that it is His will for me to retain it; but none such has ever been given. On the contrary, I have been directed to Scriptures as explicit as possible for absolute healing. Therefore I claim this, by faith in the promise. It is mine *potentially*, in God's Word; and I know it shall be in the physical fact. Meanwhile I keep constantly asking for light to see God's leading in the matter, and for apprehension to learn the lesson intended. When the lesson is fully learned I know I shall be free, even from this. Praise the Lord!

This is the meaning of a "thorn," as I see it in God's Word, whether it be a sickness or some outer trial. A lesson is to be taught. We are slow to learn, and often some slight affliction is allowed in order to gain our attention. But the lesson learned, the thorn will be removed. Most certainly, if it in any way interferes with active work for the Master. For myself, I feel that I live on the Word of God. I never dreamed that I would ever see anything except a figure in that Scripture, "man shall not live by bread alone, but by every word that proceedeth out of the mouth of God; but now I apprehend that it may be literally true. Again and again I am worn out with work; human experience says, you must wait for a good night's rest, and that will restore you. A tired man must rest. But something presses in the Lord's work, and I go to the Word. "Himself took my infirmities and bore my sicknesses" literally, actually, positively gives me physical strength; and I feel better afterward than if I had taken the suggested rest. I do not mean that all rules of health are discarded; quite otherwise. But I believe in doing what would be reasonable for a strong, healthy man under the circumstances; and when the Lord *specially leads*, I believe in doing anything. At such times I realize most marvelously that I live upon the living Word. There is nothing between my soul and hell but Jesus' blood. There is nothing between my body and death but the power of Christ. I am thus peculiarly and doubly the Lord's soul and body. Hallelujah!

(Fanatical! I do not consider this worthy of a distinct place as an objection. The cry of fanaticism has ever been a favorite with the devil. He can scare good people with that very often, when other means fail him utterly. (But it has ever been the cry against radical truth.) All real truth is radical.) The great trouble with the church of Christ to-day is that it is satisfied with half-truths, half-experiences. Our religion professes to be an "uttermost" religion, but *the church is sadly wanting in uttermost examples.* The quickest way to frighten many Christians is to urge them to believe God with that positive faith that assumes He means just what He says. Presumption! they say. What presumption? Rather let us say it is presumption to take any place lower than the one assigned to us. A true child of God does not belong in the cellar, but on the house-top, and it is *presumption to stay anywhere else.* It presumes to know better than God, and it presumes on His mercy. O, beloved, let us take the place assigned to us, as children, at our Father's table, and have perfect confidence that His blessed Word will feed us better than anything else in the universe.

So we are told that there are hypocrites who are practicing faith-healing purely to make money. This is sadly true. But what of it? Only this; it proves the existence of the real thing. The counterfeit always speaks of the genuine. Anti-Christs prove Christ always. "He maketh the wrath of men to praise him."

14.—ROMANIST MIRACLES.

We are asked how are we to distinguish between the true and the false; the evidence for the wonders at Lourdes and elsewhere is as direct as any given in modern Protestant faith-cures. What can be said about them?

Simply this. God always keeps His word, no matter who claims it. "According to your faith be it unto you," is just as true to a Romanist as a Protestant. God has always "winked at" real unavoidable ignorance. When a Romanist goes to the grotto of Lourdes, and pleads with God for healing, if *faith in God* is exercised, healing comes of course. Make no mistake about this. God is no respecter of persons. He saved Rahab *out of heathen Jericho*, and healed the Syrian Naaman, simply because they believed in Him *up to the light they had*. Lest any should stumble at this, let me give positive evidence. Fortunately I am able to speak from knowledge.

In July, 1883, Lieut. Emile Feffer, formerly instructor at St. Cyr, a

HEALING OF BODILY DISEASE. 137

professor with me in the Pennsylvania Military Academy, visited Lourdes for the express purpose of examining into the matter. He and I had talked it over several months before, and I urged him to go to Lourdes if possible. He has great reason to believe in God, having been himself wonderfully preserved and healed in answer to prayer. He is a member of the Episcopalian church. To be brief, he went to Lourdes. Under the date of July 27, 1883, he wrote me as follows:

"Four days ago I came to Lourdes with a few friends. We stopped for a moment before the grotto. There was a large gathering of people kneeling on the ground and praying, and in the midst of them was an invalid lady seated in a small hand carriage. My curiosity was aroused, and I dismounted. I drew near and upon inquiry was told that the lady, for whom they were praying, was lame. I then returned home. During the evening I thought over the matter, and determined that I would watch this case. The next day, Tuesday 24th, I went to Lourdes by rail, and attended the same services, but this time taking part in them; with very little faith, however. The prayers were offered at three different stations; the second being about ten yards distance from the first, and the third eighty yards from the second. When the party moved from the first to the second station, the lady said she felt like walking. She was helped out of her carriage and she walked the ten yards, sustained on either side by her attendants. At the next move she was not allowed to walk at all. I left Lourdes profoundly moved and interested Next day I returned with the intention of seeing the final result. This morning, at ten o'clock, the service was held. The lady walked the first ten yards without any assistance, and then sat in her carriage during the prayers. When the next move began at eighty yards, she insisted upon walking, and she did walk alone the entire distance; entered the grotto, walked around it (about twenty-five yards), sat down upon an ordinary chair, and after the service, walked out to her carriage, about thirty yards distant. These are facts which I saw. As soon as the crowd had dispersed somewhat, I approached the lady, as I desired to know the particulars from her own lips. I did not doubt her sincerity, for the emotion with which she prayed made me shiver The lady is Madame Maitre, from Bordeaux. She said: 'I have been ill for three years with an internal cancer, which has rendered me lame for the last eighteen months (incapable of walking). The physicians had exhausted every means, and declined to attempt an operation which would have certainly proved fatal. Two weeks ago I told my doctors that I would go to Lourdes, when they said that if I undertook such a trip I would die before reaching my destination. I replied that I would rather die than to live thus. So I came here; and now I am cured.' I asked, *Do you believe the Virgin Mary cured you by her own power?* '*Of course not*,' she replied, 'but she interceded.' She is an educated person, and I expected this answer. During the day I questioned more than fifteen persons, of all ages and conditions, on this point, and received the same reply."

Just after transcribing the above letter (Feb. 6, 1884), I had a long talk with my friend about his visit to Lourdes, last summer. He was thrilled through and through by the intense emotion displayed by the lady and her friends while praying; and satisfied beyond any question of their genuine faith in the power of God. He heard and saw other interesting things at Lourdes, but this will suffice. Now of course there is no disputing the fact that in some cases false miracles have been advertised by dishonest priests for pecuniary ends. Any one who is familiar with Kirwan's famous letters to Archbishop Hughes will recall the evidence therein presented on this subject. Nevertheless it is supremely absurd, and decidedly unchristian, to assume that all Romanists are liars, and all priests swindlers. That there is an immense amount of devout and simple faith in the church of Rome is a fact perfectly familiar to every well-informed person; and as that faith really *centers* in God, we should not be surprised if it secures its reward. These people have been accustomed to believe that miracles still exist in their church; while we have been brought up in the proverb "the days of miracles have passed." They are therefore predisposed to believe in the supernatural. We are inclined to doubt everything but the material. However much of corruption there has been and is in the Romish church, she has certainly one virtue which ought to put us to shame—she has not thrown away the last words of Christ, "These signs shall follow them that believe." And wherever "*them that believe*" are found to-day, there is found the fulfillment of that word which can never pass away. This settles the whole controversy. Those who do God's will are they who "know of the doctrine." The skeptic never *knows* anything about God nor His word.

He *can not*, for all spiritual knowledge comes through simple faith and asks no questions. Before we undertake to limit God's love and power to our particular ideas, we had better remember Peter on the house-top, the Centurion's daughter, the Syro-phœnician woman, and other instances in Scripture, wherein God has taught that He is no respecter of persons, but always bestows upon man "according to his faith." O, let us "have faith in God!"

15.—GLORIFYING GOD IN SICKNESS.

This is a most fertile objection. I have already treated it incidentally, and in the little tract "If it be Thy will," I endeavored to show its falsity more fully. To the query, can I not glorify God in sickness, I reply with another question. Can I glorify God in sin? How? By getting Jesus to deliver me from sin at once. But, you say, that is not exactly fair; does not God allow sickness as a sort of discipline? Ah! precisely. That is it exactly. So a father allows, or uses a whip as a "discipline." But what father or child esteems the whip in itself? Is it not an evil, so to speak? Who uses the whip a moment longer than is necessary to teach the lesson? Now I do beseech any one who may read these lines to consider this point. My brother, if you claim that God wants you to continue in sickness for his glory, you proclaim before men, angels and devils, that you have not learned God's lesson, in spite of his efforts to instruct you. Your supposed humility then really becomes genuine evidence of obstinacy. God is in a sense whipping you; and this process has been going on for a long time. You say you are glorifying God, by compelling Him to keep up the punishment. Now do you not think that the better way is to meekly and quietly learn the lesson; give up all, and take all in Jesus? suppose your child had to be whipped every day at school, would you mention the castigation to your friends to show how beautifully the child set forth the just methods of the teacher? or would you strive to reduce the child to a state of obedience? When will you learn the lesson Saul missed, that "to obey is better than *sacrifice?*"

Again, this idea of "necessary discipline," involves the fatal error of supposing that my own personal development is the chief end of life, and that something else is needed besides the blood of Christ. Now "man's chief end is to glorify God, and to enjoy Him forever," *beginning now.* In order to glorify God, in the highest sense, we must be entirely His. But we become His not through the merit of our sufferings at all, but by the sufferings of Jesus. In other words there is only one door—the door of FAITH. "Jesus Christ is made unto us wisdom and righteousness and sanctification and redemption." Surely any one can see that the very acknowledgment that we are suffering a "discipline" implies that some lesson is unlearned. But how shall we learn it? By stubbornly bearing the punishment? or by applying our whole energies to the task of closely following the delicate leadings of the spirit? If sickness must come, it is generally because the "flesh" will not die. We fail to "reckon ourselves dead indeed unto sin," and again fail to reckon ourselves "alive unto God through Jesus Christ." Truly the only real way to glorify God in sickness is to give Him a chance to manifest his power in destroying it, as one of the works of the devil.

But many a soul has been converted in sickness. True. So some men have been converted in jail, or upon the gallows. Francis Murphy, the great temperance lecturer was saved in a prison cell; but no one would argue that he should have remained there any longer than necessary. The Lord's truth is unsparing, and I must speak as before my God. It may seem a hard thing to say, but it is plain that the saintly reputation of many lingering invalids cannot be built upon their years of suffering, for these are rather the evidence either of some great sin in the past, or of a persistent lack of conformity to the will of God in one way or another. *Mark, I do not assert that every sick man is to be set down as a great sinner;* but merely to say that his sickness is by no means a correct evidence of his sanctity. The weight of inference, were it our business to judge, would bear strongly the other way. I press this point because the Lord gives me to see the greatest danger in false humility. He who is thanking God for the equanimity with which he bears his sufferings, had better ask for grace to open his eyes wide enough to see the finger of Jesus beckoning him on to a more complete self-surrender and simple faith.

I quote again from Stockmayer. "It cannot be denied that sickness itself, by the manner in which it is accepted and borne, may be a means of glorifying God. Job, by bowing at least in the beginning of his sickness unreservedly to the will of God, rendered him that service which God had from the first expected of man. And even to-day there are hundreds of God's children, who, through their patience and resignation on beds of sickness and pain, glorify God and show forth his praise. May they remain faithful so long as God gives them no further leading, nor allow themselves to be troubled by anybody."

"We are not able to fulfill the commands of God, or to respond to the demands of his holiness in such way that we may lay claim to happiness, health, and life, *as our right.* The "Accuser" is only silenced by the work and perfect righteousness of Christ. Thus Job could not prevail as long as he pleaded his rights."

"Sin has displaced our life's center, and given a wrong direction to our whole being. Instead of God, our own self becomes the center around which everything within us revolves. The work of redemption restores things again to order, and brings back the original relations. To be redeemed, therefore, means nothing less than to take again our right and true place with regard to God; to deny ourselves. . . . Heart and head, eyes, ears and mouth, hands and feet, all the members of our body, all our powers of love and thought, must be yielded to the Lord for his use. He must take the reins of our life into his hand."

"Now sickness is one of the modes of discipline which the Father employs to makes us captives to his Son, his conquered and willing subjects. The nearer a child of God is to his Father, the more jealous is the Father for his Son, that he may see in this child the full fruit of his death, and so gain a full victory over him. If therefore Satan attacks by preference the most useful and fruitful of God's servants, and seeks though sickness to rob the Lord of at least a portion of their members, it is not simply that God permits it, it is God himself who sometimes gives even these, his most blessed children, to sickness for a while, *until their self-life is thoroughly judged.*"

Hezekiah declared a great truth when, speaking of his sickness he said "O Lord by these things men live, and in all these things is the life of my spirit." But notice that he immediately adds: "So wilt thou recover me, and make me to live."—(Isa. xxxviii. 16).

"For God speaketh once, yea twice, yet man perceiveth it not. In a dream, in a vision of the night, when deep sleep falleth upon men, in slumberings upon the bed; then he openeth the ears of men, and sealeth their instruction, that he may withdraw man from his purpose, and hide pride from man. He keepeth back his soul from the pit, and his life from perishing by the sword. He is chastened also with pain upon his bed, and the multitude of his bones with strong pain; so that his life abhorreth bread, and his soul dainty meat. His flesh is consumed away, that it cannot be seen; and his bones that were not seen stick out. Yea, his soul draweth near unto the grave, and his life to the destroyers. *If there be a messenger with him, an interpreter,* one among a thousand, to show unto man his uprightness; then he is gracious unto him, and saith, *Deliver him from going down to the pit; I have found a ransom* (or atonement). His flesh shall be fresher than a child's; he shall return to the days of his youth. (A new life—a divine impartation.) He shall pray unto

God, and he will be favorable unto him; and he shall see his face with joy; for he will render unto man his righteousness. He looketh upon men, and *if any say, I have sinned,* and perverted that which was right, and it profited me not; *He will deliver* his soul from going into the pit, and his life shall see the light. *Lo, all these things worketh God oftentimes with man, to bring back his soul* from the pit, to be enlightened with the light of the living."—Job xxxiii.

Now, any one who will read these verses from the Word, cannot fail to be struck with their plain teaching. Here we are distinctly told by Elihu, the "daysman," these things come upon man as a discipline, to "withdraw man from his purpose, and hide pride from man." Then, after minutely describing physical suffering, he positively affirms that if a "messenger" or an "interpreter" sets the truth before him and he accepts it, "*then*" God is gracious to him, and *delivers* him, having "found a ransom." And with minute detail the restoration of perfect physical health is set forth: "His flesh shall be fresher than a child's: he shall return to the days of his youth." Then, not slighting the way and means of this wonderful restoration, Elihu specifies how it can be secured. Strangely enough he agrees exactly with the Apostle James. Prayer was the Scriptural "means" in the days of Job, as well as in the Christian era. "He shall pray unto God, and he *will* be favorable unto him, etc." It may be well to parallel the two directions; it will do us good to see how God is "the same, yesterday, to-day and forever."

SCRIPTURAL MEANS OF HEALING.

According to Elihu.	*According to St. James.*
B. C.	A. D.
Call for a "messenger * * an interpreter." "He shall pray." "Unto God."	"Call for the elders of the church." "Let them pray for him." "Anointing him with oil in the name of the Lord."
"And he shall be favorable unto him." "He (God) will deliver his soul from going down into the pit, and his life shall see the light." "If any say, I have sinned, and perverted right, He will deliver his soul," etc.	"And the prayer of faith shall heal the sick." "And the Lord shall raise him up." "If he have committed sins they shall be forgiven him."

Truly His word endureth forever. The way of ceremonies may change, but the way of faith, never. Let us especially notice that Elihu emphasizes the fact that all these sicknesses come solely, "To bring back his own soul from the pit." O, yes, you say; we will agree to that: sickness is necessary sometimes to keep a man from being lost. Ah! brother, read on. The old preacher was just guided by the Spirit to provide for that point. He adds, with a clearness that admits of no denial, that the discipline is not only to save from hell, but also that the patient may "be enlightened with the *light of the living.*" Hezekiah says: "The grave cannot praise thee, the living, the living, he shall praise thee, as I do this day."—Isa. xxxviii. 18–19. O, brother, do you not see your privilege in Christ Jesus?

It is true that every sick man and woman cannot, or more properly will not, be healed. There are those who have believed the evil report of the spies, and who cannot enter into the promised land, but must perforce wander and die in the desert. This is true, spiritually and physically. But no one who hears of the Gospel to the sick for the first time can claim to be of that number, unless, indeed, his resistance to spiritual leading has been so obstinate and persistent that body and soul are alike debarred from Canaan. At the same time I apprehend that not many, if any, will advance into perfect trust for the body, who do not perfectly trust for the soul. Why should they? When Jesus was on earth, visible to sense, SENSE took the stronger hold. Result; thousands were physically healed, and comparatively few thoroughly regenerated. But as soon as Christ became visible only to the spiritual eye of faith, these things were reversed. Thousands of souls believed; but few were and are healed. The reason is plain. Man realizes that sense cannot save his soul, but it is desperately hard to give up a sensible physical body entirely to the control of faith. Therefore, the supposed danger is not likely to exist. If a man can trust for bodily healing, in *real faith,* it almost necessitates a co-existent soul-faith. Experience abundantly proves this to be true; for no one has been known to trust for the body, who has not received a great spiritual blessing, even when the healing has been withheld.

A minister of the gospel, recently healed through faith, writes: "I did believe that my lameness bound me closer to the gracious Lord, but I *know,* now, that daily looking to him for health and strength, binds me a thousand-fold closer. The spiritual growth and quickening, consequent on this blessing of accepted healing, I value far more than I do my restored health itself."

But it will be objected that if God will remove a disciplinary sickness, as soon as the lesson is learned, why will He not also remove a disciplinary temptation in the same way? But the Bible says, "count it all joy when ye fall into divers temptations."

This is easily answered. We must remember that a temptation is not a sin. It is sent from the outside (in the case of a heart wholly sanctified), and we are distinctly told that, no matter what it may be, God "will provide a way that ye may be able to bear it." We are to put on the "whole armor," and with the shield of faith "quench all the fiery darts of the devil." Nothing is said about the darts piercing the armor, rankling in the flesh, poisoning the blood, and requiring to be pulled out. No, praise the dear Lord! they are all to be stopped, *on the outside.* They may keep us very busy, active in prayer, in the use of the "sword of the Spirit," and the "shield of faith," but they are to be quenched before they wound us. We "count it all joy when we fall *into* divers temptations," but by no means when we fall *under* divers temptations. How plain this makes it! Sickness is not a *dart*, but a *wound*. Satan can use it as a "dart," or a temptation, by threatening us with disease. He often shakes his dart at me, and tells me—now you are going to have a cold; don't you feel it coming? You are all worn out by overwork, and are getting low fever; you know it is creeping on you now, etc. And when he says these things, he often manages to insinuate a slight symptom of the disorder mentioned. This is the "dart." It becomes a positive *temptation to be sick*. But by God's grace I raise the "shield of faith," and cry out, "Himself took my infirmities and bore my sicknesses," and the "dart" is "quenched." At the same time I earnestly entreat the Lord to show me whether I have neglected any leading of the Spirit, and to open my eyes to behold wondrous things out of His law. And I do not "think it strange," for I know that "the trying of my faith worketh patience." If I am trusting Jesus to keep me from anything, I may naturally expect Satan to specially tempt me on that very line.

But I do not have to be sick, in order to be tried any more than I am compelled to sin. The temptations must come, but praise the Lord! they need not enter in. The three Hebrew children walked in the very midst of the burning fiery furnace, surrounded by fire, walled in by fire, walking on fire, seeing fire all around them; but the Son of God was there, and when they came out not even "the smell of fire had *passed on them.*" It had passed all around them; it had wreathed itself into terrible shapes, it had hissed and roared; but it could not pass on them, for they walked with the Son of God. We can glorify God by quenching the darts, but not so well by getting wounded and disabled, all along the line. Surely the Christian's warfare is a fight in the field, not an existence in the ambulance and the hospital. The only true way to glorify God in the midst of sin, sickness, or any temptation whatever, is to have the power of an almighty Saviour prevent them all from penetrating the whole armor of God in which we are clothed.

We sometimes hear people talk about "kissing the rod" which chastises them. This is part and parcel of the miserable delusion of Satan that God himself actually and directly wields that rod. It is very easy to substantially set forth from Scripture that sin itself may be called a rod of correction in many cases; in that the consequence is inseparably connected with the act. But who will talk of kissing sin? Or the rod may be sickness, which is admitted on all sides to be, in general, the result of sin. Shall we kiss sickness? Is it a good thing? Does not God distinctly set it forth as a curse? I do not intentionally avoid the higher meaning, however. It will be claimed that the law is holy and just and good, and that "kissing the rod" properly means a humble acquiescence in God's law. Well this is all right of course, but unfortunately it is one of those short truths that do not span the particular chasm before us. When people talk this way they forget that God's law has two grand divisions,

1. THE LAW OF DEATH.
2. THE LAW OF LIFE.

Anything, anything to beat Jesus Christ,—is the devil's everlasting maxim. He will allow us, and even persuade us to accept the law of death, if thereby we are blinded to the law of life. "Kissing the rod" simply means acknowledging God's justice in the whippings we receive. It should mean that we kiss not only the rod of justice, but also the rod of power. The rod of Moses carried death and destruction to Egypt, but life and deliverance to Israel. O reader, just resolve to kiss the rod on the other side, the side of a whole and perfect salvation from all the works of the devil in your soul and body! As a matter of fact I do not read of "kissing the rod" in the Word, but I do read "kiss the Son lest he be angry, and ye perish from the way. Blessed are all they that put their trust in him." Ah! give Jesus the kiss of trust, not merely the token of a reluctant submission.

This gives us the right view as to

16.—GOD'S WILL TO HEAL.

A lady at Old Orchard once talked with me on this subject. She assured me quite volubly of her absolute consecration to God, and her willingness to do anything for Him; but she could not help thinking it was God's will that she should continue to suffer. I asked her if she was willing to believe God. Of course she was! Well then could she believe, "Is *any* sick, let them call," etc. Here she hesitated. Now there is just one thing which ought to cause this false excuse for the absence of faith to stick in the throat. It is this: *Nearly every one of these people who say they believe or suppose it is God's will for them to be sick, have been and are diligently seeking remedies all over the face of the earth, and spending all their substance on physicians, in the direct effort to get well.* They are thus, by their own confession, placed in the position of *obstinate rebellion* against the will of God. They say it is God's will they should be ill, and at that very time are doing all in their power to defeat that will. Let all such invalids be consistent. Give up all medicines at once, and lie down in submission to the supposed will of God. When a pain comes, cry out, it is the will of God, praise the Lord for it! When you feel sick and faint, exclaim, praise the Lord for this also. Just try it for a while. Be consistent if you dare.

But that is the difficulty. These are the very people who will not dare; the very persons who will hang on to the medicine bottle with the

HEALING OF BODILY DISEASE.

clutch of a drowning man. If it were not such a terribly serious matter it would seem supremely ridiculous to stand by a sick man, hear him express his resignation to the will of God in measured terms, and then assist him to take his regular dose of some celebrated human remedy. The Lord grant that we may all be driven from this absurdly false position!

As a last resort, however, some one says: How can I know but that it is God's will for me to suffer at least for a time? And how shall I feel sure that He does not want me to use these gracious means and medicines which have saved so many lives? The answers to these are conclusive, and brief. 1. To know His will, read His word. If you do not hear Moses and the prophets, a risen dead man will not persuade you. Now God gives just one specific direction in His word to the sick, and that is a direction to get well. As to time, the only salvation in Scripture is a *now* salvation. 2. To know God's will as to means and medicines, read His word. His means and medicines are threefold,—prayer of faith, laying on of hands, anointing with oil in the name of the Lord. Generally, if you can get rid of your pride, your self-conceit, your *unbelieving heart*, and offer the sacrifice of simple, child-like *obedience*, you can be healed and saved to the uttermost *now*. God is always ready to do His work, but it must be done in His own way. We must be very, very humble to do God's work in His way. Peter and Paul were more thoroughly and deeply abused than the rest of the apostles, and we find that they alone were trusted to raise the dead. "The deepest depths lead to the loftiest heights." Even when God's will was expressed Hezekiah and Moses prayed importunately and their prayers were answered: the former for his own sickness, the latter for the sinful nation.

I am now going to venture on a startling statement. No man can *fully* and *completely* offer the Lord's prayer, who does not really desire, above all things, that God's will shall be done in his body, soul and spirit. "The sacrifices of God are a broken spirit." In order to pray "Thy will be done in earth *as* it is in heaven," I must have nothing whatever between me and God. I must be cordially willing to be deemed a fool for Christ's sake; to be called a fanatic, and to be looked upon with suspicion, even by my best friends. I must be ready to stand on God's word against my family, and relations, and even against persecution from high official sources. I must earnestly long for God's perfect work to be done in my entire being, and especially, that it be done *in God's way*. I must implicitly accept the rule of faith as the guide of my daily life in all things, small or great. And I must *believe* of course that God *is ready now* to perform His will in me, even to the uttermost. In the light of the truth, we see that God's best will for us in this life is perfect freedom from the dominion or pollution of sin, and its attendants (sickness included); and, "IF we walk in the light, as he is in the light, we have fellowship one with another, and the blood of Jesus Christ, his Son, cleanseth us from all sin." Praise the Lord!

There is not a law, given under Moses, that is plainer and more positive than the law of physical health, in Ex. xv. 26. And there is not a command, given under the gospel, more explicit and more clear in its attendant promise than the direction to the sick, in James v. 14, 15. We believe that Jesus actually " bore our sins in his own body on the tree, " and consequently we do not have to remain in sin. And we read that " Himself took our infirmities and bore our sicknesses. " How then can we possibly fail to see that " by His stripes we are healed, " in body as well as in soul ? Glory to God! for a perfect and a present salvation!

17.—THAT REVIEW ARTICLE.

In the *Presbyterian Review* for July, 1883, appeared an article on " Modern Miracles, by Rev. Marvin R. Vincent, D. D. His object was to show that the theories presented in Dr. A. J. Gordon's book, " The Ministry of Healing, " are erroneous. In the course of this article, which is exceedingly courteous throughout, he advances many objections. It may be well to notice those which he deems most important, and subject them to the proper test of scriptural logic. I will simply take them as they occur, without regard to consecutiveness of thought.

1. He quotes Trench as saying that miracles in Scripture are clustered around a few great epochs and persons, and argues that this proves that God has not intended them to be common.

Answer. So far as marked miracles over nature are concerned this may be granted (only for the sake of argument;) but with regard to the healing of sickness, a sufficient reply is found in Jesus' words, " And many lepers were in Israel in the time of Eliseus the prophet; and none of them was cleansed, saving Naaman the Syrian."— Luke iv. 27. This was spoken in Nazareth, where "he did not many mighty works *because of their unbelief.*"—Matt. xiii. 58. Here Christ clearly gives the reason why more miracles were not performed—UNBELIEF. Again, the very epochs he cites—Moses, Elijah, Babylonish captivity, present the truth he widely misses, that *when men are thrown desperately upon God, and God alone,* the kind of faith springs up which allows "mighty works" to be done. " All things are possible only to him that believeth. " Dr. Vincent says himself, on p. 476, " Supernatural interventions are not lavished in unnecessary and wasteful profusion. *They come only at the call of need.* " Certainly; and as we have just seen, desperate need begets desperate faith, and then miracles are not in danger of being "wasted, " as they would be if cast before unbelievers.

2. He alludes to Dr. Gordon's citation of healings and miracles among all struggling and persecuted churches; as the Moravians, Huguenots, Covenanters, Friends, Baptists, Methodists, Waldenses, etc. He then attempts to answer this by saying, " the great revivals which have

HEALING OF BODILY DISEASE.

taken place in this country do not confirm Mr. Gordon's sweeping statement that miracles "everywhere" attend "a revival of faith."

Answer. This is very wide of the mark. Miracles do not specially attend a "revival of faith" which has no possible faith in modern miracles. How absurd to imagine that any class of men, who discredit the supernatural entirely, will ever be healed miraculously, no matter how much their spiritual faith be revived. If Dr. Vincent will take the pains to follow the already wonderful history of the "revival of faith" for physical healing, that has been rising all over Christendom for the last forty years, he will find that miracles of healing are multiplying with the most astonishing rapidity.

3. "Granting they spring up around the cradle of a new-born faith, they follow the great general law of retrocession which marks the display of miraculous energy along the line of Christian development."

Answer. If they do, what is proven? Why is it that spiritual power and interest recede after a time of revival? It will be very hard to show that God arbitrarily withholds the power when we read so many promises in Scripture. Dr. Vincent says that the miracles have fallen off in much greater proportion than the spiritual manifestations. Well, suppose that men naturally lose faith in the active, *present* benefits of Christ's salvation, while clinging to the more vague, *future* deliverance from hell. Who will venture to say this is not so? The truth is the present fruits of salvation require a vivid, present renunciation and faith. *Thousands trust God for eternity, who cannot possibly make up their minds to trust Him for time.* How few, alas! realize the present cleansing from all sin, which is their blood-bought privilege! Is it any wonder then that so many have failed to know Jehovah Rophi?

4. Dr. Bushnell is quoted as saying, "What is wanted is a full, consecutive inventory of the supernatural events or phenomena of the world."

Answer. No, what is wanted is unquestionable faith in God. There are too many calls for somebody to indorse God's notes of promise. But why did not Dr. Vincent quote from Bushnell, when the latter gives case after case of modern miracles? See "Nature and the Supernatural," by Horace Bushnell, last chapter.

5. "It is very easy to point out multitudes of cases where every evidence testifies to a high degree of living faith, but where these signs do *not* follow, and never have followed them which believe; and these cases are in the vast majority over those in which miraculous energy is developed or claimed."

Answer. This is the most unfortunate argument possible. It is a clear case of argumentative suicide. The truth is this "vast majority" never had any faith whatever in the "signs;" never dreamed of asking God for them, as the apostles did (Acts iv. 29, 30); never thought of taking Paul's direction literally "covet earnestly the best gifts,"—(1 Cor. xii. 31); and, in short would, with one voice, unite with Dr. Vincent in saying, "The days of miracles have passed." Think of the most spiritual man you please; one who walks near to God. Then try to imagine the sick being healed in answer to his prayers, when he frankly expresses his entire disbelief in the present application of Mark xvi. 17, James v. 14, 15, and 1 Cor. xii. How are the signs to follow those who do not and never did believe *in the signs?* The apostles did believe in them, and they specially asked God to send them *through them*. When the "vast majority" do this and fail, then Dr. Vincent's argument will be in order.

6. Dr. Gordon having stated that raising the dead was not included in the "signs," Dr. Vincent argues that we cannot account for the resurrection of Dorcas.

Answer. Jesus, himself, healed every day, but he only raised the dead three times. This of itself indicates an exceptional quality in this miracle. The apostles only performed it twice, so far as we know. This confirms the thought. The true reply is that the Spirit evidently directed Peter and Paul upon these special occasions. Peter only spoke *after* he had "kneeled down and prayed." Dr. Gordon quotes from "Scot's Worthies" the testimony as to the raising from the dead of a young man, in answer to forty-eight hours continuous prayer, by the covenanter, John Welch. Dr. Vincent does not notice that; I presume he does not believe it. Dr. Gordon aptly says, "If we are startled to ask in amazement—'are such things possible in modern times?' we might better begin with the question, has such praying and resistless importunity with God ever been heard of in modern times?" *If we can get a miraculous faith,* the miraculous work will be easy enough to credit.

7. Dr. Vincent quotes John xiv. 12, and adds: "If that promise is literally applicable to the healing of the sick in the church of all ages, it is equally applicable to the other works performed by Christ, and true believers in the modern church ought to do greater works than these and more of them."

Answer. Will Dr. Vincent produce the "true believers" who have actual faith that the Lord calls them to do these "greater works"? Certainly "true believers" *ought* to do many things; but where are the "true believers" to be found? But, is it not perfectly clear that all such signs and wonders must, of necessity, be under God's control and not man's? Dr. Vincent like Dr. Cuyler, makes the common mistake of supposing that these miraculous powers are to be under the immediate direction of the believer. Did Paul work as he pleased? Did Moses perform a single miracle undirected by God? Surely Christians ought not to be so blind on this point. Let the skeptic be assured, that a real "true believer" will do any mighty work whatever for God's glory, *when God directs him to do it.* Two things are absolutely essential, both of which are totally ignored by objectors. First, a Christian who really has faith for and in the miracle. Second, the direction of the Spirit to perform it. In the case of praying with the sick, we have the plain command, "Is *any* sick," etc. But for the rest we have no word which says *all* these signs shall follow *every* believer; but rather the contrary, for Paul speaks of the "Spirit dividing to every man severally *as he will*."— 1 Cor. xii. 11. As to the special signs of tongues, drinking deadly things, resisting the bite of serpents, etc., see "Supernatural Gifts of the Spirit."*

8. "It surely requires no argument to show that the Lord's Supper, prefigured in the formal institution of the Passover, and solemnly *enjoined* on the Church as a perpetual observance, stands on a different basis from the healing of the sick. The following statement of Mr. Gordon is simply monstrous: 'In St. James' Epistle we find healing recognized as an ordinance *just as* in Paul's Epistles to the Romans and Corinthians we find Baptism and the Lord's Supper recognized as ordinances. As signs they could never lose their significance till the Lord comes again.'"

Answer. The Lord's Supper was "prefigured in the formal institution of the Passover." Granted. But who knew that under Moses? It was only "prefigured." Whereas, healing by the power of God was much more "prefigured." It was set forth in whole chapters of the law; it was formally "enjoined upon the church" (Israel), in company with the rest of the law, as continually binding. It was enunciated in the most positive of plain language in Ex. xv. 26. It was repeated again and again, see Ex. xxiii. 25; Lev. xxvi. 15, 16, 40; Deut. v. 33; and vii. 15, and xxxii. 39; 1 Sam. ii. 6. When Christ came He said that he "came not to destroy the law, but to fulfill." This special law of healing, by God's power alone, was almost the first one He set forth. He made it His daily business. Even where people had so much "unbelief" that He could not do "many mighty works," He healed a few sick people. He handed over this healing commission to the twelve, then to the seventy, and finally to "them that believe." Miracles of healing were the first He wrought, according to Matthew, Mark, and Luke, and the commission to heal constitutes the last codicil of His New Testament, accompanying the declaration "all power is given unto me in heaven and earth," and, "Lo, I am with you alway, even to the end of the age." The Acts of the Apostles refer to this twenty times to one reference to the Lord's Supper, and the proportion is in its favor in the Epistles. James "solemnly enjoins" this ordinance upon the "twelve tribes scattered abroad;" and even the Revelator, as we have seen, omits to mention sickness in the list of the tribulations left behind on earth. Healing by faith was not only "prefigured," but was *practiced* all along the ages before Christ, and since that time has been continuously known in the church to "them that believe." It is true Christ stopped the ceremonial law but He only strengthened and enlarged the moral and spiritual law.

9. Dr. Vincent attempts to weaken the force of the argument by citing cases of recovery through the effect of imagination, etc. Again he

---

* Willard Tract Repository, Boston.

does good service in substantiating some of the Romish miracles. He says of these, "The fact remains, cures are wrought (at Lourdes and elsewhere) and the testimony to the cures is abundant, and as respectable as that which attests the work of Dorothea Trüdel or of Dr. Cullis."

Answer. Nobody discredits the force of the imagination. Many people have been cured in that way who did not trust in God. With them we have nothing whatever to do at present. We are speaking about those who do trust. Suppose it be shown that a man, whose imagination could not possibly be spurred into sufficient activity by love of life, family ties and affections, physical sufferings or physicians' remedies, suddenly takes hold of God by faith and rapidly recovers. And suppose it be admitted that his imagination was the agent used in his restoration to health. What then? Who should have the glory? I do not know what particular medicine God uses in each case, but if I happen to discover its name, shall I transform the medicine into the physician? But this whole line of argument begs the question. There are plenty of cases where imagination could by no possibility have operated in the least. Read of the scalded child in "Pastor Blumhardt," of the many cures of cancer, of broken limbs healed in a night, of blind eyes thoroughly restored, of cut and shrunken tendons renewed, and of the many, many testimonies so rapidly multiplying on all sides.*

10. He asserts that Christ "never despised natural agencies, but used them freely."

Answer. For proof of this remarkable statement he offers the water changed to wine at Cana, and the net used in the miraculous draught of fishes. Strange blindness that cannot see the test of faith given to those about our Lord. The use of the water in itself proved His power over nature, while it gave occasion for faith in those who stood by. The net was not necessary to get the fishes into the boat; God's power could have caused them to leap in; but it was necessary to try the disciple's faith. They had "toiled all night and taken nothing," and now Jesus told them to cast just where they had been dragging. They might well have said, Lord, there are no fish here, we have tried already; but somehow their faith stood the test, they obeyed orders without any theorizing, and of course received their reward.

11. He thinks that miracles would be "cheapened" if given as "ordinary remedies for sick headache or colic."

Answer. Never despise the day of small things. Praise the dear Lord! there are no little things with God. If he did not take his best care of the atoms, the worlds would go to smash. Did our good brother ever think God's providential care is "cheapened" by counting the hairs of his head, or by taking care of a little sparrow when it falls to the

---

* See numerous publications in Willard Tract Repository Catalogue. This answer meets Dr. Buckley's arguments from "phenomena" alone.

ground? How gloriously "cheap" this healing power was when Jesus "healed all that had need of healing," and when "as many as touched were made perfectly whole!" The Saviour, who can note that a man is "carrying a pitcher of water," can surely listen when His children suffer with a sick headache. "Except ye become as little children." How the church needs that truth to-day. "What true mother ever thought her love "cheapened" by listening to the childish troubles of her boy? Bless the Lord, salvation is so cheap that it is absolutely *free!*

12. "If indeed, society, after the lapse of these Christian centuries, can be redeemed only by a second manifestation of God in the flesh, then it may be frankly conceded that it needs physical miracles to attest and effectuate the work of redemption. (Then the work of the Holy Spirit is branded with failure, and He is proved impotent to fulfill His promise to convict the world of sin, of righteousness, and of judgment." —John xvi. 8–11.

Answer. When will Christians, as a body, give up the idea that the church is destined to convert the world? "Evil men and seducers shall wax worse and worse," "In the last days perilous times shall come," 'As it was in the days of Noah, so shall it be also in the days of the Son of man. They did eat, they drank, they married wives, they were given in marriage, *until the day* that Noah entered into the ark, and the flood came and destroyed them all. Even thus shall it be in the day that the Son of man is revealed." The leaven (always a symbol of death and destruction) works till the whole is leavened. The tares and wheat both "grow together till the harvest. These and a multitude of other Scriptures are totally ignored. The quotation from John xvi. 8–11, is most singularly unfortunate. It contains a plain declaration that the Holy Spirit shall "convict" (that is the real meaning of the Greek) *the world* of sin, of righteousness, and of judgment. We may well quote Christ's question, "When the Son of man cometh shall He find faith on earth?" A world "convicted" of sin, righteousness and judgment, certainly has the greatest possible need of miracles of salvation. The Holy Spirit is working hard to-day to "convict" the world, but the world listens to the siren song, "we are growing better every day," and refuses to acknowledge the conviction. Christians shut their eyes to their lack of real, earnest, simple faith; and eloquently discourse about all these "Christian centuries," and of the development of "Christianity." It would not be very hard, in looking over the "Christian centuries," to show that the tares have lived up to their reputation, and grown faster than the wheat. The most remarkable development in real Christian experience seems to be the development of unbelief, and of innumerable schemes for limiting God, and discrediting the plain sense of His word.*

---

* It may startle most readers to know that the Mohammedan missionaries to-day secure three to six converts to every one converted to Christianity.

Our brother seems to forget the many prophecies which distinctly affirm that the "second manifestation" will be preceded and attended by miracles, much more astounding than any that even Moses ever saw. In view of these tremendous facts, may we not as well ask whether the marked revival of miracles of healing in modern times is not one of those signs which surely indicate the speedy coming of the Lord? Let us lift up our heads, for our redemption draweth nigh; that redemption of soul and body together for which Paul longed, and for which "the whole creation groaneth and travaileth in pain until now, waiting for the adoption, to wit, the redemption of our body." Let us not despise our physical part, but only look for his perfection, echoing the wish of the apostle, " not for that we would be unclothed, but clothed upon."—2 Cor. v. 4.

"The judge standeth at the door. We are even now touching on the last scene of this awful mystery, and therefore we ought to be looking for the immediate appearance of the gifts."

18.—THE CENTURY ARTICLES.

In June, 1886, there appeared in the *Century* magazine a lengthy article from the pen of Dr. Buckley, editor of the *New York Christian Advocate*, entitled "Faith-Healing and Kindred Phenomena." In the same magazine, in March, 1887, side by side with the article which forms the introduction to this book, appeared a second article by the same author. These articles excited a great deal of attention, and were quoted far and wide. Very little space is needed here for their consideration. The writer proves that many people are cured by faith in magnetism, spiritualism, quack medicines and appliances, Romanist shrines, "faith-cure," etc. He then attempts by induction to establish a common rule from all these cases or "phenomena;" and this rule or law is simply *faith* —a belief in the thing or power in question.

I submit to every logical mind that all this is entirely outside the subject, and absolutely foreign to the true and only ground for the debate. The doctrine of Divine healing has never been and is not now based upon any "phenomena" whatever. Like the doctrine of soul-healing or salvation, it is not inductive at all, but deductive. It does not start with the special or particular and reason to the general; but begins on the general promises of God and deduces therefrom the special application to the individual. It will thus be seen at a glance that this objector, so able in philosophy, has fallen into the egregious error of totally mistaking the kind of argument applicable in the case.

I answer Dr. Buckley, therefore, by saying that when he steps upon the real ground of debate, and writes something truly philosophical, it will be time to consider his argument. But as yet he has written nothing whatever on the subject of Divine-healing. He has not considered the Scriptures for a moment. Yet the Bible is the only foundation upon which we build for a moment, and the overwhelming promises are the only materials with which we build. (As a minister of the Gospel of Christ, he ought to know better than to follow the lead of the infidel in attacking an avowed *Scriptural* belief through its abuses and excrescences. He ought to know that Robert Ingersoll argues in that way, but a Christian starts always upon the promises of God.

19.—WHY INFANTS SUFFER.

A minister of the Gospel asks this question: "The atonement of Christ removes the curse of sin, so that children, who have not come to years of accountability, are in a relation to God analogous to that of the believer. If the atonement is for the physical curse as well, why are not such children saved from sickness?"

God said, "I the Lord thy God, am a jealous God, visiting the iniquity of the fathers upon the children, unto the third and fourth generation of them that hate me, but showing mercy unto thousands that love me and keep my commandments." The "mystery of iniquity!" Who can know it? (Entailed depravity and entailed disease are our portion in this "estate of sin and misery." But Jesus has offered a full and free salvation to "whomsoever will." It is true that justification by faith places the believing soul where he was in infancy, guiltless of actual trangressions, because pardoned, and not held responsible because of the atonement of Jesus Christ. But the inbred sin remains in the believer's heart after full justification, just as it is in the child's heart from birth. The fully sanctified soul, however, emerges into a new condition, wherein is not found this inbred sin in the soul. The "old man is crucified with Christ," and the "body of sin destroyed," and the believer is no longer a "babe in Christ" but a "new man."

The atonement removes a parent's *responsibility* for sin in the case of infants, but it does not remove the sinful state, or inbred sin, as manifested in temper, selfishness, etc., even in the youngest child. The root is there, and *and it will sprout*. So it is with disease. Certainly the atonement will not prevent a child from inheriting a diseased constitution, but it does provide, as in the case of sin, a way of escape through faith, when years of accountability are reached. And just as the inbred sin manifests itself in the outward temper of the child, so the inbred sickness, weakness, or imperfection of constitution, may show itself in outward sickness, colic, cramps, indigestion, etc. The child is not intelligently responsible for the sickness, as a grown person generally is, just as it is not intelligently responsible for the temper. But the temper will come, and so will the sickness. One child may inherit a terrible temper, another, a terrible disease, or weakness. The two stand on precisely the same platform, and may be eventually reached through the atonement in precisely the same way.

An adult is generally responsible for sickness through neglect of the laws of health, extending from early childhood in most people. A cold is caught from thoughtless or reckless exposure. Dyspepsia comes from smoking, over-eating, rapid eating, or improper food. Diphtheria and inflammatory rheumatism are often contracted from drinking impure water. But again, parents are very frequently responsible for sickness in their children. Christians will probably never fully learn the laws of *holy procreation*, until they reach the experience of full salvation for the body, as well as for the soul. A volume might be written on this point, but we pass it. Even if a child be naturally healthy, it is often physically wrecked by want of care, or too much care; by stuffing at all hours, and hot-house nursing. But in all such cases, we can easily see that sickness is the result of sin—the sins of the parents visited upon the children. Finally, however, there may exist the same reason for sickness in a child as that given by Jesus for the blind man's affliction, in John ix. 3, "Neither hath this man sinned, nor his parents, but that the works of God should be made manifest in him." The Lord may foresee that without the subduing power of affliction the soul would never be saved; and the "works of God" are manifested in delivering to-day, where faith exists, just as much as in the time of Christ's work in the flesh.

In connection with this point the question arises, what of the pains of motherhood? Does the gracious work of Jesus cover this severe physical suffering? "To the law and to the testimony." "And Adam was not deceived, but the woman, being deceived, was in the transgression. Notwithstanding she *shall be saved* in child-bearing, if they continue in faith, and charity, and holiness, with sobriety."—1 Tim. ii. 15. The word "saved" is precisely the same word as is used in Acts xvi. 31, when Paul told the Philippian jailer, "thou shalt be saved," and is used in scores of places with a similar meaning. Paul evidently meant that the jailer should be saved then and there from his sin: the jailer so believed, and was so saved. But Paul says that the mother, on certain conditions of conduct, shall be saved in child-bearing. What could he mean but a full and present salvation? A mere preservation from death would hardly seem to warrant the strength of the assurance, for if a woman continue in sound health and strength, there is no need of apprehension. But let us look at another point. Paul has just compared the transgression of Eve with that of Adam, thus evidently reverting to the sad history of the fall. He recalls the fact that the woman was first in sin, and we see rise before us the primal curse of the sin upon the guilty pair. God spoke in judgment upon the serpent, and then in prophetic love of the promised seed, who should "bruise" the serpent's head, before one word of reproach or direct condemnation was addressed to fallen man. But next, he turned to the woman, saying, "I will greatly multiply thy sorrow and thy conception; in sorrow thou shalt bring forth children; and thy desire shall be to thy husband, and he shall bear rule over thee." Manifestly recalling all this, Paul declares, "Nevertheless she shall be saved." But note the conditions, "*if she continue in faith, and love, and holiness, with sobriety.*" Christ was "made a curse for us," and He has made possible a complete deliverance from the law of sin and death; and, therefore, he has provided a release from the primal curse, the direct consequence of sin.

This is a high and delicate experience, and therefore we see set before us *very high conditions.* But the mother who knows the fullness of Christ, who is filled with the faith and perfect love of God, and who *continues* in these, nay confidently claim life, by faith in the atonement of her Saviour; and freedom from all excessive sickness and weakness, and a safe, natural, and easy delivery. Some cases might be cited in experimental proof upon this point, but I prefer to leave it on God's word alone. The mass will scout the very idea; the few who fulfill the conditions, and who *simply believe,* will be saved. Praise the Lord!

20.—WHY NOT INSTANTANEOUS?

Before I was healed myself, I had an honest impression that if God chose to heal any man in these times, He would do a perfect work, and make the thing complete at once. I argued that Jesus Christ healed in this way when upon earth, and that there should be no difference now. I see very differently to-day, not because my own cure was gradual, but because the Lord has opened my eyes. As a matter of fact, there are a few cases of healing recorded in the Bible which might be called gradual. *

1. Miriam. She was smitten with leprosy. Moses prayed, "Heal her now, O God, I beseech thee." But the Lord said, "If her father had but spit in her face, should she not be ashamed seven days? Let her be shut out from camp seven days, and after that let her be received in again." Here we see that God declined to answer the direct letter of the prayer, "to heal her *now,*" because, by His law, she required seven days of purification. This is exceedingly significant. Many a Christian comes for bodily healing to-day, with a very imperfect idea of the depth and breadth of spiritual renunciation and consecration required by the *law of perfect love.* Hence the healing is gradual, that the soul may learn, and learning, may be purified through faith by the blood.

2. In the raising of the Shunamite's son, there were stages which make it a gradual case. See 2 Kings iv.

3. King Hezekiah was healed, during three days.—2 Kings xx. 5.

4. Job's boils did not vanish instantly; at least there is not the slightest indication in the record of such an event.

---

* The Lord took a quarter of a century to heal Sarah of barrenness. Sarah was one of the doubting kind. She laughed at God's power. But after twenty-five years it was by faith that she received strength to bear a son. Heb. xi. 11. This surely was gradual enough.

5. When David said, "I shall not die, but live, and declare the works of the Lord"—(Psalm cxviii. 17), it would seem that he expected to recover from illness, or felt that he was recovering.

When we come to the miracles of Jesus, it might be argued with perfect fairness that it is entirely possible that many were gradually healed. Such statements as "Jesus went about all Galilee . . . healing all manner of sickness and all manner of disease among the people"—Matt. iv. 23; and "Jesus went about all the cities and villages . . . healing every sickness and every disease among the people"—Matt. ix. 35, cannot be used to prove that all these cures were instantaneous. On the contrary, reasoning from experience, we would be inclined to say that the comparatively few cases of healing, specially recorded in the text, were the most remarkable ones. Why were they selected out of such multitudes of instances? Humanly reasoning there could be only one cause—the desire to specialize the most extraordinary. No one, who believes only in the general inspiration of the Scriptures, can object to this line of argument. I give it for the benefit of such objectors. I cannot say I believe it myself. There is, to me, a better reason. Still it has strength, for we read that when the whole multitude sought to touch the hem of His garment, "as many as touched were made perfectly whole"—Matt. xiv. 36. Why did not the Apostle add some such note in either of the cases previously cited? But I do not care for this; it is contrary to my own belief in the original verbal inspiration of God's Word.

6. In Mark viii. 22-25, we have the case of the blind man whose eyes Jesus touched twice before he was fully healed.

7. John iv. 49-52 gives us a marked case. The nobleman asked for life. Jesus said, "Thy son liveth." He did not say he was entirely well; and so the father learned from the servants that he "began to amend" at the very time of Jesus' words. This case illustrates the fact that God often gives no more than we ask. Modern experience furnishes many instances where God has granted wonderful improvement; whereupon the patient has confessed to a lack of faith, or even inclination to ask for complete healing.

8. Jno. ix. 1-7. Here we have a strong case. Jesus laid His divine touch upon the blind eyes, but they did not open. "Go wash in the pool of Siloam." When this was done, the man "came seeing." There is a world of education here for the inquiring soul. When we can give the simple testimony of *absolute unquestioning obedience*, "I went, I washed," it will not be long before we will joyfully add, "I see." We can see plainly that though the touch of God had been given, the healing was delayed until the man had carried out to the letter the commands of Jesus. Many would be healed to-day if they would only give up all, or do all, or take all that they feel to be required in the Word. But the pool of Siloam appears unnecessary, or repugnant to the reason or the heart, and they will not obey fully. The Spirit whispers, "go wash;"

but they rebel. *My brother, you must be clean in order to see.* "Light is sown for the righteous." He who carries a pack upon his back must bend over, and sees only the ground. Get rid of your burden of doubts, fears, hesitatings, pride; and you will walk erect in the light of heaven.

9. Lazarus. It seems to have escaped every one's mind that this friend of the Lord's was prayed for while sick, but notwithstanding, he grew worse and finally died. "His sisters sent unto him saying, Lord, behold he whom thou lovest is sick."—Jno. xi. 3. Oh! what a prayer that was! It thrills me through and through as I read it. What simple faith, what absolute confidence, what perfect trust in the love of Christ! "Lord, behold he whom thou lovest is sick." Glory to God! Why cannot we believe that way? Has not God filled His Word with declarations of his love for me? Do I not read " God so loved the world that He gave his only begotten Son, that whosoever believeth in Him should not perish but have everlasting life?" Did not Jesus give His life a ransom for me? Did He not *first* love me? Has He not promised to "withhold no good thing from them that walk uprightly?" And am I not trusting the blood to cleanse me now from all sin? Does not the Spirit witness with my spirit that I am a child of God? Is He not Jehovah Rophi still? Did not Jesus bear my sicknesses and my sins for me? O, when these things are so, how can I fail, if sickness comes, to just go to Jesus and confidently cry "Lord, he whom thou lovest is sick?" God always honors child-like faith such as this.

True they said "Lord, if thou hadst been here my brother had not died." Legalist Martha spoke it partly in remonstrance, but Mary in the same loving confidence in the loving Jesus. The lesson of the whole event is plainly set forth, "This sickness is not unto death, but for the glory of God, that the Son of God might be glorified thereby." "And I am glad *for your sakes* that I was not there, to the intent you may believe." Said I not unto thee. that, *if thou wouldest Believe*, thou shouldest see the glory of God?" " I knew that thou hearest me always, but because of the people which stand by I said it that they may believe that thou hast sent me." These verses show that the Lord may withhold the visible answer until the time best adapted to glorify His Son. And they show that a sick one may recover, after some time, and after many prayers, in order that those "which stand by may believe." It does not argue anything against being kept from sickness at all. That experience belongs to another plane altogether. We are now considering those who first seek healing though faith. My heart disease was cured gradually, but since that event I have been enabled to praise God for the instantaneous cure of other complaints. Upon one occasion I suffered for two days with cold, fever and chill. I prayed constantly, and rested in Jesus alone. At last faith seemed to be given for actual grasping of the promise; the Word was given me, and *suddenly* the chill and all sickness left me. I threw off the thick quilt in which I had been wrapped, and praised the Lord for complete deliverance. Glory to His name!

10. The case of Epaphroditus, Phil. ii. 26, 27, seems to speak of an illness of some duration; yet it was God who "had mercy upon him," and raised him up, in answer to Paul's prayers in his behalf. Stockmayer says, "would that God's servants who are obliged to suspend their work in the Lord's vineyard, whose heads are wearied and nerves overstrained, would wait upon the Lord until it becomes clear to them what has not been of the Spirit in their work or in their life, until the Lord can fulfill (Isa. xl. 31) in them. Would that instead of quitting their posts in discouragement, they would 'humble themselves under the mighty hand of God; that he might raise them up in due time,' (1 Peter v. 6).

"These remarks on Isa. xl. do not contradict the fact that the condition of a child of God on earth remains a condition of *weakness*. We run our course here below in the midst of the greatest weakness (1 Cor. ii. 3). Suffering and privation are our portion (2 Cor. vi. 10, xii. 10). The life of Jesus will be made manifest in our body only so far as we are always bearing about in the body the dying of the Lord Jesus (2 Cor. iv. 10). As long as we are in this tabernacle we do groan, being burdened (2 Cor. v. 4). We wait for the redemption of our body (Rom. viii. 23), but at the same time God must show his strength perfected in our weakness, and for this reason must have our members free for his disposal. As sure as we walk by faith we become in very deed strong just where we feel ourselves weak. and we are able to do all things through Christ which strengtheneth us" (2 Cor. xii. 9, 10; Phil. iv. 13).

11. Trophimus was certainly a gradual case, as Paul was compelled to leave him behind at Miletum. 2 Tim. iv. 20.

These are surely enough to demonstrate that healing in Bible times was not always instantaneous. When Jesus Himself healed, He was guided by an infallible judgment and perception. "He knew what was in man." The Apostles may have been granted an inspired insight, in many cases at any rate. "Seeing he had faith to be healed," testifies to this inspiration in one instance at least. (Acts xiv. 9.) But we know that Paul sometimes lacked the "mind of the Lord." It is therefore entirely possible that he occasionally failed to heal immediately, as he certainly did fail in the case of Trophimus.

We have already seen that there are many reasons for gradual healing to-day. All allow that sickness is a discipline. But manifestly the disease cannot be removed if the patient refuses to yield to the divine purpose. If we are slow in learning the lesson set us, why should we wonder at the slow removal of the teacher? Truly "God speaketh once, yea twice, yet man perceiveth it not." Let any one who doubts the need of gradual healing, carefully read and ponder upon the thirty-third chapter of Job. No words of man can make it plainer. "The entrance of Thy words giveth light."

HEALING OF BODILY DISEASE. 159

Finally, some people say that they know such a Christian, one of the salt of the earth, who has prayed and prayed and prayed, yet has not recovered. I reply. No one can tell when any man has "touched" Jesus, except Christ and the individual soul. No man can see and prove the union, the absolute consecration, the simple faith. The Jews doubted the union between Jesus and God, and thus brought upon themselves the reproof "Ye receive not our witness." Like Jesus we can "speak the things that *we* do know;" but they can not be proved any other way. If we "touch the hem of his garment," we will know it. Therefore we find three vital reasons for an imperfect or a gradual healing.
 1. The absence of the complete "touch."
 2. Imperfect consecration, requiring time for the entrance of the light, and the deepening of the work.
 3. Not comprehending, nor apprehending God's plan. "The law is a schoolmaster to bring us to Christ," and the Word distinctly teaches, as we have seen, that sickness comes from violation of the law. But when we come to Jesus, when the conditions are *all* met, when we touch, we are certainly healed. Praise the Lord!

CHAPTER VI.

FULL SALVATION.

"And the very God of peace sanctify you wholly, and I pray God that your whole spirit, and soul, and body be preserved blameless unto the coming of our Lord Jesus Christ."—1 Thess. v. 23.
 "Beloved I wish above all things that thou mayest prosper and be in health, even as thy soul prospereth."—3 John 2.
 "We know that whosoever is born of God sinneth not; but he that is begotten of God keepeth himself, and that wicked one toucheth him not."—1 John v. 18.

Salvation is a big word. To my apprehension, and in my experience it has marvellously expanded during these last five years of communion with God. It is a perfect word, and represents a perfect work. As we have seen, Salvation has four sides. Now the number 4 has always had the special significance of perfection, in connection with mankind. The old giant, who owned Hebron, was called Arba; and Rev. Alfred Jones, in his dictionary of Scripture names, tells us that the word means "quadrangular," and that he was so called on account of the perfection and strength of his form. He also says that the Romans used a quadrangular stone as a symbol of wisdom and strength of mind. Dr. Milo Mahan, in his "Mystic Numbers," gives it special prominence in connection with mankind and the earth. The *four* quarters of the world, the *four* feet of the highest order of beasts, the *four* elements, *four* rivers of Paradise, the *four* gospels, *four* camps of Israel, the *four square* city of the redeemed. It is the figure of the *Cosmos* in its universality and order; the idea being that of a concentrated and orderly, not of a vague universality. Prof. Asahel Abbott says, that four always relates to man as a spirit immersed in matter. It typifies God in a sensible form, revealing himself to the senses of his creatures. Hence the Pythagoreans swore their great oath by Four (the Tetractys), "that hath revealed to our souls the fountain of ever-flowing nature." Man has a dual nature, and each half is itself a duality. We may divide thus:

Soul. { Spiritual, - Inbred Sin, or Depravity. (Nature / Defects)
       { Moral, - - Committed Sin, or Transgression.

Body. { Physical, - Sickness, or Disease.
       { Mental, - - Sorrow, or Affliction.

} SALVATION.

Here we see the comprehensive sweep of the Atonement. Jesus Christ died to save men wholly. Strange to say, all Christians allow that two out of the four great deficiencies in our nature—the moral and the mental—are embraced in the *present* scope of the Great Sacrifice. A large number of Christians are willing to accept a third—the Inbred Sin, or depravity; but the church has almost lost sight of the possibility of deliverance from the fourth. Committed sin can be very properly placed under the head of the moral law or nature; and sorrow or affliction is manifestly a mental trouble. These, all agree, can be handed over to Jesus *at the present moment.* But just here a vast majority of the church stops short, in experience, if not in theory. The wonderful power of the Atonement to cleanse from all the SIN which was inherited as an inborn taint of corruption, is totally unknown to multitudes who worship God in sincerity and truth. One half the Atonement is therefore overlooked, slighted, and absolutely discredited by the majority of the Church to-day. These halves are not mathematically divided, for which we have reason to be devoutly thankful, and in God's mercy, we have held to the primarily essential portion of our Saviour's work. Yet the other half exists. Thanks to the power of the truth, thousands of witnesses have testified, and do testify, to the reality of the death to inbred sin; and one very large branch of the church* emphatically proclaims this item of faith in its official utterances, while some others, at least *allow* it. But few, if any, bodies of Christians, since the days of the Waldenses, have included faith in Christ for bodily healing in their church creeds.

Many a Christian, to-day, thinks the four evangelists good enough and amply sufficient for his daily reading, and neglects the rest of God's word altogether. Well, he can be saved of course, but will his soul ever grow fat? How Paul prays for the Ephesians, that they "may be able to com-

---
* Methodists.

HEALING OF BODILY DISEASE. 161

prehend with all saints what is the breadth, and length, and depth, and height; and to know the love of Christ, which passeth knowledge, that ye might be filled with *all the fullness of God.*"—Eph. iii. 18, 19. The Church is sadly in need of *quadrangular* Christians to day.

Dr. Vincent seems to think it a "huge impertinence" for any one to say that unbelief is at the root of the church's failure to grasp a complete salvation. (Impertinent or not, it is true.) I remember that unbelief seriously hampered the twelve men who absolutely left their earthly all and followed Jesus in the flesh. Even when striving to do the Master's work, they were prevented by lack of faith. "Lord, why could not we cast him out? Because of your unbelief." Pastor Otto Stockmayer says, in "Sickness and the Gospel," p. 39: "Why do we not take the position of redeemed and sanctified which the work of Jesus Christ gives to us? Why is the discipline of sickness necessary to make us listen to our God, and walk in his ways in all things and at all times? Why, even in sickness, are we so slow to gather the lessons it brings us? Why has not God yet been able to make of us intelligent and powerful fellow-workers?—It is because of our unbelief. . . . . It did not occur to the Jews in the synagogue of Nazareth that, if in the time of Elijah all the widows in Israel were not miraculously helped like the one of Sarepta, if in the time of Elisha all the lepers of Israel were not cleansed like Naaman, all the fault was attributed to their unbelief.*—Luke iv. 25-27. In the same way, the Christians of to-day seem to ignore the power of the Saviour whom God has given them, and the fullness of the salvation which that Saviour has procured for them."

Why is it that even the best Christian people to-day fall so frequently below the Bible standards or examples? Why is it that so few ministers of the Gospel are able to make Paul's language their own? How many can say "Thanks be unto God that *always* causeth us to triumph in Christ?" Why is it so few can testify to a vivid personal knowledge of the distinct baptism of the Holy Ghost? Why is it that many of the most learned doctors of divinity, equipped with every weapon of reason, knowledge, wit and oratory, utterly fail to lead souls to the Saviour? Is our God dead? Is the power that attended the work of the apostles, of Whitefield, Wesley, Jonathan Edwards, Asbury, and others, an arbitrary gift to a few? Is a personal experience like that of Paul, Fénelon, Madame Guyon or Mrs. Edwards, something absolutely beyond the average Christian? O reader, what is it that bars the way? What can it be, but UNBELIEF? Paul emphatically enjoined upon the church to "covet earnestly" the miraculous gifts of the Spirit, which he took special pains to enumerate. Modern teachers say, do not covet any such thing, you cannot have them; it is preposterous for any man in these times to talk

---

* I remark that when Jesus told them the truth, on this point, they considered it a 'huge impertinence," and attempted to take his life.

of a supernatural gift. And then they think it a "huge impertinence" if they are accused of unbelief. May the dear Lord lift the veil that is wound about so many of His children, when they read the Word.

FULL SALVATION.—How my whole being thrills with love and praise as I think of the rounded completeness of the finished work of my Jesus! Christ met and conquered every foe known to the human race. Yes, every one. Even death suffered defeat at His hands.

It is not a conjecture which leads Stockmayer to say that "when the church has realized the victory over sickness, she will be in a condition to pass on to the victory over death. Enoch and Elijah are not remembered as they should be. I cannot believe for a moment that these two were arbitrarily chosen by Jehovah to exemplify His power. Of course this end was accomplished beyond a doubt, but there is something deeper than that. I see in these two saints a glorious proof of the infinite possibilities open to the child of God. Two men of mortal mould have, by God's grace, lived so near to Him, kept His commands so inviolably, been so zealous in His work, worshipped Him in such absolute devotion, and above all, manifested such transcendent faith, that "the wicked one touched them not." Even over death they were triumphant. The fire of the Spirit burned so intensely in their souls and bodies, that even the mighty prince of darkness could not approach them near enough to cast his fatal dart. In a moment, in the twinkling of an eye, they passed away from earth, to be with the Lord. So the day is coming when, instead of two, many who "are alive and remain shall be caught up to meet the Lord in the air." Will it be solely because an arbitrary date, set in the mind of God, has come? or may we not believe that, when that date does arrive, the children of the King will be walking with uplifted hearts, *really believing* that their redemption draweth nigh? Five out of ten virgins were ready with lamps trimmed and burning when the bridegroom came. The Lord grant that the proportion may hold good when the glad cry is heard, "Behold the Bridegroom cometh, go ye out to meet Him."

"It is the object of the present dispensation to prepare for the Lord Jesus a bride, *who is able to understand him*, and who will reign with him. The Lord desires a people for his own possession, not a people to cringe as slaves, but a people who will boldly enter with full purpose of heart, mind, and will, into the lines of God's purposes and ways, whenever the Holy Ghost opens before them new vistas and possibilities. The late Pastor Blumhardt said, 'The promises of God are not self-fulfilling, their realization depends upon man. The fulfillment of what God has promised is always more or less dependent upon man's free will, whether he really deserves that which has been promised to him or not.' Yes, the Lord seeks a people who will understand him."

"Furthermore it is a striking sign of our times that positions of prominence, such as that of an Apostle Paul or even that of a reformer, are more and more rare. The sound of the footsteps of our approaching Master more and more rises above every human sound. 'Every mountain and hill is brought low.' We must be in our own eyes simply vessels and instruments, our entire personality, yea even that individuality which God has committed to us, and which is precious in the sight of God, must first pass through death and resurrection before the Master's image and mind can be impressed upon us sufficiently clearly to be recognized by those afar off. We must die and be raised again before the light committed to us can find its way into our brother's heart, and become the common property of the body."

"Through all the outward divisions of the church of Christ, there is growing up between its *living* members a deep and mutual heart intelligence, there is a bond formed which incloses the different members, shielding and upholding them to a degree which Paul in his time did not enjoy."*

Let us "comfort one another with these words." Surely the great awakening to the willingness of Jesus to save the body from the powers of evil, is another and mighty token that the day of our redemption is at hand. Salvation is becoming more and more a positive reality. Religion begins again to mean something more than a profound mental apprehension of doctrine, and a keen sense of legal distinctions. The grammar of experience is being revised, and we see the possibility of living in the present tense, the first person, the singular number and the possessive case. Abstract nouns and nouns of multitude give place to distinctive proper names: the personal pronouns are limited to I and me, and the verb is known in its full sense—*to be, to do, and to suffer* (*or experience*) *anything and everything in Jesus*. Let us not "be fools and slow of heart to believe *all* that the prophets [have spoken," but let us, like the noble Bereans, "search the Scriptures daily whether these things are so."—Acts (xvii. 11, 12). It is wonderfully significant that when they thus searched daily, we are told, "*Therefore* many of them believed." Very often those who cry, "search and look, for out of Galilee ariseth no prophet," are, like the Pharisees, totally ignorant of the true meaning of Scripture, as well as of the real evidence in the case.

A short time ago I read of a woman in China, who, after hearing of the wonderful Jesus and his work, asked if she could not be healed of lameness; only to be sorrowfully informed by the missionary that the " days of miracles have passed." In contrast to this, read the following, from "China's Millions."

" One day when our native helper, Mr. Yao, was preaching in the chapel, an old beggar-woman, of over seventy years of age, came to the door and listened to what was said about the person and power of the Lord Jesus Christ. She returned to her home and told Mrs. Chang, a

---

* *Stockmayer.*

blind neighbor, that which she had heard, and proposed, next day, to lead her around to the chapel and ask the teacher if Jesus could open her eyes. The old woman, accordingly, appeared at the chapel next day, with her blind friend, Mrs. Chang, and told the preacher their object in coming. After a long conversation, Mr. Yao told the blind woman that if she had faith to be healed it could be done. They accordingly kneeled down and prayed that God would have mercy upon them and regard their prayer. This was repeated next day, and again on Sunday, when Mrs. Chang's eyes were improving. She was beginning to see again. By the Sunday following, her sight—of which she had been deprived three years—was perfectly restored, and she now wished all to join her in praising God for what he had done. Within a fortnight after the day she was first led to the chapel and asked to be cured, her eyes were opened and she could see as other people. No medicines were used, nor were any other means than those of prayer and faith, employed to bring about this end. The simple woman believed implicitly that Christ had the same power to heal to-day as He had eighteen hundred years ago; and she sought and found in Him what she desired."

Now which of the missionaries held up a perfect Saviour? "According to your faith be it unto you." David said, "I have set the Lord always before me (can we say that?) because he is at my right hand, I shall not be moved. Therefore my heart is glad, and my glory rejoiceth (this is the spiritual experience); my flesh also shall rest in hope (dwell confidently—margin.) Here we have the physical security. Young translates this verse,

> " Therefore hath my heart been glad,
> And my honor doth rejoice,
> Also my flesh dwelleth confidently."
> Ps. xvi. 9.

Perfect submission and consecration to the Lord Jesus will inevitably bring about that mysterious union with Him, in which He, with the Father and the Spirit, will take up His abode in our souls and bodies. Nothing short of this is *complete* Christianity. *Christ must be formed in us.* The spirit must be in us. We must enter the holiest through the veil of His flesh, and abide continually in the very presence of God. Instead of being appalled at the height of the standard, let us remember the infinite promises of an infinite Saviour, and enter into that marvellous life of faith wherein, as little children, we believe God without a question, and enjoy the benefits that can only flow through faith.

CHAPTER VII.
REVIEW AND CONCLUSIONS.

"Hear the conclusion of the whole matter."—Eccle. xii. 13.
"In meekness instructing those that oppose themselves."—2 Tim. ii. 25.
"I will speak of Thy testimonies also before kings, and will not be ashamed."—Ps. cxix. 46.
"But when they shall lead you, and deliver you up, take no thought beforehand what ye shall speak, neither do ye premeditate: but whatever shall be given you in that hour, that speak ye; for it is not ye that speak, but the Holy Ghost."—Mark xiii. 11.

Jesus Christ came into the world to save sinners; to save them now from every sin, from all inbred depravity, from outbreaking sickness and from the inworking germs of disease.

If we sin, it is because of at least temporary unbelief or through ignorance; and if we are sick, the reason is generally similar. It may be that the unbelief is manifested in our refusal to see the leadings of God's Spirit, but all is best summed up in the one word—unbelief. "Are not these evils come upon us because our God is not among us?"—Deut. xxxi. 17.

Sickness and sin are alike the work of the devil. Neither is ever "necessary," in any true sense. God permits Satan to try us simply because we *will not* listen to His voice, and as an occasional discipline. Bodily illness is *allowed*, therefore, as a corrective, or better, as the taskmaster's lash to make us weary of bondage, and ready to follow the leaders God sends. In precisely the same way we fall into sin, not because it is "necessary to keep us humble," but because our stiff necks will not bend. As in the case of Joseph, God brings good out of evil, for the smart of our sins leads us to cry unto God, whereupon He delivers us out of our distresses. All this tends to open us by degrees to the great truth, that salvation is meant for our whole being—body, soul and spirit. I hope this conclusion is clear. Sin and sickness *may* be used or allowed as corrections. They are not *necessary*, however. We can be free from either, or both, as soon as we find Jesus, through faith, as the complete Burden-Bearer. If we are falling under either it is not always a sign that we are being kept humble, but rather may be that we are not yet humble enough to give up everything and believe everything.

The physical body is not a cage; it should not be considered an embarrassment at all. On the contrary, the man who says he could be good if it were not for his bodily appetites, simply acknowledges that his "heart is not right" before God. The heart is the fountain, and if that be purified thoroughly, all the bodily appetites will work normally and properly. The body is to be offered to God as a sacrifice, just as much as the soul. We will never be glorified until our bodies are changed. Our bodies are, or should be, actual temples of the Holy Ghost, and not merely "halls of theology."

Instead of neglecting the most minute laws of health, we are bound the more to observe and do all the "statutes."

The rigid observance of the Biblical bill of fare is absolutely as imperative on us to-day as it ever was on the Hebrews. We need not wonder at the prevalence of diphtheria and other blood poisons when everybody eats swine's flesh, and other "abominations to the Lord."

Any one may be healed who is drawn of the Spirit to seek healing. The promise is to "any sick among you." At the same time there is a "sin unto death." In this case, however, it is about certain that true faith will be sensibly wanting. This "sin unto death" may be fully pardoned, and consist with a deep spiritual experience of God's love, as in the case of Moses.

The "means" of healing laid down in James, present a perfect way. We must consecrate all to Jesus, relinquish everything contrary to His will, and be absolutely ready to be, to do, or to suffer all things for Him.

Physicians are mercifully provided in general for those who cannot trust God alone. No one can thus trust to God who knowingly withholds anything, however slight. Medicines, of course, cannot share God's glory. They stand upon precisely the same ground with the physicians, and serve to demonstrate the abounding love of God to an unbelieving world.

The whole tenor of Scripture is to the effect that God is the Healer of sickness as well as of sin. Under the old dispensations this was abundantly and repeatedly set forth, even to the extent of a special direction for an "atonement" offering in the case of many diseases. Under the new dispensation, this feature of physical healing was most particularly emphasized, in word and deed; and we have the special assurance that Jesus came to fulfill the law and not to destroy it.

The Scriptures for the vicarious Atonement for sin are no more explicit than those for sickness; the same words or phrases being used for both. Jesus is positively said to have borne our sins and our diseases; and this statement is abundantly exemplified and expounded, as we have seen.

We must exercise sanctified common sense and not fly to the extreme of expecting God to enable us to bid defiance to the laws of health, unless *most unmistakably* led of the Spirit to do so temporarily. Such leading is rare.

The devil is a beaten foe, and does not know half as much as we have supposed. He is not God, and cannot tell the future. Nevertheless he must not be despised, but ever regarded as an enemy whom only Jesus can overcome.

Close communion with God develops the faculty of receiving actual life for soul and body, an inspiration or in-breathing of the life of Jesus. And this life becomes a "well of water springing up into everlasting life."

HEALING OF BODILY DISEASE.

Jesus started His church with a double charter which has never been revoked. "Preach the gospel and heal the sick." The Apostles set the example of asking for "signs and wonders" to attend their work; and Paul distinctly enjoins the church to "covet" these miraculous gifts "earnestly," while James plainly directs their use in the healing of "any sick."

Sickness may be sometimes a means of grace. So may trials arise from others' sins. Indeed "thine own wickedness shall correct thee." (Jer. ii. 19). Obviously then this does not make sickness a good thing.

The "body is for the Lord," and is not a worthless lump of clay. If a human body was good enough for the Son of God, we ought not to complain of ours.

All sickness was and is included under the "curse of the law." This is again and again declared in Scripture. But "Christ hath redeemed us from the curse of the law, *being made a curse for us.*" Either this declaration is false, or Jesus bore my disease for me, just as he bore my sins. If I am compelled to bear them also, then His work was incomplete. But He declared, with his dying breath, "It is finished."

The miracles of Jesus were not merely to prove His divinity, but were the natural outflow of that divinity, when brought into close contact with suffering humanity; and their continuance testifies to the Headship of the risen Saviour in His connection with the Church.

He who "touches" Jesus, always receives life. Satan could not inflict sickness upon Job till God gave His permission; and this permission was given solely to lead Job to a deeper death of self. As soon as the lesson was learned, the sickness was taken away. So we can be sure that God will not allow Satan to whip us after we have apprehended and received the intended instruction. "Before I was afflicted I went astray, but now have I kept thy word."—Ps. cxix. 67.

The body, which gives us so much trouble, is not the body of flesh, but the "body of sin." When this is crucified we can live the resurrection life in Christ, and the body of flesh will be in perfect accord with the divine will.

The dietary laws of Moses are for our good to-day, just as much as they were for the Jews. He who thinks he can slight the stomach, as of small account, opens a thousand doors to disease and suffering.

The devil kills a great many good people long "before their time."

Evil is always ready to come. God "sends" it by simply withdrawing the hedge he sets about us.

Healing may be instantaneous, but is more likely to be gradual, because of the imperfect consecration and faith in so many patients. Gradual restoration gives the opportunity for education.

A sin which has caused sickness is necessarily forgiven when the disease is removed. This James specially declares, v. 15.

There is no more necessity for us to be sick than to sin. If then we are wholly the Lord's, and rest in His Word, we may enjoy health of body and of soul. This requires the closest attention to the voice of God. We must not dare to slight the least of His commands. *There are no little things in the life of faith.* And we must give God the glory.

We may be tempted with sickness, just as we are tempted with sin. By faith in Jesus one may be resisted just as well as the other. The temptation will then be useful, and we may "count it all joy." Paul's "vile body" was simply his body in a "low estate,"—not yet glorified.

Trophimus was undoubtedly healed, but not until he was separated from Paul, according to the divine purpose.

Paul's thorn in the flesh, if a sickness, was certainly from the devil. It did not hinder his work, and there can be no doubt it was removed by the power of God alone. This thing was allowed as a precautionary measure, to teach him the deepest humility, and of course was removed when the lesson was learned.

Spiritual blessings invariably precede or accompany bodily healing. Faith is always the vehicle for God's bounty.

"Chastening" requires the presence of Satan. There are no tears in heaven, no "chastening," no trials. Sickness, death and sin are always unrelenting enemies, and emanate from the devil.

Divine-healing does not affect the necessity of dying, provided our time arrives before the Bridegroom cometh. We are not, however, to look for death as a friend, but earnestly "hasten the coming of the Lord," keeping the glorious possibility of translation constantly before our eyes.

Apostolic gifts cease only from lack of apostolic faith.

The days of miracles have not passed. On the contrary we may expect greater wonders than the world has ever seen, for such is the express declaration of the Word. The day of the Lord hasteth greatly, and the miracles preceding and attending His second advent will be more remarkble than anything ever recorded in the past. The supernatural always slumbers when faith lies sleeping, or dead.

The only "means" *needed* for the sick, are the Scriptural ones of "laying on of hands, anointing with oil," and "the prayer of faith." The Bible never advises us to trust in any one or anything but in God. He who would know God's power must walk humbly in God's pathway.

Those who reject God's ways are influenced by ignorance, or by the idea that they are wiser than the written Word; by pride, or by unbelief. Like the Jews they become very angry when told the plain truth concerning themselves.

There is not the faintest hint in Scripture that oil was commanded or used as a medicine, rather than as a symbol. We have abundant testimony to the existence of thousands of remedies at the beginning of the Christian era.

The "Elders of the Church" are God made Elders, and not merely or-

HEALING OF BODILY DISEASE.

dained of man. Before proceeding in any special work for God, we should be very sure that we are called of the Spirit, and that we are in no way influenced by personal ambition.

There is no doubt of the existence of "gifts of healing" in the church to-day. These gifts never were exercised at the discretion of the possessor, nor ever used for the mere purpose of proving anything for the benefit of unbelievers of any grade.

The foundation of the doctrine of faith-healing is the Word of God, and not visible results. *Apparent* failures count for nothing. "Heaven and earth shall pass away, but my word shall never pass away."

The devil is the sole author of the notion that he cannot now "possess" men's bodies, as in former times. He is very anxious to have men think lightly of him. Despising an enemy gives him a great advantage. That was how David came to kill Goliath.

Paul's experience with his thorn, like Job's sickness, is not an exception, but a representative case. Both are paralleled constantly in individual cases to-day.

God always honors faith, even if it be clouded and enveloped in ignorance. It is "according to *thy* faith," not according to the faith of Moses or the apostles. Each man's faith is his own, and no matter how ignorant, if he trusts God, God saves him. See the case of Rabab and that of Naaman.

We can glorify God in sickness by showing His wonderful power to sustain; but we can glorify Him better by giving an opportunity for His delivering power. *Jesus came to preach "deliverance to the captives," not exactly to feed them in prison.* A long continued affliction *may* indicate an obstinate refusal to follow Jesus entirely.

It is just as possible to refuse the passage of Jordan for sickness, and to be turned back to struggle with disease and to die in the wilderness of affliction, as this experience is possible in spiritual matters.

We must walk in the fire in this world, but if Jesus walks with us, the smell of fire need not pass upon us.

God's rod is a rod of power and deliverance, as well as of destroying might. There is a law of life, as well as a law of death. When we talk of the law, we should remember the life side as well as the other. God condemns according to one, and saves by the other.

(Let people who believe it is God's will that they shall be sick, prove their belief by relinquishing all efforts to get well; give up their medicines and save the money spent on physicians.)

The way to find God's will is to read His Word, in the Spirit of Paul, "believing all things which are written in the law and the prophets."— Acts xxiv. 14.

The petition "Thy will be done," can only be perfectly offered by one whose spirit, soul and body have been placed absolutely in Jesus' hands.

"Signs" never have followed, and never can follow those who do not believe in the "signs." They follow those who, like the apostles, pray for God's miraculous power, and heartily believe it will be manifested.

The evidences of miraculous power always multiply when faith becomes concentrated, simple and absolute.

God may use an infinite variety of agents or laws for the recovery of the sick. He may use the patients' imagination or anything else. The only question is, who produced the effect? If God did it He should have the glory.

A miracle is not a violation of natural law, but the superposition of another law. God's laws are never *violated;* they cannot be. It is a natural law that anything material will be attracted towards the earth. An inflated baloon, however, leaves the earth, but not in violation of gravitation. On the contrary it is because of gravitation drawing down the heavier air all around the balloon. The balloon is attracted, according to law; but another law steps in, and through their combination a very different effect is produced.

The proper definition of a miracle is, anything which transcends human power. It would be just as great a miracle for a man to jump one hundred feet as one million miles, because both are absolutely impossible *to man.* All the talk about a miracle being a reversal of some great natural law is fundamentally absurd. There is every reason to believe that natural laws are never reversed, but only modified through combinations with other laws. The idea that a miracle consists in the performance of inherent impossibilities is most absurd of all. God is the perfection of harmony and equity. Two and two, added together, give four. This is truth; and as God, who changes not, is, or holds the essence of truth, we simply testify to this attribute when we say no miracle can or will ever change this numerical relation. Thoughtful men need to open their eyes to this fact. God answers prayer through the operations of law. Indeed He has established *the law of prayer;* "If we ask: anything according to his will, he heareth us." If He heals the sick, it is through and according to law. If He opens a pathway through the sea it is by the operation of law. (Ex. xix. 21). If mighty changes are made in the topography of a continent, such as those prophesied in Zech. xiv. 4, it will be according to law. A few years ago a mountain split in two in far distant Alaska; and a dozen mountains rose out of the waters of of the straits of Sunda. Wherein will the dividing of the Mount of Olives be more distinctly miraculous than these? We cannot tell how the bones of a child are formed, nor how the acorn expands into the oak; but we know both are facts. So far as we are concerned they are just as miraculous as the instantaneous restoration of the withered arm.

Why should we undertake to make time the test of the miraculous, when the Actor is He with whom "a day is as a thousand years, and a thousand years as one day?"

HEALING OF BODILY DISEASE.

The only foundation for Divine healing is in the written Word; not in cases or "phenomena." There are always abuses of every good thing.

We must not be discouraged if the answer appears to be delayed, but diligently seek for possible hinderances in ourselves. "Though it tarry, wait for it, for it will surely come." Healing in Scripture was not always instantaneous. It is, moreover, extremely probable, that the most remarkable cases were narrated in detail.

We may be gradually healed because of imperfect faith, incomplete consecration, or heedlessness of the Spirit's leadings.

The church is sadly in need of *Quadrangular Christians:* those who have found out that Salvation has four sides— committed sin, inbred sin, mental trouble and bodily sickness.

The church, like the apostles, can not cast out devils or perform other wonderful works, *because of unbelief.* The average Christian misses the rounded experience of the saints solely through unbelief. He will not believe it to be his duty to at once consecrate *everything* to God; or he will not believe God's promises to be in the present tense.

The way to "hasten the coming of the Lord," is to really believe He is coming, and to act accordingly. The day is drawing near when faith will be necessary to a part in the first resurrection.

Even translation will be through and according to the *law of faith.*

He that believes that Jesus is not coming, however devout he may be, will surely be left behind. The wise virgins were those who watched. *Watching means expecting.*

If the world is to be converted, apostolic faith and power are needed.

When Satan says "The day of miracles has passed" *he* means to insinuate that God is dead. He chuckles prodigiously over any departure from a supernatural faith in a supernatural God, ever present and ready to literally perform His promises.

Holiness is undoubtedly much more important than bodily healing; but we should never forget that the "day of our redemption" will never come till each "spirit, soul, and body" is "sanctified wholly" from every touch of evil.

Beloved, let us not be left behind for want of asking. Let us pray for grace, for faith, for power, for love, for fire, and even for the miraculous manifestations of a miraculous Saviour, that we may "speak the word with all boldness," and that men, especially Christians, may be convinced that our "glorious Lord" is not chained by His own decrees, nor disposed to alter the meaning of His own language.

Finally; I am "preaching peace by Jesus Christ."—(Acts x. 36.) Peace from all sin. Not a rest from conflict, but a rest from defeat. Peace from all sickness, yes, peace from all inward taint of evil. "Preaching peace by Jesus Christ." What a glorious Saviour we have! What a perfect salvation! How transcendent His glory! how deep His mercy! how unsearchable His love! How free is His grace! how boundless His compassion! how inexhaustible His resources! how enduring his promises! "The eternal God is thy refuge, and underneath are the everlasting arms."—(Deut. xxxiii. 27.) How strong are those arms! How mighty is His power! Jesus paid it all, all the debt I owe; then why should I be striving to pay a portion of it over again? I fly to the mighty Jesus; to Him who has "all power in heaven and earth," and I find "perfect peace" when my "mind is stayed" upon Him alone. I do not find this peace perfect when I "put confidence in men" for a portion of my safety. I want Jesus to have all the glory, and so I trust the "everlasting arms" to hold me without tying myself up by means of man's devising. Thus I have peace. And oh! such peace! How profound; how unfathomable! "Preaching peace by Jesus Christ." Praise the Lord for what follows. Peter adds, "He is Lord of all." Yes, I am determined He shall be the Lord of *all*. "That word, I say, ye know, which was published throughout all Judea, and began from Galilee, after the baptism which John preached: *How God anointed Jesus of Nazareth with the Holy Ghost and with power; who went about doing good, and healing all that were oppressed of the devil; for God was with him. And we are witnesses of all things which he did.*"

This is the kind of peace I preach. Peace that brings freedom from the touch of the devil. How glorious it is to know Jesus as a perfect Saviour in the present tense! "My soul doth magnify the Lord" (Luke i. 46) for all His benefits toward me. "He hath given me rest round about." "He loved my soul from the pit of corruption."—(Isa. xxxviii. 17, margin). "God is the Lord which hath showed us light."—Ps. cxviii. 27. "Light is sown for the righteous, and gladness for the upright in heart."—Ps. xcvii. 11. "For the Lord God is a sun and shield; the Lord will give grace and glory; no good thing will He withhold from them that walk uprightly."—Ps. lxxiii. 23. "I will go in the strength of the Lord."—Ps. lxxi. 16. "Let God be magnified."—Ps. lxx. 4. "The God of Israel is He that giveth strength and power unto His people." "Unto God the Lord belong the issues from death."—Ps. lxviii. 35, 20. "O bless our God which holdeth our soul in life."—Ps. lxvi. 9. "O Thou that hearest prayer, unto Thee shall all flesh come."—Ps. lxv. 2. "I will cry unto God most high; unto God who performeth all things for me."—Ps. lvii. 2. "It is better to trust in the Lord than to put confidence in man."—Ps. cxviii. 8. "Thy God hath commanded thy strength."—Ps. lxviii. 28. "Call upon me in the day of trouble; I will deliver thee, and thou shalt glorify me."—Ps. l. 15. "I will praise Thee forever, because Thou hast done it."—Ps. lii. 9. "Come and hear, all ye that fear God, and I will declare what He hath done for my soul."—Ps. lxvi. 16. "For this God is our God forever and ever; He will be our guide even unto death."—Ps. xlviii. 14. "O clap your hands all ye people; shout unto God with the voice of triumph."—Ps. xlvii. 1.

HEALING OF BODILY DISEASE.

Oh, this peace! how it deepens and broadens and flows!—Isa. xlviii. 18, and xxvi. 3, and lxvi. 12; Ps. cxix. 165; John xiv. 27.

"MY PEACE."

When Peace like a river flows over my soul,
   Away, to the darkness infernal,
My troubles, my cares, and infirmities roll;
   I bathe in the waters eternal.

I drink from the river of life, as it flows
   Straight down from the city resplendent;
The Peace of my soul toward infinitude grows,
   My joy is supreme and transcendent.

"O not as the world giveth, give I to thee;"
   My Jesus, the only Peace-Giver,
Thy Spirit alone bringeth sweet liberty;
   "My Peace" floweth on like a river.

"My Peace,"—what a token of infinite Love,
   My deepest devotion commanding;
Unchanging, and pure, gracious Heavenly Dove,
   "My Peace" passeth all understanding.

"My Peace" like a river flows over my soul,
   No shadow my path is o'er-casting;
But billows of light in omnipotence roll,
   I joy in the life everlasting.

My mind, ever stayed, dearest Lord, upon Thee,
   Beside the still waters I'm growing;
I'm trusting, rejoicing, restful, and free,
   "My Peace" like a river is flowing.

" Glory to God in the highest, and on earth, peace, good will to men."—Luke ii. 14. "His name shall be called Wonderful, Counsellor, The Mighty God, The Everlasting Father, The Prince of Peace."—Isa. ix. 6. " Beloved *now* are we the sons of God." Let us claim our heritage, for our Father saith " all that I have is thine." Let us be QUADRANGULAR CHRISTIANS.

"LET EVERYTHING THAT HATH BREATH PRAISE THE LORD."

APPENDIX A.

JOHN WESLEY ON DIVINE HEALING.

"Is any among you sick let him call for the elders of the church, and let them pray over him, having anointed him with oil in the name of the Lord; and the prayer of faith shall save the sick, and the Lord shall raise him up, and if he have committed sins they shall be forgiven him." James v. 14, 15.

"This single conspicuous gift, which Christ committed to his apostles (Mark vi. 13) remained in the church long after the miraculous gifts were withdrawn. Indeed, it seems to have been designed to remain always, and St. James directs the elders, who were the most, if not the only gifted men, to administer it. (This was the whole process of physic in the Christian church till it was lost through unbelief. That novel invention among the Romanists, practiced not for cure, but where life is despaired of, bears no resemblance to this.

"And the prayer of faith shall save the sick. From his sickness; and if any sin be the occasion of his sickness, it shall be forgiven him."— *Wesley's Notes on New Testament.*

"*Sunday, May* 10, 1741.—But at our love feast which followed, besides the pain in my back and head, and the fever which still continued upon me, just as I began to pray, I was seized with such a cough that I could hardly speak. At the same time came strongly into my mind—'these signs shall follow them that believe.' I called on Jesus, aloud, 'to increase my faith' and to 'confirm the word of his grace.' While I was speaking my pain vanished away, the fever left me, my bodily strength returned, and for many weeks I felt neither weakness nor pain. 'Unto Thee O Lord, do I give thanks.'"— *Wesley's Journal*, Vol. I. p. 210.

"*Wednesday, November* 12, 1746.—In the evening at the chapel my teeth pained me very much. In coming home Mr. Spear gave me an account of the rupture he had had for some years; which, after the most eminent physicians had declared it incurable, was perfectly cured in a moment. I prayed with submission to the will of God. My pain ceased and returned no more."—*Journal*, Vol. I. p. 382.

"*Tuesday, April* 6, 1756.—One was informing me of an eminent instance of the power of faith. 'Many years ago,' said she, 'I fell and sprained my ankle so that I never expected it would be quite well. Seven years since, last September, I was coming home from the preaching on a very dark night, and stumbling over a piece of wood, fell with the whole weight of my body upon my lame foot. I thought, 'O, I shall not be able to hear thy word again for many weeks.' Immediately a voice went through my heart, 'Name the name of Jesus, and thou shalt stand.' I leaped up and stretched out my foot and said, 'Lord Jesus Christ, I name thy name; let me stand.' And my pain ceased and I stood up, and my foot was as strong as ever."—*Journal*, Vol. I. p. 599, 600.

"*Monday, May* 2, 1757.—An account of a widely different nature, 1 received about this time, from Ireland:—Thomas B., about three miles from Tyrrel's Pass, was at the point of death from a violent rupture; while they were praying for him in the societies, he was at once restored to perfect health."—*Journal*, Vol. I. p. 630.

In the second volume of his Journal, on Saturday, December 27, 1761, he records the case of Mary Speciah, who was at once healed of several tumors in the breast, in answer to prayer. Upon this case Mr. Wesley makes the following comment:—

"Now here are plain facts: 1. She was ill. 2. She is well. 3. She became so in a moment. Which of these can with modesty be denied?"

On Sunday, May 17, 1772, he writes:—

"Dr. Hamilton brought with him Dr. Munroe and Dr. Gregory. They satisfied me what my disorder was, and told me there was but one method of cure. Perhaps but one natural one; but I think that God has more than one method of healing either the soul or the body."—*Journal*, Vol. II. p. 373.

"*Friday, July* 26, 1772.—The next day I read over Mr. Eilse's ingenious 'Treaties on the Hydrocele.' He supposes the best cure is by a seton or caustic, but I am not inclined to try either of them. I know a Physician that has a shorter cure than either one or the other."—*Journal*, Vol. II. p. 381.

"*Wednesday, May* 24, 1782.—Mr. Floyd lay in a high fever, almost dead for want of sleep. This was prevented by the pain in one of his feet, which was much swelled, and so sore it could not be touched. We joined in prayer that God would fulfill his Word and give his beloved sleep. Presently the swelling, the soreness, the pain, were gone, and he had a good night's rest."—*Journal*, Vol. II. p. 559.

On Thursday, October 15, 1787, he records the case of Mr. Kingsford, who was healed in answer to prayer of a malady of many years, continuance.

On Thursday, October 7, 1790, he narrates the case of Mrs. Jones, who, after having been confined to her bed for two months with a most severe case of *Prolapsus uteri*, helpless and hopeless, was immediately cured upon commending her case to the Lord, and adds, "I think our Lord never wrought a plainer miracle, even in the days of his flesh."

"I was desired to visit one who was eminently pious, but had now been confined to her bed for several months, and was utterly unable to raise herself up. She desired us to pray that the chain might be broken. A few of us prayed in faith. Presently she rose up, dressed herself, came down stairs, and I believe had no further complaint."

"My old disorder returned as violent as ever. A thought came into my mind, 'Why do I not apply to God in the beginning, rather than in the end of my illness?' I did so and found immediate relief, so that I needed no further medicine."

"My horse was exceeding lame, and my head ached more than it had done for some months. (What I here aver is the naked fact. Let every man account for it as he sees good.) I then thought, 'Cannot God heal either man or beast by any means or without any?' Immediately my weariness and headache ceased, and my horse's lameness in the same instant; nor did he halt any more either that day or the next. A very odd accident this also."

"When I came home they told me the physician said he did not expect Mr. Myrick would live till morning. I went to him, but his pulse was gone. He had been speechless and senseless for some time. A few of us immediately joined in prayer. (I relate the naked fact.) Before we had done, his sense and speech returned. Now, he that will account for this by natural causes, has my free leave; but I choose to say, This is the power of God."

Sunday, July 1, 1759.—"While the society was gathering, I went to a young woman, who was some days since struck with what they called madness; and so it was, but a diabolical madness, as plainly appeared from numerous circumstances: however, after we had been at prayer, she fell asleep, and never raged or blasphemed after."

Monday, July 2.—I rode to Durham, and went at once to the meadow by the river side, where I preached two years ago. The congregation was now larger by one-half; but the sun was so scorching hot upon my head, that I was scarce able to speak. I paused a little, and desired that God would provide us a covering, if it was for his glory. In a moment it was done; a cloud covered the sun, which troubled us no more. Ought voluntary humility to conceal these palpable proofs, that God still answereth prayer?"—Vol. IV. p. 31.

Tuesday, July 17.—"I had been very ill the preceding week: wherefore last night I had recourse to God in prayer; and this morning, instead of rising with difficulty at eight or nine, as I had usually done, I rose with ease at five; and instead of losing my strength in a mile or two, I walked eighteen without weakness or weariness."—Vol. IV. p. 37.

Wed., July 18.—"The work of God, however, quickly began among them that were serious; while not a few endeavored to make sport, by mimicking gestures of them that were wounded. . . . However, in a while many of the scoffers were weary and went away, the rest continued as insensible as before. I had long been walking round the multitude, feeling a jealousy for my God; and praying Him to make the place of His feet glorious. My patience at last began to fail, and I prayed, 'O King of glory, break some them in pieces, but let it be to the saving of their souls!' I had but just spoke, when I heard a dreadful noise on the farther side of the congregation; and, turning thither, saw Thomas Skinner coming forward, the most horrible human figure I ever saw. His large wig and hair were coal black; his face distorted beyond all description; he roared incessantly, throwing and clapping his hands together with his whole force. Several were terrified, and hasted out of his way. I was glad to hear him, after a while, pray aloud. Not a few of the triflers grew serious, while his kindred and acquaintances were very unwilling to believe even their own eyes and ears. They would have got him away, but he fell to the earth, crying, 'My burden! My burden! I cannot bear it!' . . . His agonies lasted some hours; then his body and soul were eased." Vol. IV. p. 38.

Sat., Jan. 30.—"Walking between one and two in the morning I observed a bright light shine upon the chapel. I easily concluded there was a fire near; probably in the adjoining timber yard. If so 'I knew it would soon lay us in ashes. I first called all the family to prayer, then going out, we found the fire about a hundred yards off, and had broke out while the wind was in the south. But a sailor cried out 'H'vast! 'H'vast!' the wind is turned in a moment!" So it did, to the west, while we were at prayer, and so drove the flames from us. We then thankfully returned, and I rested well the residue of the night." Vol. IV. p. 537.

APPENDIX B.

The Case of Mrs. Rebecca S. Fravel.

Only the merest outline of this case can be given here. *Liquor was the cause of the trouble.* Sometime in 1875 this lady was attacked because she would not deny her religious convictions, and most horribly injured. She was choked into insensibility, her back broken, the bones of the legs broken, the right hip and right shoulder dislocated, and her whole body covered with terrible bruises. In this condition, when the merest spark of life remained, after being examined by several physicians who refused to attempt to do anything for her, she was raised up by the power of God alone, and walked, besides using her right hand in signing her name, within twenty-four hours after the injuries were inflicted. Many of her friends and acquaintances, near Cincinnati, Ohio, were and are familiar with these facts, and medical testimony was given under oath concerning her injured condition. I am personally acquainted with the lady, and have had the privilege of meeting with several of her intimate friends. The evidence in the case is full, clear and voluminous, and no hasty sketch like this can begin to give any idea of the wonderful and continued manifestations of God's hand in her experience.

APPENDIX C.

THEOSOPHY AND ESOTERIC RELIGIONS.

The educated world is filled with strange doctrines and writings. The past is being resurrected in a way that would have appeared incredible a few years ago. If any man had appeared as a prophet at the close of the civil war, and predicted that in less than twenty years thousands of educated men and women in the United States, England, the Continent and in India, would be positive outspoken advocates of Buddhism, that they would teach and believe that man's soul passes through an infinity of incarnations or transmigrations, and that by becoming an "adept" through fasting, absolute continence ("forbidding to marry"), and the refusal to eat any animal food ("commanding to abstain from meats," 1 Tim. ii.) a man may be able to recover the recollection of his previous incarnations—that they would talk of "astral spirits" and "compel their souls" to go to any part of the universe at will, *à la* mesmeric mediums—that they would sink the Eternal Son of God to a level with a vast crowd of "Christ's," or those who have in any age "suffered for humanity,"—that they would deny utterly the vicarious atonement and scoff at the blood, prating of a general state of "at-one-ment," with the supreme powers of the universe *at*tained by discipline and the "knowledge of the truth;" not *ob*tained as a "free gift,"—that they would proclaim to the world that the Bible is a very limited record of truth, and that the real custodians of the "higher mysteries" have been, not the Prophets, not the Apostles, not Jesus Christ, but the disciples and priests of Buddha, and especially a certain set of mystics avowed to be secluded in the mountains of Thibet, and only to be found and approached by an initiate,—that they would revive and rehash the "philosophies" of the Rosicrucians, the Fire-worshippers, the Stoics, the Gnostics, and other ancient errors, mixing in a liberal supply of the Canaanitish worship of the "host of heaven" (always in Scripture referring to the demons or "gods")—that they would prate of "spiritual affinities," between men and women, write and talk of the exaltation of woman, the advent of a "Female Messiah,"—the "Second Eve," who is to save the world,—that they would darkly whisper of a strange form of "spiritual adultery," of the possibility, for women at least and perhaps for some men, of enjoying a sexual gratification with unseen beings, thus reviving the frightful sins of Canaan when we read of women who were "*the mistress of a demon*" (1 Sam. xxviii, 7 Hebrew), and yet teaching this horrible depravity under the guise of a mystical interpretation of Solomon's Song,—that they would start publication houses under the name of "Culture," and issue books professing to be the depositories of all "truth" as preserved by the "mystics,"—that "esoteric" religion would be held up as vastly superior to the simple religion of the cross, intelligible to a child as well as a scholar,—that they would fill the periodicals of the day with articles and advertisements of the new-old religion,—that they would openly publish and commend the theory and practice of the "occult arts,"—that they—but merciful and long-suffering God! can'st thou endure much longer?

If, I say, such a prophet had appeared twenty years ago, who would have believed him? Indeed who can credit the statement that these awful things are now received and taught by multitudes all over Christendom? *Nevertheless, it is true.*

For years I have seen a rising tide of this filth of perdition, sweeping up and around our people, and bearing many, many Christians away upon its deceitful flood. Understand that all these works and books *begin* with accepted truth, and thus win assent; but soon the poison appears, skilfully interwoven with truth, until at last the mask is dropped entirely. The anonymous authors of "The Perfect Way, or The Finding of Christ" do not tell the reader in the first chapter that "*Jesus Christ could never have been but for Buddha,*" but they write it down plainly enough after two hundred pages of arch seduction unrivalled since the "days of Noah."

The Mind Cure, and Christian Science, do not teach at first that by Jesus' death comes no virtue: but they teach it plainly enough at last, and in their monthly journals scoff and sneer at the idea of God "getting His fill of plenty of blood."

Oahspe, or the New Bible The Book of Life by Sidartha; The Perfect Way or The Finding of Christ; Esoteric Buddhism; The Esoteric Magazine · Occultism and the Mystic Arts; Theosophy by Madame Blavatsky The Christian Science Magazine; these, and many other publications, swarm all around us. The bottomless pit is open and the entire brood of hell seems determined to sweep out upon the human race. Every one of these works without exception, no matter how high sounding may be its opening passages, carries a sting in its tail—(Rev. ix. 10). Every one without exception makes war upon the fundamental truths of our holy religion—the Blood of Jesus Christ, the atoning sacrifice for sin. Every one of these, without exception, is a part of the very spawn of hell. Many of the ablest scholars have testified in amazement that such works as Oahspe, and The Book of Life, could not have been written by any one man; that no single individual could gather such stores of knowledge. Be this as it may in our days "knowledge shall be increased" —(Dan. xii. 4), and unfortunately such knowledge "puffeth up"—(1 Cor. viii. 1), and whether human or devilish it is all bent to the one end of uplifting man, and pulling down Jesus.

Those who "lack understanding" are deceived. "To the law and the testimony," (not to the priests of Buddha), "if they speak not according to this word, it is because there is no light in them"—(Isa. viii. 20). "The knowledge of the holy is understanding," and that knowledge leads to faith. And when men talk of "new light for this age," let us remember that the Spirit's office is to bring to mind what *has been* said, not to transcend the written word; and that for the last times, not "not new light," but *great darkness* is predicted. Finally, remember that, "*Faith cometh by hearing, and hearing by* THE WORD OF GOD—(Rom. x. 17).

APPENDIX D.

MY CONFESSION.

"In all thy ways acknowledge Him, and He shall direct thy paths."—PROV. iii. 6.

For several years I have longed to write this little book. When I was led to surrender my whole soul and body into the Lord's hands, I found Him abundantly able to save to the uttermost. My God, for Christ's sake, forgave me all my sins, cleansed me from all unrighteousness, and healed my body of mortal disease, as related in the tract, MIRACLES OF HEALING. This was in September, 1879. As the months went by, a thought slowly formed itself in my mind. It seemed exceedingly radical; different from every idea and belief of my life; widely at variance with the accepted views of Christians, and, on the whole, rather a dangerous matter. But I could not get away from it; so I took it to the Lord, and earnestly prayed for His guidance, and for the light of the Word. The more I prayed and studied, the deeper became the conviction that the thing was of the Lord. At last, I ventured to speak about it to a few friends, and together we talked it over, only to deepen the impression already formed. This thought was, that *the Church has been limiting the atonement of Jesus Christ.* Do not start, dear reader. There is no doctrine of Restitution hidden here. I believe that Jesus died only for the "Whosoever will." I began to believe that my Divine Master not only took upon himself my sins, but also bore my bodily sicknesses, and that I might, through simple faith, be free from the latter, just as well as from the former. To the man who believes that he must continue to sin as long as life lasts, there can be no parallelism of course; but, I had come to see that my Jesus is able and willing to save me from my sins, and was trusting Him for it. He had forgiven me my past offences, and He had healed my past sickness—heart disease. I was trusting Him to keep me from sinning; then why not trust Him to keep me from being sick, if Matt. viii. 17 and Psalm ciii. 3 have any present application?

The great question was, "Is it the truth?" How I prayed the dear Lord to keep me from error! There was not a single published word upon the subject, for the literature of Divine-healing was confined to Dr. Cullis' first volume of "Faith Cures," and "Dorothea Trudel;" beside such more general works as Horace Bushnell's "Nature and the Supernatural." I could not, therefore, get any help from man, and this fact threw me absolutely on God. I trusted in Him, and strove hard not to lean to my own understanding. But, in this way at least, I did not publicly acknowledge Him; that is I did not profess my faith on the subject. In the course of two years, however, I was led into a firm belief; and then the conviction grew upon me that I must make public confession. At this point the devil was ready. He said, "Now if you do profess such a thing, *even if it is true,* you will not have strong enough faith; you will get sick immediately; and bring the profession into disgrace, and yourself to confusion." I only prayed, O Lord, make me sure of the truth, and I will confess it; I have nothing to do with consequences; that is Thy part.

Well, Jesus made me sure, and about two years ago I publicly announced my belief, in a meeting held in St. George's Hall, in Philadelphia. A very short time before this confession I was attacked with severe griping pains and internal disorder. I resisted in faith, and called on my friend and brother in Christ, G. W. McCalla. He laid hands on me, anointing me with oil in the name of the Lord; we both claimed immediate deliverance from the threatened trouble, and the Lord entirely healed me. In order to prevent my profession of faith, however, the devil referred to this attack. He argued in this wise: "It is true that you have not been sick of any account these two years and more, but you have had slight attacks of cold, etc. Now you had better not take such radical ground, for if you do you will be sure to catch a heavy cold; you know you always have one or two in a winter, and thus you will get into trouble." I said, "Jesus has the keeping part, I have the believing and confessing."

So the rubicon was crossed, and the declaration of my faith made public to a few. At that time I wanted to write something on the subject, but for various reasons it was not done. And now, after two years of trusting and keeping, I begin to write down what I believe God has done for my soul and body. Meanwhile several have spoken and written this very item of faith—the keeping power of Jesus to save from bodily sickness; but it is a matter of regret that some of these have been led into the mistake of disregarding all natural laws, maintaining that a man need scarcely sleep or eat if the work of the Lord presses upon him; but that God is bound to take care of him through any amount of physical exertion. This I apprehend to be a grave error. Moses and Elijah fasted forty days and nights, but in each case a special, clear, and unmistakable manifestation of God's hand and will made the way plain before them. If the Lord wants me to work for days without natural rest, He will make the duty plain by *supernatural* indications. When He does so, I will work, and trust Him for the consequences.

This, then, is my confession. I believe that Jesus " bare my sins—all of them—in his own body on the tree;" and I believe that " he took my infirmities, and bore my sicknesses." Now if He bore them for me, I am not necessarily obliged to carry them myself; so I just believe it and cry, from my inmost being, Praise the Lord! Of course, I know that I am professing faith in an item of experience which can not be hidden from the eyes of those about me. A man may sin and feel condemned in his own heart, and no one know anything about it; but he can not be seriously ill without the fact becoming apparent. All this I have counted. That is I have counted it all over into the hands of my Saviour and Physician. I have nothing to do with the future; I live by present breath for the body, and present faith for the soul. But I do boldly avow my belief that *Sin and Sickness are from the devil; while Holiness and Health are from God.* If I sin, it is because the devil gets the advantage in my soul, and if I am sick, it is because he gets the advantage in my body. From many sins no sickness *directly* results, and many sicknesses, like those of Job and the man born blind, are not the *direct* consequences of sins. But all the same the devil gets the advantage in the body. In neither case, however, does any absolute necessity exist.

This little book, the writing of which has been singularly blessed to my own soul and body, is now committed to the work which Jesus may have for it to do. And to His name be all the praise!

PENNSYLVANIA MILITARY ACADEMY,
March, 1884.

Just three years after the writing of the above I was taken with a severe attack of brain prostration. With the greatest difficulty I continued in my college work in addition to my editorial labors on "The Kingdom." For eight years I had been incessantly at work, and always using the brain. This was a mistake—an honest one, for I really did not think I was overworking; but it was necessary for me to learn a lesson in the school of health. July 14, 1887, at Mountain Lake Park camp meeting, in answer to prayer by Mrs. Hammer, Mrs. Sharpe, Mrs. Denman, and Rev. Stephen Merritt, according to Mark xvi. 18, the Lord was graciously pleased to entirely heal me, so that I was enabled to endure the severe exertion of camp preaching without the least evil result.

In the light of the reasons and conditions developed in this book, such experiences will offer no argument against the Scriptural doctrine of Divine-healing. The *conditions* laid down for our observance are very particular and absolutely rigid. These conditions have been overlooked by the majority in their eagerness to obtain the gift. It is ever so. We are all apt to jump over the intervening objects in order to reach our aim, and all too frequently we thus leave dangerous foes in the rear, and ourselves unprotected from their assault. In revising this book I find these conditions all there, and clearly stated; but not emphasized as they should be in order to guard against the weakness referred to. *I therefore warn every reader to pay special attention to the conditions attached to the promises* quoted from the Scriptures. By so doing you will escape the error of many critics who have written against our beliefs during the last five years. Very many cases of healing have come to my knowledge as direct results from the reading of the first editions of this book, and some from my article in the Century magazine, for March, 1887. But all such cases are directed into other channels, and a few which were embodied in former editions are omitted from this revision, for the reason that the only proper ground for this discussion lies in the Word of God.

The old-time, cast-iron, fatalistic Calvinism arose from the too exclusive study of cases, i. e., the study of men and men's contradictory experiences. Arminianism on the other hand came from the study of the promises of God. Perhaps a careful combination may be advisable, but certain it is that he who studies *cases* of healing or salvation will soon find himself trembling upon the verge of fatalism, while he who studies the glorious "whosoever" will quickly throw wide all the possibilities of the vicarious Atonement to the race.

Praise The Lord!

Yardville, New Jersey
November 19, 1887.

GLOSSARY OF SCRIPTURE TEXTS.

GENESIS.	PAGE
i., 3	89
i., 29	79
iii., 16	80
xx., 7–17	32
xviii.,	32
xviii., 14	24, 72
xx., 17	11, 68, 82
xxv., 21	11, 32
xxx., 1–2	11, 32
l., 20	111

EXODUS.	
xv., 26	11, 32, 46, 115
xix., 5–6	81
xix., 21	170
xxxiii., 22–25	12, 98
xxiii., 25	46
xxiii., 26	86
xxxiii., 25	93
xxxiii., 18–23	18, 23, 76
xxxiv., 6	76

LEVITICUS.	
xi.,	77
xi., 44	79
xii., 6, 28	79
xiii.,	80
xiv.,	80
xv.,	77, 80
xv., 31	81
xxi.,	80
xxvi., 15, 16	12

NUMBERS.	
xii., 13	12, 87
xvi., 47–48	12
xx., 12	106
xxi.,	34
xxvi., 9	12

DEUTERONOMY.	PAGE
iii., 26	87
iv., 40	83
v., 29, 33	12
v., 16	32
v., 33	83
v., 88	67
vi., 24	77
vii., 12, 15	12, 33, 95, 98
vii., 9	95
vii., 15	46
viii., 3	50
xii., 25–28	88
xxii., 7	33
xxiii., 1	81
xxviii., 15–16	88
xxviii., 58–62	13, 67
xxix., 22–24	83
xxx., 6	24
xxx., 20	57
xxxi., 17	165
xxxii., 39	34, 46, 92
xxxiii., 27	172
xxxiv., 7	75

JOSHUA.	
xxiii., 14	12

1 SAMUEL.	
ii., 6	34, 67
xxviii., 7	177

2 SAMUEL.	
xxiv., 25	12

1 KINGS.	
iii., 14	85
viii., 37–39	82
viii., 56	12
xxii., 34–35	43

2 KINGS.

	PAGE
iv., 40	90
v.,	82
xx., 1–11	14, 120
xx., 5	82
xx., 12	14

2 CHRONICLES.

vi., 28–30	82
vii., 12–14	35
vii., 13, 14	13
xvi., 12	83
xvi., 12, 18	14
xviii.,	64, 67
xx., 15	14
xxiii., 31	14
xxx., 20	82
xxxii., 31	36

JOB.

i., 10	54, 110
xiii., 4	83, 100
xxxiii., 4	100
xxxiii., 14–30	14, 30, 174
xliii., 8	87

PSALMS.

vi., 2, 5, 9,	36, 82
xxvii., 1	18, 82
xxx., 2, 3	18, 82
xxxiv., 7	54, 110
xxxiv., 19	69
xli., 2	36
xli., 3	13, 82
xlvii., 1	172
xlviii., 14	172
l., 15	172
liii., 9	172
lv., 22	82
lv., 23	86
lvii., 2	172
lx., 11	82
lxii., 22	89
lxiii., 28	172
lxv., 2	172
lxvi., 9	172
lxvi., 16	172
lxviii., 20, 28, 35	172
lxx., 4	172
lxxi., 16	172
lxxvi., 10	111
lxxviii., 20–22	36
xc., 3	67
xc., 10	86

PSALMS.

	PAGE
xci., 1–6	13, 69, 82
xci., 36	36
xcvii., 11	172
ciii., 2–5	13, 82
ciii., 2, 3	21, 179
ciii., 3	26
ciii., 1–5	38
cv., 37	12, 46, 95
cvii.,	39
cvii., 20	47, 82
cxviii., 8	172
cxviii., 17	82
cxviii., 27	172
cxix., 67	167
cxix., 71	96
cxix., 165	172
cxxx., 8	21

PROVERBS.

iii., 6	178
iii., 7, 8	39
iv., 20, 22	29, 39
ix., 11	29, 40
x., 27	40
xii., 28	39
xiv., 27	40
xvi., 17	40
xvii., 22	83, 119
xxiii., 20	73
Song of Solomon	177

ECCLESIASTES.

vii., 17	29, 90
vii., 12, 17	40

ISAIAH.

vii., 20	70
viii., 20	178
ix., 6	178
xxvi., 3	172
xxxiii., 24	40
xxxviii., 17	172
xl., 29–31	40
xliii., 25	21
xliv., 22	21
xlv., 7	64
xlviii., 18	172
liii	41
liii., 3, 4, 5, 10	14
liii., 6, 12	21
lvii., 18	47
lviii., 8	47, 100
lxvi., 12	172

GLOSSARY.

JEREMIAH.

	PAGE
vi., 7	43
viii., 22	47, 83
x., 19	43
xi., 1–10	96
xvii., 5–14	14, 47, 82
xxx., 13	83, 119
xxx., 17	47
xxxii., 27	14, 47, 73
xxxiii., 6	47, 82
xlvi., 11	47, 83, 119

EZEKIEL.

xviii., 24	22
xxxiii., 12	22
xxxiv., 4–16	48, 82
xxxiv., 2–16	14, 97
xxxvi., 25–29	24
xlvii., 12	83, 119

DANIEL.

ix., 24	66
xii., 4	178

HOSEA.

iv., 17	111

MICAH.

vi., 13	14, 48
vii., 19	21

HABAKKUK.

iii., 19	48

ZECHARIAH.

iv., 10	96

MALACHI.

iv., 2	14, 48, 82

MATTHEW.

i., 21	48
iv., 1–11	49
v., 17	113
vi., 24	73
viii., 16, 17	14, 41, 45, 93, 179
ix., 12	83
x., 1–12	51, 83, 115
xiv., 36	50
xvii., 20	53
xviii., 29	53
xxiv., 35	53
xxviii., 18, 20	84
xxviii., 19	17

MARK.

	PAGE
ii., 17	83
v.,	68, 83
vi., 5	15, 51
vi., 12, 13	51
vi., 13	174
vii., 13	116
viii., 14–21	114
ix., 28, 29	53
xiii., 11	165
xvi., 17, 18	17, 52, 84, 114, 181

LUKE.

ii., 14	173
iv., 23	83
iv., 27	15
v., 31	83
viii., 43	83
ix., 1–6	51, 83
ix., 1–16	15
ix., 56	51
ix., 56	53
ix., 62	73
x., 1–19	15, 51, 83, 115
xiii., 11–17	65
xiv., 4, 5	65

JOHN.

i., 4	39
iv., 14	50
vi., 51	56
vi., 63	50
xi	109
xiv., 27	172
xv., 7	53
xvii., 15	54
xvii., 18	53

ACTS.

ii., 38	17
iv., 17	28
iv., 29, 30	15, 52, 54
x., 15	77
x., 36	171
x., 38	65
x., 48	17
xiii., 39	21
xix., 5	17
xix., 11, 12	120
xx., 31	103
xxiv., 14	89, 169

ROMANS.

iii., 23–25	21
iv., 25	21

GLOSSARY.

ROMANS.
	Page
vi., 6	72
viii., 10–28	17, 73, 94
viii., 11	16
ix., 17	111
x., 17	32, 178
xii., 1	73
xii., 3	84
xiv., 14	78

1 CORINTHIANS.
ii., 5	54, 84
iii., 16, 17	54, 74
iii., 22, 23	114
v., 13, 20	74
v., 5	86
v. and vi	54
vi., 13	16, 74
vi., 19, 20	55
viii., 1	178
x., 8	55
x., 13	24, 114
x., 25–27	78
xi., 1, 4, 16	102
xi., 30	16, 88
xii.,	114
xii., 28	16, 84
xv., 23–32	18
xv., 44	55

2 CORINTHIANS.
i., 8–11	105
i., 20	18, 55, 84
ii., 14	24
iv., 8–11	105
v., 1–4	73
v., 7	56
vi., 4, 5, 9	105
x., 4, 5	24
x., 10, 11	104
xi., 15	69
xi., 30	103
xii., 9	73

GALATIANS.
iii., 13	17, 56
iii., 17	95
iv., 13, 14	103
i., 14	16
ii., 5–8	106
ii., 22	74
iv., 8	58
v.	56

GALATIANS.
	Page
v., 23	45
vi., 3	33, 114
vi., 12	67

PHILIPPIANS.
i., 20	75, 101, 104
i., 22	104
ii., 25–27	84, 101
iii., 6	97
iii., 17	102
iii., 21	101

COLOSSIANS.
i., 27	57
ii., 4	57
ii., 14	92
ii., 17	75
iii., 4	18
iv., 12	57
iv., 14	83

1 THESSALONIANS.
i., 6, 7	102
ii., 10	102
iv., 3	46
v., 23	75

2 THESSALONIANS.
iii., 9	102

1 TIMOTHY.
i., 20	86
ii.,	177
iv., 4	78
iv., 14	120
v., 23	120

2 TIMOTHY.
i., 6	120
ii., 1	120
iv., 20	101

HEBREWS.
ii., 8	18
ii., 14, 15	66, 67, 112
iii., 6	74
vii., 25	24
ix., 22	81
ix., 27	17, 112
ix., 28	18
x., 9, 10	46
x., 22	81

GLOSSARY.

HEBREWS.	PAGE
xi,	69
xi., 6	84
xi., 11	32, 57
xiii., 6	114
xiii., 8	84, 116

JAMES.	
i., 5	114
ii., 17	84
v., 13	85
v., 14, 15	16, 90, 115, 174
v., 16	18, 78, 86

1 PETER.	
ii., 5	74
ii., 24	15, 21, 43, 45, 93
iii., 15	100
ix., 9	81

2 PETER.	
i., 20, 21	31
iii., 2	96

1 JOHN.	PAGE
i., 7	24
iii., 8	67
v., 11, 12	47
v., 14–17	39
v., 18	85

3 JOHN.	
i., 2	95

JUDE.	
9	75
12	90
24	24, 100

REVELATION.	
i., 6	81
ii., 10	63
v., 10	81
ix., 5, 6, 20	63
xvi., 2, 9–11	64
xx., 6	81
xxii., 18, 19	115

www.ingramcontent.com/pod-product-compliance
Lightning Source LLC
Chambersburg PA
CBHW020240170426
43202CB00008B/161